# The Customer Care and Contact Center Handbook

Also available from ASQ Quality Press:

*Online Customer Care: Strategies for Call Center Excellence*
Michael Cusack

*Analysis of Customer Satisfaction Data*
Derek R. Allen and Tanniru R. Rao

*Customer Centered Six Sigma: Linking Customers, Process Improvement, and Financial Results*
Earl Naumann and Steven H. Hoisington

*Customer Satisfaction Measurement Simplified: A Step-by-Step Guide for ISO 9001:2000 Certification*
Terry G. Vavra

*Improving Your Measurement of Customer Satisfaction: A Guide to Creating, Conducting, Analyzing, and Reporting Customer Satisfaction Measurement Programs*
Terry G. Vavra

*Measuring Customer Satisfaction: Survey Design, Use, and Statistical Analysis Methods,* Second Edition
Bob E. Hayes

*The Trust Imperative: Performance Improvement through Productive Relationships*
Stephen Hacker and Marsha Willard

*Customer Satisfaction Measurement and Management*
Earl Naumann and Kathleen Giel

To request a complimentary catalog of ASQ Quality Press publications, call 800-248-1946, or visit our Web site at http://qualitypress.asq.org .

# The Customer Care and Contact Center Handbook

Garry Schultz

ASQ Quality Press
Milwaukee, Wisconsin

*The Customer Care and Contact Center Handbook*
Garry Schultz

**Library of Congress Cataloging-in-Publication Data**

Schultz, Garry, 1958–
   The customer care and contact center handbook / Garry Schultz.
     p. cm.
   Includes bibliographical references and index.
   ISBN 0-87389-561-4 (Hardcover, Case bound : alk. paper)
   1. Customer services—Handbooks, manuals, etc.  I. Title.

HF5415.5 .S4444 2002
658.8'12—dc21                       2002151130

10 9 8 7 6 5 4 3 2 1

ISBN 0-87389-561-4

Publisher: William A. Tony
Acquisitions Editor: Annemieke Koudstaal
Project Editor: Paul O'Mara
Production Administrator: Gretchen Trautman
Special Marketing Representative: David Luth

ASQ Mission: The American Society for Quality advances individual, organizational, and community excellence worldwide through learning, quality improvement, and knowledge exchange.

Attention Bookstores, Wholesalers, Schools, and Corporations: ASQ Quality Press books, videotapes, audiotapes, and software are available at quantity discounts with bulk purchases for business, educational, or instructional use.
For information, please contact ASQ Quality Press at 800-248-1946, or write to ASQ Quality Press, P.O. Box 3005, Milwaukee, WI 53201-3005.

To place orders or to request a free copy of the ASQ Quality Press Publications Catalog, including ASQ membership information, call 800-248-1946. Visit our Web site at www.asq.org or http://qualitypress.asq.org .

Printed in the United States of America

♾ Printed on acid-free paper

**American Society for Quality**

Quality Press
600 N. Plankinton Avenue
Milwaukee, Wisconsin 53203
Call toll free 800-248-1946
Fax 414-272-1734
www.asq.org
http://qualitypress.asq.org
http://standardsgroup.asq.org
E-mail: authors@asq.org

# Table of Contents

# Table of Figures

# Acknowledgments

First off, I would like to thank the thousands of Customers I have dealt with throughout my career. This book would be nothing without the lessons I learned—often the hard way—from conversations I've had with Customers. While there was often some fire and brimstone in the conversations, the overall experience has been, and continues to be, very positive.

I would like to thank my wife Jackie for allowing me the luxury of time and space to write the book, and for the near constant stream of Tim's (those of you in Canada know Tim's makes the best coffee) she supplied.

Thank you to George Pappas for taking the time out from his incredibly busy schedule to read the manuscript and write the foreword, and to Lorne MacDonald (Mac) for reading the drafts, commenting, rereading the drafts, commenting, and so on. You are a very patient man and were a constant source of support during the long review process.

As for Jenna, my daughter, perhaps you assisted in simply allowing me access to the computer to write the book . . . but I don't need to acknowledge that (it's my computer!). I do, however, dedicate this book to you (and yes that means you have to read it now).

Lastly, thank you to the reader for buying the book and for putting up with my flippant sense of humor which is sprinkled throughout. Some believe that humor has no place in business—that is poppycock, humor can make the most somber business fun. I hope you enjoy the read ahead of you.

*Garry*

# Foreword

There is no doubt in my mind that the ability to deliver world-class customer care has become a prime, if not *the* prime, differentiator among corporations. Those who deliver will prosper; alternatively, those who do not deliver will soon be abandoned by their most precious asset, their customers. No customer, no revenue, no business.

I first met Garry Schultz when he was representing a young company with a revolutionary new product. In the vernacular found in the book, Garry had *new product release* challenges and I was the COO in charge of a key *enabling* technology. They were very exciting times. What first impressed me about Garry was his unrelenting focus on the customer. The customer's best interest was always Garry's driving force. I was pleased to see that this customer-centric focus is retained throughout the book.

*The Customer Care and Contact Center Handbook* is an ambitious book, and it impressed me as such. The reader is introduced to how the customer has an impact on almost every department in a corporation: engineering, finance, marketing, sales, quality assurance, and so on. The intercorporate relationships and sanctions necessary to successfully deliver on customer satisfaction are presented well, and actionable guidance is given on how to shop ideas to ensure success. *The Customer Care and Contact Center Handbook* makes it clear that the contact center is not a stand-alone operation and must be in the mainstream.

I found the text to be realistic in scope. The concepts are reasonable and can be implemented with relative ease. Few of the systems outlined require securing a large budget or applying a disproportionate degree of effort. These attributes secure the likelihood of the ideas actually being implemented.

Perhaps the most useful part of *The Customer Care and Contact Center Handbook* is chapter 4 in which business metrics are discussed. I am not the first to say "what gets measured gets managed," but I stand by it. The sections on performance, support, financial, and product metrics alone are worth the price of the book. The examples (plots and graphs) provided are clear and would, in their brevity and ease of interpretation, delight any executive.

There is a sentence in the opening pages of the book that struck me and I will repeat it here as it is the key:

*Above all, Customers must be treated with respect, and do not forget to apply a little common sense.*

I wish Garry success with this book.

George Pappas
COO Cingular Interactive

# Introduction

Providing quality Customer care is a hot issue. High-technology start-ups and old-school industries have taken note of the power the Customer of the millennium can exercise. Every second business magazine has a cornerstone article on Customer care. Executive after executive appear in press and on television expounding on the Customer care theme—clichés abound. The themes are not new . . . some of the parameters have changed but the core issue remains the same: "satisfy the Customer." This book is a road map to satisfying the Customer by creating a positive Customer experience. The ideas and concepts come from the 20 years the author has enjoyed in Customer services.

## FORMAT

*. . . what it is . . .*

The book is laid out in a logical fashion progressing from theory to practical application. It takes the reader from a description of the challenges and the current climate in Customer services, to structure, and then to execution and systems. A brief outline of the chapters follows.

*Chapter 1—Creating a Contact Center.* Chapter 1 outlines who the target audience for the book is, why contact centers are needed, the current climate in Customer support, and introduces a set of important factoids that underscore today's Customer support challenge. It concludes with a listing of the key defining points that require attention in the creation, maintenance, and growth of a contact center.

*Chapter 2—Contact Center Structure.* Chapter 2 introduces the concept of the business model and discusses how to align the corporate business model to contact center operation. It then moves on to detail key concepts that must be understood for the contact center to thrive. A discussion of strategic accounts is followed by one on escalations. The impact of business partners and enabling technologies on the contact center is touched on and then explored in a series of subchapters titled "We Don't Do Windows I, II, and III." Outsourcing criteria is then discussed and contact center structure (physical as well as psychological) is presented and explored. The chapter wraps up with details on hiring, compensation, and employee retention.

*Chapter 3—Standard Operating Procedures.* Chapter 3 focuses on the creation and maintenance of procedures. Audits are discussed and a continuous improvement program is put forward. The chapter wraps up with a discussion of crisis management and provides examples of the data points that must be anticipated and managed in the contact center.

*Chapter 4—Performance Metrics.* Chapter 4 introduces contact center metrics, definition through interpretation. A continuous improvement cycle is presented and discussed at length. A generic support call is analyzed from start to conclusion. Reports are discussed and ample examples of performance, support, financial, and product metrics reports are provided. Each metric report is dissected as to utility, interpretation, corrective action, and long-term ramifications. The chapter wraps up with a discussion of service level agreements (SLAs).

*Chapter 5—Training and Testing.* Chapter 5 outlines one of the most important and most neglected aspects of contact center management—training. A recommended training sequence is presented followed by recommendations on partnering, testing, and final graduation to a fully accredited Customer support representative. The chapter wraps up with an introduction of call recording and its applicability to quality initiatives.

*Chapter 6—Systems.* Chapter 6 details the systems and tools needed for a world class contact center to operate. Data flow through the organization is explored to some depth. System purchasing criteria for standard systems found in a contact center are detailed and concrete guidance is given in regards to selection criteria. The chapter concludes with a discussion of system progression within an organization from paper-based mom-and-pop operation to fully automated enterprise resource planning (ERP) centric mega-corporation.

*Appendix A—Acronyms and Terms.* Appendix A is a glossary of terms found in the text. Note that appendix G is also a glossary of terms, however appendix G is dedicated to financial terms whereas appendix A contains general terms. Furthermore, all entries in appendix G are cross-referenced in appendix A. Therefore, always check appendix A for definition of a term, since if the term is actually to be found in appendix G the reader will be directed as such.

*Appendix B—Job/Role Descriptions.* Appendix B contains details on every position found in a contact center.

*Appendix C—FMECA.* Appendix C presents the failure mode effects and criticality analysis tool. Perhaps one of the most powerful tools in the manager's tool kit, the FMECA can be used to anticipate the impact of new products and/or product changes on the contact center's operation.

***Appendix D—The Five Whys of Quality.*** Appendix D discusses this other analytical tool. It is somewhat whimsical compared to the FMECA, but no less powerful.

***Appendix E—Organizations.*** Appendix E outlines some of the organizations that are of relevance to contact center professionals.

***Appendix F—Alpha/Beta Testing.*** Appendix F introduces the concepts of Alpha and Beta testing, and their applicability and impact on and in the contact center.

***Appendix G—Finance for Contact Center Managers.*** Appendix G is a primer on financial concepts and what they mean to the contact center manager. This is by no means meant to be a definitive guide to the world of finance, but rather a good introduction to the terminology and applicability to the contact center manager. Note that all definition entries in appendix G are cross-referenced in appendix A.

***Appendix H—SOP Template.*** Appendix H presents a template to be used in the creation of standard operating procedures (SOP). An example of a complete SOP is provided.

***Appendix I—Selected Readings.*** Appendix I contains a number of references to excellent books on contact center and Customer care in general.

# 1

# Creating a Contact Center

## OBJECTIVE

*What may be learned in this chapter.*

This chapter introduces the challenges facing contact center managers and personnel. A central theme regarding the propensity of Customers to continue to raise their expectations is introduced and explored.

This chapter covers the following topics:

- Description of the target audience for this book

- Why contact centers are needed

- The current climate in Customer support

- An exploration of the continued evolution of Customer demands on contact centers

- A listing of the key defining points that require management related to the creation or growth of a contact center

- Lists of questions which will assist contact center management in focusing and understanding the challenges inherent in any contact center operation

## THE NEED

*. . . very, very loudly . . .*

The need to provide quality care is certainly not a new challenge. What is new is the power brandished by today's Customer; power facilitated and enhanced by the Internet. Today's Customers have the power to not only take their individual business elsewhere, but to start/join/engage in openly published and easily accessible forums. They have the power to complain very, very loudly—so loud that the inhabitants of the corner offices and crystal palaces hear and take notice. For a business to succeed it must treat Customers with honesty, integrity, and fairness while respecting their intelligence. This sounds simple, yet it is not—it is in fact very, very difficult.

Customer expectations may have gone too far. Recently, I was at a gas station waiting in line to pay for my purchase when the credit card belonging to the individual in front of me was rejected. It wasn't the gas station clerk that rejected the card, it was the financial service provider at the other end of the modem link. But the individual, the Customer, took it as a personal affront. He was deeply offended by the clerk! He paid with cash but then demanded a gratis car wash for his trouble. The clerk was not prepared to extend a free wash after being verbally abused for ten minutes by the Customer. I would like to think that this is an isolated instance of consumer to business abuse, but evidence indicates it is a growing trend. Have we, as Customers, gone too far?

Then there is the case of an escalation I took from one of the frontline representatives of a contact center of which I was the director. A very senior IT manager from one of our major accounts was very upset and was demanding a full credit plus a punitive penalty. He proceeded to tell me that the support our contact center provided was the absolute worst he had seen in the entire high-technology sector. I was intrigued by his comments and conducted a full investigation with a view to corrective action. What I uncovered was that the Customer's IT manager in charge of supporting my company's solution at the Customer's site had recently resigned from their organization. Subsequently, the Customer experienced a failure of one of the supporting systems that enabled my organization's solution.

The failure was with a popular e-mail platform; the fix was well documented and published by the e-mail platform's technical support team. The tricky part was that this failure manifested itself by rendering my company's solution inoperative. When the enabling system failed, the senior manager contacted his former employee for support; the employee told the senior manager that a command line switch had to be run to correct the situation. But, he had forgotten the syntax of the command line switch and suggested to his former boss that he call the vendor (my organization's contact center). The IT manager, not being overtly technical, interpreted this as he was to call my contact center and we were to *"throw a switch."* When his people called our contact center to inform us that they were down and we needed to "throw the switch," our people were dumbfounded. Our contact center got them up and running by assisting with restoration of the e-mail platform, but not before the Customer had concluded that we were ineffective, evasive, and simply didn't know what we were doing; "... the worst support he had ever seen . . ." Here is the kicker: even after I politely took the Customer through the sequence of events and clearly demonstrated that the failure was not with my company's product, he still demanded a full credit plus additional credit for opportunity-loss. I did not extend the full credit but instead took the time to explain the situation until the Customer had the eureka moment and understood where the breakdown was. Some may conclude that it would have been more economical to simply extend the credit, but then precedent would have been set—and the contact center would have had to live with the consequences for all time.

Finally, there is the case of a class-action suit brought against a major video rental business. In a nutshell, the prosecution contended that the video renter was gouging the public for late fees. Now it is true that approximately 17 percent of the video renter's revenue is based on collection of late fees, but it is the Customer who takes on the burden of returning the video within the agreed upon and clearly indicated time frame. The case was settled, but suffice to say the lawyers were the only beneficiaries of the class action. Is this a breakdown of Customer care? Or have Customers been allowed to expect too much from business?

Entitlement disorder is a term psychologists have coined to label the root of some of the more aggressive and disruptive behavior found in society today. Leonard Ingram of the Anger Institute suggests, "Our society wants instant gratification. We can't wait. We're unable to be tolerant. We confuse democracy with entitlement and think every little slight is a trampling of our civil rights." Observe the behavior of the Customers in an average contact center and you too will bear witness to an epidemic of "entitlement disorder."

Have we gone too far with the idea that the Customer is always right? The Customer must be served. The Customer is central to success. The Customer drives the bottom line. The Customer demands to be treated with respect. But where is the line drawn between a reasonable response and disproportionate retribution for a perceived or actual slight?

These are hard questions, and this book doesn't have all the answers. What lessons can we draw from these anecdotes? Simply that communication and understanding are key—keep the lines open with the Customers and listen very carefully to everything they have to say. The Customer care playing field is continuously evolving and only the fleet will be able to retain their footing. Hopefully the ideas presented in this book will guide the reader to staying ahead and upright.

*Author's note:* On the capitalization of "Customer." Long ago, when I was still active in the field, oscilloscope in one hand, DVOM in the other, I realized that the true source of my pay package was not the company I was working for. The company was only an intermediary. I realized the source was the Customer—they paid me—epiphany event! My whole attitude towards Customers changed and, out of respect and to remind myself of who was boss, I began capitalizing the "C" in all my correspondence. As I climbed the corporate ladder I have kept this habit and have been pleasantly surprised by how many times I get challenged on the capital "C." Every time I'm challenged I get an opportunity to tell the epiphany story, which spreads the message, which reinforces the most important underlying concept—above all, Customers must be treated with respect, and do not forget to apply a little common sense.

# TARGET AUDIENCE

*And who are you?*

The target audience for this book is anyone who wishes to understand the parameters related to Customer care and the creation and maintenance of a Customer satisfaction–driven, world-class contact center. The book will be of use to an individual who has been tasked with the creation or overhaul of a contact center. The methods and lessons found in the book may be applied to any Customer care professional that has world-class support and Customer satisfaction as their primary goals.

The book can be of use to people in the following scenarios:

> As the author is committed to delivering the best possible value, suggestions for improvement are welcome. Please feel free to send your suggestions and comments to Garry Schultz c/o ASQ Quality Press, or to contact Garry directly, e-mail him at jaxschultz@rogers.com

- New VPs, directors, supervisors, and managers in the contact center environment

- Established VPs, directors, supervisors, and managers who are searching for new ideas to supercharge their contact center

- Anyone wishing to move up the corporate ladder from within the contact center (or otherwise)

- Those that have a need to start a contact center from scratch (such as release of a new product that demands Customer support services)

- Those that are considering outsourcing their support challenge

- Those enrolled in a business college or university that have need of a definitive guide to contact centers in the real world

- Professors and teachers of contact center and business unit methodologies and operations

## THE EVOLVING CUSTOMER RELATIONSHIP

*. . . meet ⇒ exceed ⇒ delight ⇒ anticipate ⇒ ?*

A number of publications have given a great deal of exposure to the idea that "the Customer is in control" or "the Customer is king." Many of these publications have positioned this as a (heads up, incoming cliché) *paradigm shift*, as a new idea. I beg to differ. Quality minded businesses, in it for the long run, have long held the Customer as the key and the driver to their long-term success.

Contact center mission statements have evolved from "meet the Customer's expectations" to "exceed the Customer's expectations" to "delight the Customer." I propose that if product and service providers treat the Customer with respect—more as a partner than a consumer—and apply common sense, then all will prosper. The relationship should be more symbiotic than parasitic. In fact, it has been oft said that all businesses need to do is *apply common sense* in every transaction and success will follow. As you read through this book there will be parts that you no doubt have come across before. That is because this book is based on applied common sense, universal truths in business.

If the corporation and, most particularly, the support operation: treat the Customer as a partner; do not underestimate the Customer's intelligence as they are a savvy and sophisticated group; do not attempt to suppress data the Customer base have a right to be aware of as consumers of the product/service; and treat the Customer as the most valued data source for product improvement and evolution (no one knows better than the Customer base), then the operation is on the road to success.

Remember and practice these precepts and Customer satisfaction is bound to follow.

## CUSTOMER SATISFACTION IMPACT FACTOIDS

*Account retention is crucial.*

The following bullets accentuate the need to provide world-class support services:

- The American Management Association estimates that 65 percent of the average company's business comes from repeat customers.

- The Technical Assistance Research Program (TARP) estimates that it costs five times more to attract a new customer than it does to retain an old one.

- There is a nine times greater chance of losing a customer dissatisfied with some aspect of the product or service (including post-sale support).

- Research conducted for the Office of Consumer Affairs indicates that 91 percent of dissatisfied customers will never do business with the offending company again.

- Greater customer loyalty is created by solving a customer problem than if there was no problem encountered at all.

The first four bullets clearly illustrate that Customer satisfaction has a real impact on the bottom line performance of a product/service. The lesson is to treat the Customer base with profound respect for the entire lifecycle of the product/service. The last bullet is included because it is interesting in its implications and utility—support-contacts spawned by design would make a fascinating product feature.

## CONTACT CENTER DEFINITION

*And what is it we are attempting to build?*

The simplest definition: the contact center will provide support services for a product or service. However, there are many models and nuances that differentiate one contact center from another. Each model, or operational mode, has its own set of demands on both the management layer and the personnel dealing with the user base.

To better understand the various operational models, review the following list of operational modes and choices that serve to differentiate one contact center from another:

- Method of contact—What methods or modes of contact are to be supported?

  - Facsimile—general query and sales orders?

  - Phone—general query, sales orders, and support issues?

  - E-mail/Web—general query, FAQ, sales orders, and support issues?

  - Online chat—ICQ chat (instant messaging) , general query, sales orders, and support issues?

  - VoIP (Voice over Internet Protocol)—general query, sales orders, and support issues?

  - Walk-in (over the counter)—returns, general query, sales orders, and support issues?

  - Wireless interaction—up-sell, content refresh, general query, and support?

- Pre-sales support (in addition to post-sale)—Will the contact center be called upon for support services during the sales cycle?

- Twenty-four/seven versus standard nine to five business hours—What are the hours the contact center will operate? Are after-hour or holiday support services needed?

- Incoming versus outgoing calls (mixture perhaps)—Is there a telemarketing or telesales component to the contact center? Will the contact center participate in, or drive, up-sell and account penetration programs?

- Traveling versus non-traveling personnel—Will contact center personnel be expected to travel:

  - To Customer sites for installation support or training sessions?

  - To trade shows to assist with assembling/dismantling or manning the corporate booth?

  - To speak at seminars?

  - In a pre-sales capacity (for example: installation services)?

  - To Customer sites to conduct courses and training sessions?

Once the reasons for travel are delineated, understand and define the frequency for each travel mode.

- Cost center versus profit center—Is the contact center expected to realize a revenue stream?

- Product maturity—How stable is the product? Is it just out of prototype? or has it taken its definitive form?

- What is the expected lifecycle of the product? Are there multiple releases, maintenance releases, and patches?

- Technical demands on contact center personnel—What is the level of technical sophistication demanded by the product? Can the local community provide the needed staff? Do the local colleges provide training courses for contact center personnel?

- User demographics:

  o Define which languages must be supported—English, Spanish, French, and so on.

  o Response expectations—What is the degree of mission-criticality of the supported product? Will Customers demand immediate resolution to an issue? or one hour turnaround time (TAT)? or one day turnaround time? and so on.

  o Technical sophistication—What degree of technical knowledge will the average user possess?

- Enabling technologies—Does the supported product rely on any technologies outside the direct control of the corporation?

- Return processing—Will there be a return stream for the product?

- Billing/invoicing—What is the billing model and what are its complexities?

Many of these areas are expanded upon and explored in this book, others are self-explanatory and require no further discussion. Depending on the target product and support services, some of these areas will have a huge impact on the design and subsequent long-term management of the contact center while others will have minimal impact. It is up to the reader to determine which areas require an in-depth understanding and which areas can be given cursory attention. It is strongly suggested that each section be given adequate attention so that the reader's knowledge of contact center operational modes has as few gaps as possible. It is very difficult to know that which you do not know.

# 2

# Contact Center Structure

## OBJECTIVE

*What may be learned in this chapter.*

The structure of any system is very important to its success. Structure refers to the philosophical constructs as well as the physical placement of teams. This chapter introduces and focuses on the philosophical issues first, and then moves to the more mundane physical attributes that are desirable in a contact center.

This chapter covers the following topics:

- Business models and how they relate to contact center operations

- Key concepts that need to be internalized by all contact center management

- Definition and discussion of the importance of strategic accounts

- Definition and discussion of the issues surrounding issue escalation

- The impact of enabling technologies and partnerships on the contact center

- Hiring, compensation, and employee retention

- The chapter contains a number of lists of questions, which will assist contact center management in focusing and understanding the challenges discussed

## UNDERSTAND THE BUSINESS MODEL

*What is the vision? What direction is the product headed?*

Regardless if the task is to create a contact center from the ground up or if the reader is in a managerial position in an expanding contact center, it is imperative one understand the underlying corporate business model. For instance, if the corporate strategic plan is to operate as an original equipment manufacturer (OEM) in a tiered distribution chain, the contact center may have very little, if any, interaction with the actual user base. In the original equipment manufacturer example, incoming contacts would be from the contact center associated with the distribution chain, that is, business-to-business not business-to-consumer.

Key business model design criteria must be gathered in order to build a contact center that best fits the requirements of the corporation. Before embarking on designing the contact center, ascertain and understand the following:

- Long term—Who *owns* the relationship with the end user of the product or service? Will the contact center deal directly with the end user of the product/service? or is another company acting as the Customer-facing support point? The ramifications are huge; the Customer owner has a great deal more detail work as compared to a company simply providing product in a supply chain. Consider:

  ○ The owner of the Customer relationship will need systems to support a database of the users. This database could potentially be hundreds of thousands of records. Further, the database must contain pertinent details of each Customer and transaction. To be an effective tool it must be easily accessible and searchable in real time. A full help desk database system is mandatory. Compare with a company simply providing product (such as an OEM); they have only one Customer, the distribution channel.

  ○ Call entitlement and enforcement—Is the Customer at the source of the contact entitled to support services? Is the warranty valid? Has the product been abused or used improperly? Is there a return policy and if so what are the operational parameters of the policy? Again, a need for a comprehensive database that supports real-time lookup is called for. The product provider may have a return policy (perhaps complicated by a repair capability) in place with the distribution tier—the underlying logistics need to be understood and managed.

  ○ Billing and invoicing—This is an area overflowing with Customer dissatisfaction potential. Understand that: consumers are relatively tolerant to manuals seemingly written by technical writers with English as a third language; consumers will overlook a couple of bugs in the software; consumers do not mind that the hardware may fail within the warranty period providing you have a fair and expedient return policy; however, consumers have very little tolerance to any anomalies when it comes to invoicing. If the product is a service or contains a recurring billing component the issue is even more pressing. Address issues with billing and invoicing as a matter of highest priority.

    The Customer owner needs to have systems and staff to handle incoming contacts on billing and invoicing. Compare with a company simply providing product, they have only one Customer, they likely have only one bill and one collectible—to the distribution channel.

- Short term—Product maturity drives another aspect of Customer ownership. If the product is in its infancy than it behooves the company to own the Customer relationship. This is to facilitate the gathering of performance data in as direct a communication path as possible. This is the only way to respond to issues with the product in good time (best time); having an intermediary between the company and the Customer only serves to slow down the response time. As the product moves from infancy to adolescence to maturity, the contact center's proximity to the Customer can be reevaluated as the particular market niche demands.

- Forecast data—What story does the sales forecast tell? Does the forecast predict the user base will grow like a rocket? or will adopters of the product come in at a trickle? This data is needed so that the contact center can be adequately staffed before the call volume demands it.

- User's perspective—What challenges does the product itself present to the user?

  ○ Installation challenges—The key parameter is how many contacts are generated during an average installation phase. The worst case is a one-to-one ratio—each Customer attempt to install the product spawns one or more contact events. The further the product is from a one-to-one contact ratio the better. Consider the following: What is the target out-of-box-experience the product management team envisioned for the product? Consider these very different contact center design drivers:

    * Is the target for the user up and running in two minutes?

    * Is there a professional services component to the deployment of the product?

    * What is the prerequisite skill set to install the product?

    * Is the product directed at the man on the street or specialists?

    * Is the product a consumer product or is it an enterprise product?

    * Is the product designed to be used in a stand-alone mode with one user or is it an enterprise (companywide) solution?

    * Are special tools required to install the product?

    * Is access to secure areas required? For example: Is there a need to access firewall or router ports?

    * Alternatively, is access to areas that the common user usually does not access, such as a telephone company junction box, needed?

    * Are ancillary cables or interconnects needed that are not supplied? For example: S-video cables are needed to optimally connect the latest generation video players; ask your mother if she has an S-video cable in the house.

    * How user-friendly is the installation manual? For example: has it been written with the target audience in mind?

&ast; How tolerant is the product to installation gaffes? For example: does the installation clean up after itself? If interconnected incorrectly does the product burst into a plume of smoke?

&ast; Will the product interfere with other products likely to be in the same environment? For example: wireless devices have been known to cause odd behavior in other devices.

- Back-office issues—What are the daily operational challenges the installation and use of the product presents to the end user? Has the product had thorough testing of its ergonomics? As an example: are tools needed to access the battery? Is the product suited to the environment it is most likely to be used in?

- Cost center or profit center—One of the harsh realities of support services is that senior management and the executive often view support as a necessary evil. Post-sale product support is often viewed as an overhead the company is burdened with. It is not desirable to position the contact center as a cost center as cost centers only erode the bottom line. The sooner the contact center can be positioned as a profit center, with a recognized revenue steam, the better. For more information on financial concepts as they relate to the contact center see appendix G—Finance for Contact Center Managers.

- Product maturity—Related to the comments above on "short term," the contact center's ability to be profitable is linked to product maturity. Products in their infancy typically do not have the market share or mind share to support billing for support services. Companies do not penalize early adopters of products by charging them for a service they are actually rendering to the company—providing invaluable feedback. When the product is in its infancy the contact center should be positioned as the authoritative source of product health metrics and opportunities to improve the product as a whole. As the product moves through its lifecycle the contact center should adjust its position to respond and capitalize on revenue opportunities.

---

One corporation had a marketing team adamant in the belief that in order to be competitive, support services had to be available twenty-four/seven. Research into the belief uncovered two facts: marketing's stance was based on the opinion of the VP of marketing (one individual), and the Customer base was resoundingly uninterested in twenty-four/seven support as the product did not lend itself to use outside of business hours. Additional research uncovered the fact that the VP of marketing had come from a firm that was in an overcrowded and fiercely competitive consumer market—with few similarities to the current market. It is best to discard preconceived notions when joining a new team; the business model may be significantly different from the previous environment.

- Customer requirements and needs—Visit the Customer base to proactively solicit their opinion on what services they want and when they need them to be available. Conduct frequent survey exercises and learn from the user community. Just as importantly, conduct surveys on those accounts that choose the competitor's products. Understand what the Customer's key drivers are and respond accordingly.

- Asset management—Is there an asset management component that is provided? If so what controls are in place? How is configuration information gathered? Are there open loops in the system?

There are other factors, but an understanding of the points above will provide a great deal of guidance in determining the type of contact center needed.

# DEFINITION OF SERVICES

*What it is . . .*

This section provides the reader with the framework for defining which services the contact center under construction or study will provide. A number of the key concepts are presented and elaborated on.

## Key Concepts

There are a number of concepts that demand discussion before a definitive list of contact center services can be compiled. Those that have experience on help desks and in support services will be familiar with the majority of the concepts below. The audience for this section is made up of the peers of contact center management—the sales, marketing, engineering, and development departments, finance, and the CEOs. Those that have not made support services a study often need to be calibrated to the realities of supporting Customers.

The concepts are presented in alphabetical order. The label for the concept is followed by a description, then by an example of the application of the concept.

### All Things to All Men—Procedural Concept

Description: The contact center provides specific services. There may be a range of services available, such as Bronze, Silver, and Gold service levels, but the salient thing to bear in mind is that the services are well defined and structured.

Application: Personnel in the contact center are often asked to provide non-standard services to Customers. More often than not the nonstandard service request originates from a member of the sales team. To effectively manage resources, contact center management must know what to expect. Special requests are very disruptive as they:

1. Remove resources from their prime job to service the request, forcing other team members to pick up the slack

> To keep requests for nonstandard services to a minimum, publish a brochure or specification sheet that outlines the services provided. Ensure that the sales team understands what is provided and what is not. Also, initiate a protocol where sales (or others) may request additional services to be considered for the mainstream contact center services suite.

2. Establish precedence with the Customer—do it once and do it forever

3. Create mistakes—specials, by definition, are not governed by protocol and procedure

The services the contact center provides should be thought of with the same discipline as the features and benefits of the product. A member of the sales team would not dream of visiting a software engineer and nonchalantly mentioning one of their accounts would like the financial reporting portion of the product rewritten to their satisfaction.

If a change is needed in the product, in this case the services the contact center provides, a protocol should exist that intelligently handles the enhancement request. A Procedure Change Request (PCR) is submitted which leads to an investigation into the feasibility and universality of the change and either an approval to proceed or a refusal (with justification). The change must go through testing, validation, verification, and finally a Procedure Change Notice (PCN) to be realized. The PCN is then packaged and messaged to all parties including the Customer.

**Sales Differentiator—Value-Add Sales Concept**

Description: The services provided by the contact center should be leveraged as part of the product story.

Application: Build a world-class contact center and then market it as such. There are few products where the consumer of the product does not care about the post-sale support.

- Work with the marketing team to create sales collateral focused on the post-sale support services.

- Create a standard services template document for the sales team that details the services and performance metric targets in use by the contact center.

- Provide the sales team with training so that they understand, in detail, what the contact center does, how it does it, and what the Customer can expect of the contact center.

- Include in the standard services template document all aspects of relevance to the Customer. This should be done so that the Customer can refer to the document for details on any transaction or service the contact center provides that they are entitled to; the Customer's expectations are calibrated.

*Standard Services Template*

The contact center standard services template should include the following sections:

Objective—Outline the purpose of the document.

Responsibility Matrix—Detail exactly *who* is responsible for *what* (see Figure 2.1, Responsibility matrix example). Figure 2.1 is an example of a responsibility matrix between a reseller, a Customer, and a contact center.

Terms—Define terms that have a bearing on the contact center. For example, when does the warranty commence; at the ship event, at the receive event, or at the deployment event? What are the shipping terms? What constitutes an out-of-warranty condition and how are the costs calculated.

Help Desk Structure—Outline the structure of the contact center help desk. Provide a graphic depicting the flow of contacts through the operation. Figure 2.2, Help desk structure, depicts a very basic structure.

Pursuant to the objective of instilling confidence in the capabilities of the contact center, the standard services template should include information on the systems that are in use in the contact center. Document the corrective action protocol, the continuous improvement mechanisms that are in place, and so on.

Escalation—Detail the escalation process for issues that are not resolved via the standard channels. See Figure 2.3, Escalation path, for ideas regarding escalation procedures.

Order Entry—Detail how follow-on orders will be handled. Include examples and copies of purchase orders and any other documentation necessary to process an order. If materials are online, include the Web link address (URL).

| | Customer | Reseller | Contact Center |
|---|:---:|:---:|:---:|
| Installation/deployment | ✓ | | |
| First tier support | ✓ | | |
| Second tier support | | ✓ | |
| Third tier support | | | ✓ |
| Initial fault diagnosis | | ✓ | |
| Verify failure return candidacy | | | ✓ |
| Return ticket generation | | | ✓ |
| Ship replacement | | | ✓ |
| Repair/replace device | | | ✓ |
| Update install (client side) | | ✓ | |
| Update install (service side) | ✓ | | |
| Out-of-warranty costs | ✓ | | |

**Figure 2.1**  Responsibility matrix example.

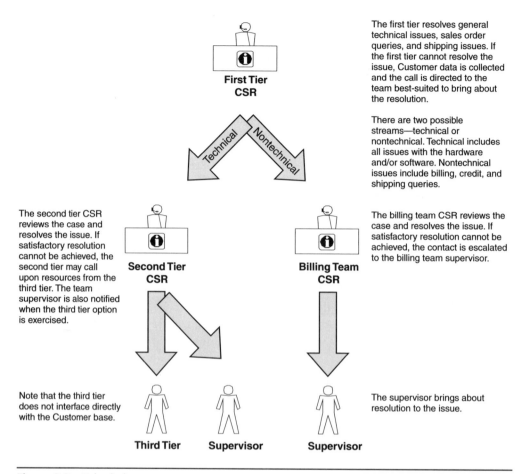

The first tier resolves general technical issues, sales order queries, and shipping issues. If the first tier cannot resolve the issue, Customer data is collected and the call is directed to the team best-suited to bring about the resolution.

There are two possible streams—technical or nontechnical. Technical includes all issues with the hardware and/or software. Nontechnical issues include billing, credit, and shipping queries.

The second tier CSR reviews the case and resolves the issue. If satisfactory resolution cannot be achieved, the second tier may call upon resources from the third tier. The team supervisor is also notified when the third tier option is exercised.

The billing team CSR reviews the case and resolves the issue. If satisfactory resolution cannot be achieved, the contact is escalated to the billing team supervisor.

Note that the third tier does not interface directly with the Customer base.

The supervisor brings about resolution to the issue.

**Figure 2.2** Help desk structure.

Returns—Detail the product return procedure. Include examples of any paperwork or URLs that are needed.

Contact Information—Collect telephone numbers and contact details (e-mail, instant message service address, and so on) for all pertinent members of the team supporting the account such as, the contact center project manager, the Customer's project manager, the account manager (sales), support teams, and so on.

Performance Metrics—This is most important section. Document all the performance metrics that bear relevance to the account. For example, include:

- Hours of operation
- Holiday support services
- Support desk rings before pickup target
- Support desk problem resolution time target

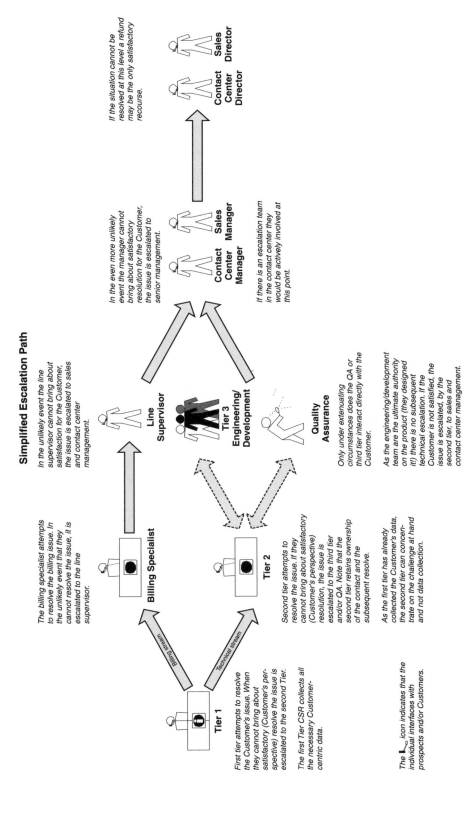

**Figure 2.3** Escalation path.

- Order entry turnaround time (the time between when they place an order and when the product arrives)

- Failed product return turnaround time (the time between when the Customer returns a failed product and when they receive either a replacement or the fixed original unit)

- Software update frequency and access details

Glossary—Include a glossary of all technical terms or terms that may be subject to interpretation used in the document itself.

To further get the message across, and as a value-added service, visit prospects with the sales team and take a portion of the presentation time to expound on the capabilities of the contact center. Provide tours of the contact center facility for Customers and prospects. Display the controls and capability built into the systems in the contact center. Publish performance metrics so that the Customer base can appreciate the excellence of the full product experience.

### First Contact—Performance Concept

Description: "First contact" refers to the very worthy target of resolving all issues on the "first contact." That is, no call-back is needed, no research time is required, and the CSR had the answer at hand in real time.

Application: Self-explanatory for the most part. A related concept is "Top $x$ Issues."

### Perspective on Failure Modes—Empathy/Understanding Concept

Description: Product failure modes and how they are articulated through an organization is a Pandora's box of misunderstanding and misinformation, particularly when there is that healthy passion about a product that marks the most successful ones.[1] This concept is one the contact center managers must understand when conversing with their peers in other departments.

Application: It is given that the contact center is the definitive source for performance data on a product. The contact center will be expected to generate raw data if not full reports on a product's performance in the field. Be as precise as possible and remove as much subjectivity as possible from the performance reports. Review Figure 4.21, Data plot, top failure modes, on page 143 and consider the following.

The target audience for product performance reports is made up of quality and engineering teams, subsequently, it is important to clearly indicate the data source. The discerning quality engineer will want to know the source for the failure modes as there is often a huge difference between what the Customer may claim and what the actual failure mode is. In most support cycles, there are three "opinion" or perspective points on any given failure:

1. What the Customer claims. For example: ". . . it's making a terrible noise when I power it up."

2. The CSR diagnoses: "It is probably the hard drive, please take the unit into our repair depot."

3. The depot repair technician's repair action: "One of the front panel control cables was rubbing against the power supply fan; securing the cable to the panel raiser rectified the problem."

From this example there are three separate, potential failure mode areas: noisy, the hard drive, and an unsecured cable. And the repair technicians may be wrong—there very well may be a cable rubbing against the power supply fan but perhaps the hard drive doesn't start to "make a terrible noise" until it has burned in for twelve hours. All three perspectives are important to report on and analyze. As follows:

1. Quality engineer: The quality engineer is interested in that there may be issues with securing internal cables. An analysis of the frequency of the issue and an analysis of the potential fixes and their cost implications should be conducted. The quality engineer would also be interested in the Customer's original comment, "terrible noise." An astute quality engineer would be interested in what constitutes a "terrible noise," and they would then want to quantify and qualify the noise.

2. Contact center: The contact center manager needs to know if additional training is needed and, as per the quality engineer, if an analysis of the frequency of misdiagnosis is needed. The manager also needs to know if the frequency of this failure is high enough that the knowledge base needs to be updated with a description and action for this failure mode.

    The contact center manager perceives a number of ancillary concerns, such as: to better serve the Customers, is it possible to isolate the cable noise and sample it as a digital sound file (.wav format)? The sampled .wav file could provide the CSRs with a reference they could listen to when talking a Customer through the issue. And, being that the cost to resolve this issue impacts the contact center hardest, a recommendation for a Customer self-fix kit, for those that are inclined, could be made available; a small kit with a tie-wrap, a drawing, and detailed instructions could be fabricated.

3. Engineering: The engineering department typically does not give a wit for what the claim was or what the CSR thought it was. The design engineer does care, however, that the cables are working themselves loose for both the noise issue and the potential hazard of the insulation becoming eroded and shorting to the frame.

    To conclude this example, the design engineer puts his head together with the quality engineer and concludes that a $0.0025 tie-wrap is the fix. As the material cost is minimal and the impact on the assembly line is equally minimal, the engineer proceeds with an Engineering Change Notice (ECN) and any new product rolling off the line is secured with said tie-wrap.

One simple failure, but three separate perspectives on what it is. It is critical to understand who the audience(s) is, their needs, and the proper perspective regarding the data points being delivered.

### Resource Pool—Customer Satisfaction As a Function of Resource Planning Concept

Description: This concept has more relevance based on the size of the contact center; small operations are not as affected as the larger contact centers.

Optimal use of the resources at hand is the goal of all managers. In a contact center environment, contact volume, timing, and resolution are tracked and analyzed, and resources (personnel and tools) are deployed appropriately. But as with most statistical analysis exercises, averages and majority trends are the key data points; one-offs[2] and exceptions compromise the analysis. Consider that it is very difficult to meet service level agreement (SLA) performance metrics when the Customer base does not follow established channels.

There are two prevalent methods for approaching one-offs: attempt to accommodate them, or convince Customers to use the contact center as a pool of resources.

Application: One-offs and exceptions refer to any action that does not follow standard channels; they are, by definition, operationally disruptive. For statistical analysis to effectively drive staffing levels over time, it must be assumed that the contacts will be distributed equally across the staff. The most common one-off situation is where a Customer gets into the habit of calling the contact center and requesting to speak with a specific CSR. This is undesirable because the potential for Customer dissatisfaction is actually increased by the one-to-one relationship because at any given time the CSR the Customer is looking for is:

- Already on a call. Therefore, the Customer must be put on hold. The result is dissatisfaction.

- Not available due to training, vacation, shift change, break, sick leave, and so on. The result is dissatisfaction.

- Not available due to job transfer (a tenacious Customer will often try to raise a CSR known to them). The result is dissatisfaction.

The more tenacious the Customer is, the more disruptive they become, and the more Customers engaging in this behavior the more difficult it is to have adequate staff on the phone system queue. If the Customer leaves a message for their special CSR to call them back, the CSR has to log off the phone queue system, place the call (with the attendant telecommunications charges), and deal with the Customer not being available and being put on hold. This is not scalable and certainly does not serve the Customer base as a whole.

Sales staff tapping into specific CSRs further exacerbates the situation. The result is the same; the analysis models driving the staffing levels are compromised. Additionally, as the sales staff tend to pick the stars of the contact center for their special Customer issues, the overall Customer experience suffers.

The solution is simple. Convince the Customer base and sales staff to use the contact center as a "pool of resources." Once used as a pool, the contact center management can confidently publish SLA performance metrics and then staff to meet those performance metrics.

The alternative is to condone and support the one-to-one relationship. The restricting issues are scalability, critical mass, and the impact on performance metrics. The question that must be resolved is, how many one-to-one relationships can a CSR support? If the revenue margins are high enough, one-to-one can be supported and the company can remain profitable. The cost, however, is very high. Perhaps the one-to-one capability is extended only to strategic accounts in which case we are full circle back to the contact center being structured as a "pool" for the nonstrategic accounts.

## Empowerment

Employee empowerment is a term that has come into vogue in the past few years. The idea behind empowerment has a great deal of merit; provide the Customer-facing personnel with the authority to grant the Customer what they are entitled to. If the Customer was overbilled, empowerment allows the CSR to issue a credit immediately. In the event that the Customer was misinformed and subsequently dissatisfied with the performance of the service, empowerment provides the CSR with the authority to issue a full credit immediately. In brief, empowerment is the CSR being able to act on the idea of "I can take care of that for you right now." Empowerment is a great concept, but the road to enabling employee empowerment is a difficult one.

There are many difficulties in enabling empowerment, not the least being *real-time decisions* require *real-time systems*. There are two lists below that outline the challenges. The lists are divided into two broad categories: Customer verification (Customer- and system-centric) issues and integrity verification (trust-centric) issues.

### Customer Verification

Before the CSR can issue a correction credit they must verify that the caller:

- Is in fact a legitimate Customer—A lookup in the Customer relationship management system (CRM) must be initiated.

- Is registered for services—In the event Customer registration is mandatory before services are extended a lookup on the registration database is needed.

- Is entitled to a credit—If the Customer's account is past due then a credit is premature. A lookup on the financial accounts receivable database is needed.

- Has, in fact, been billed-in error—The CSR must ascertain if the Customer's claim is legitimate. A lookup on the billing engine system (financial system perhaps) in tangent with a lookup on the subscription management system is needed. The CSR must then correlate the data from the two systems.

*Integrity Verification*

Then there is the challenge of human nature in the presence of monetary gain. Can the following issues be mitigated?

- Has an opportunistic Customer found a technical loophole that enables them to legitimately issue credit requests before the credit can be validated?

- Is a CSR in collusion with an alleged Customer?

- How much should a CSR be able to authorize? $10, $100, or $1,000? What happens once the CSR's threshold is exceeded?

The CSR must balance these Customer and system issues while speaking to the Customer. Management must grapple with the trust issues.

There are many difficulties and many more will surface as the corporation learns, but employee empowerment is a necessary attribute—Customers demand it. As with many aspects of the personnel comprising a contact center, the degree of discretion allowed the CSRs is tempered with trust on the part of the management team.

Some existing operations are far too rigid and regimented to support any degree of empowerment. A forklift overhaul may be the fastest route to a successful overhaul in such cases. Consider the following points:

1. The latitude given to a CSR must be well documented.

2. The training program must train and test so that CSRs are confident of the latitude they are provided, and how and when to exercise it.

3. The management team must expect and contend with mistakes, for they will be made. Corrective action plans are necessary if the mistake run rate is inordinately high.

**Abuse Standards—Procedural Concept**

Description: The CSRs need to have a firm understanding of what is acceptable behavior on the part of the Customers.

Application: CSRs take a great deal of abuse. They should know that they can expect and rely on management's full support in the event that a situation cannot be defused and the Customer resorts to verbal abuse. Management must stand behind the staff. Scripts should be created for abusive situations complete with the actions open to the Customer, documentation procedure, and the protocol for raising flags and warnings in the CRM system. Note that situations where Customers become abusive are an excellent use of the ability to record and play back contacts.

**Service Level Agreement (SLA)—Total Quality Management (TQM), Customer Satisfaction, and Sales Concept**

Description: World-class contact centers have published performance targets. These include target metrics such as: number of rings before the phone is answered, maximum time a Customer will be on hold, target turnaround time on an issue that is not resolved on first contact, and so on.

The document where the performance targets are detailed is known as a service level agreement or SLA. Some business models support one universal set of performance targets while other, usually more specialized, businesses define performance targets for each account. Some business models demand that each account may have its own discrete SLA.

At a minimum, every contact center should have a baseline SLA. The baseline SLA details the minimum performance targets all Customers can expect. The baseline document also serves as the starting point for those accounts that demand, and are willing to pay for, specialized performance targets.

Application: There are four areas to understand about SLA administration and application.

*Baseline*—The baseline SLA defines the performance targets for all personnel in the contact center. Each manager and supervisor focuses on ensuring that his or her team is meeting or exceeding the baseline. Once a baseline metric is being comfortably met, there is opportunity to raise the bar and tighten the metric (continuous improvement concept).

*Sales*—The baseline SLA defines the performance targets that the sales team can put forth to allay any concerns the prospect may have regarding post-sale support. In this context, the SLA can assist in closing deals.

*Customized*—In extreme cases the sales team can leverage the baseline SLA and use it as a starting point to define, under the guidance of contact center management, a specialized SLA that precisely meets the requirements of the target account. Proceed with caution, however, when negotiating customized SLAs as Customers can be very creative in their requests.

If a customized agreement is the only way to secure the business, it is highly desirable to have all costs associated with the tighter performance metrics absorbed by the account. The astute contact center manager will proceed with caution as what appears to be a minor incremental change to the baseline SLA can spawn hidden costs. A unique SLA needs to be managed, administrated, measured, and reported on—the costs accumulate quickly. In this context, the SLA defines special circumstances and is a potential revenue stream.

In the event that the customized agreement is too difficult to execute, "No" is a plausible answer to the request for enhanced services. As difficult as it may be, especially for the sales team, sometimes it makes more sense to walk away from the business.

*Penalties*—In the most extreme cases, the SLA may invoke penalty clauses for nonperformance. For example, if the service level falls below threshold $x$ for time $y$, the contact center will credit the account $z$ dollars. Penalty clauses usually are more common in direct service providers (an Internet service provider for instance) than in contact centers, but some accounts the contact center serves may demand penalties.

## Statistical Deviation—Customer Satisfaction and Sales Concept

Description: Contacts, on occasion, will fall outside the SLA targets. If the management of the contact center has established reasonable performance targets, deviation from the targets should be infrequent and minor. There will, however, be times when the performance metrics are off target. Two reasons jump to the forefront: the contact center itself has experienced a failure, or the contact statistically falls outside the target but, when averaged, is acceptable.

Application: Every contact center manager has heard claims of outrageous on-hold time and experience has shown that exaggeration is rampant (review the PBX log for the actual on-hold time). To allay this, for it is very real and common, the contact center management team must educate the Customer base. Statistical techniques and application of averages must be understood by contact center management and sales personnel so that when confronted, they have a plausible explanation for the alleged violation.

In the event a Customer confronts the contact center management with a claim of a breach of the SLA, the data surrounding the claim must be analyzed. It must be clear when communicating with Customers (and the sales team) that performance targets are based on statistical averages. There will be instances where a Customer may be on-hold for an excessive period (beyond the published performance metrics), but the statistical average on-hold time can still remain within the published bounds.

## Top *x* Issues—Continuous Improvement Concept

Description: The Top *x* Issues report lists the top issues in order of frequency of contact. The report answers the question, What issues are the CSRs dealing with most often? In practice, the number of issues ($x$) is defined as how many issues the organization can focus corrective action on. The most popular number is ten—ergo the "Top 10 Issues."

Application: The first challenge is to put a system in place that captures the reasons Customers are contacting the contact center and then quantifies and qualifies the reasons. One approach is to assign codes to the most common reasons for contact so that the CSRs can quickly key the code into a help desk system or a database or spreadsheet.

The target is to eradicate the top reasons Customers call in (that is, complain). Once the data is gathered it can be analyzed for root cause and a corrective action can be effected to reduce the core reason (cause). Often the root cause analysis will reveal a number of causes that are easy and economical to remedy. These easy/economical remedies are often labeled "low-hanging fruit." Do not hesitate to pick the low-hanging fruit immediately and concentrate on the more challenging causes soon after.

Classifying and dividing the issues into areas of expertise can assist with managing the corrective actions. For example: the top 10 issues for an example product could be classified into the following:

- Product failure—The product has a failure mode that many Customers have experienced. This could be anywhere in the lifecycle of the product, from installation to event-driven (such as changing the battery) to normal use. The engineering and development teams own this type of corrective action; it is the engineering and development teams' job to design the failure out.

- Training—The Customer *perceives* a failure that can be mitigated by educating the Customer. This is particularly true in situations tagged as *finger problems.* A finger problem is where the Customer is doing something they should not that is directly or indirectly causing the failure. An example of a finger problem is the continued failure of a starter motor in a car. On analysis it surfaces that the Customer is in the habit of engaging the starter motor (turning the key as if starting the car) while the engine is running. This action causes premature wearing of the motor and subsequent failure. The technical writers (those who write the user's manual) and the training team own the corrective action. The remedy is to document and train the user base better.

- Documentation—The Customer follows the documented procedures yet the desired result does not follow. The technical writers own the corrective action; the manual set is first to be reviewed for technical accuracy. Second order is to review the manual set for usability. A usability analysis focuses on the content in the context of the target end users—can the manual set be interpreted correctly by the prime target?

- Billing—The Customer's bill is in error. The finance or operations department owns the corrective action.

Tracking and eradicating the top issues drives continuous improvement. Customers will be delighted when the top failure modes are eradicated, however, a new set of top issues always surfaces—hopefully not as universal or serious as the original top issues, but issues nonetheless.

If the corrective action lies outside of the direct influence of the contact center, there may be push-back on applying the resources to affect the remedy; that is, the issue's corrective action owner will not assign resources to rectify it. To overcome the objection, the contact center manager must leverage two aspects: the hidden cost of Customer dissatisfaction and the hard cost inherent in dealing with the issue. If the sum of these two costs is greater than the objector's cost then it simply makes good business to effect the corrective action. Collect the data in the format needed to convince the objector and the issue will be addressed.

See "Top Ten Issues," page 142, for information on refining and training staff to deal with the top issues. See Figure 4.21 Data plot, top failure modes, page 143, for an example of a graphic plot of top issues.

### Business Rules—Procedural Concept

Description: Business rules refer to the protocol(s) that control the processing of transactions.

Application: The optimal application of business rules occurs when the actions initiated by contact center personnel are governed and enforced by the system (software application) being used. Management defines the rules, and personnel are trained as to what these rules are, but it is the underlying software application the personnel use to process business that executes the rules. By design, the personnel using the systems are disallowed from making procedural mistakes, and the decisions most crucial to the business are actually made by business rules embedded in a software application. The better the rules are defined, the better the system operates.

An example: Review Figure 2.4, Business rule example.

This example rule is focused on approval for credit. The regional manager can approve a transaction below $10,000, however, a transaction above $10,000 demands a full credit check and financial search to be conducted on the prospect.

In long form: *if a transaction value is greater than $10,000, a full credit check must be conducted to prove the prospect's liquidity before credit is extended. If the transaction value is less than $10,000, the regional manager may approve the credit.*

There are two ways of enforcing the rule: train personnel on the rules and hope they get it right, or hard-code[3] the rules into the order entry system thereby removing human error from the procedure.

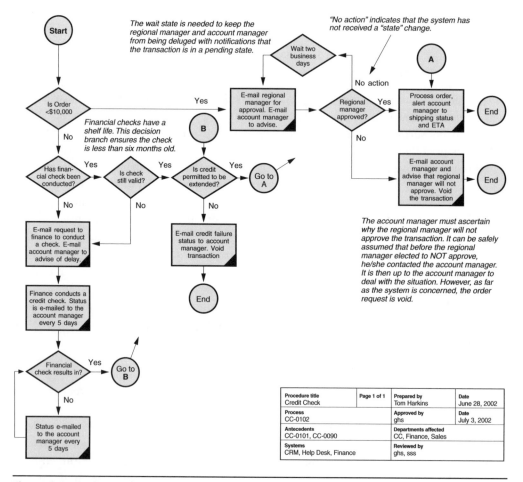

**Figure 2.4** Business rule example.

Expanding on the example, the order entry system could be programmed so that when an order is keyed into the system it automatically checks the monetary value and, depending on a hard-coded threshold, the system can do one of three things:

1. If under the threshold ($10,000), send a note via e-mail to the appropriate regional manager informing them that their approval is needed, and send an additional e-mail to the account manager so that he or she knows the deal is pending the regional manager's approval.

2. If over the threshold and a financial search has already (recently) been conducted deeming the account a good credit risk, process the order and send notes to the account manager and the finance department alerting them that the system self-processed a credit decision.

3. If over the threshold, send a note to the finance department requesting that they conduct a full financial search on the account *and* send a note to the account manager alerting them that the order is pending (they then contact the Customer to explain the delay and align expectations). The system retains the order in limbo (pending) until finance clears the credit. As an added customer-centric value-added feature, the system can remind all parties on a regular basis that this business remains pending (nothing falls through the cracks).

Review Figure 2.4, Business rule example, again but this time consider that all the decisions—all the diamond shaped branch points—are made by the software application and not order entry personnel.

Apply similar logic and business rules to all transactions, from taking calls to requisitioning spares, and fewer mistakes will be made. Customer satisfaction will increase.

### Negativity—Stress/Mental Health Concept

Description: The personnel working in a contact center environment are subjected to negativity on a regular basis. Customers complain, sales complains, and, on occasion, senior management may complain as well. The contact center is the closest thing resembling a lose/lose dynamic in a corporation. The key to managing the stress of this negative environment is to understand it and face it.

Application: Star contact center managers are those that inspire confidence, motivate, and nurture a healthy culture in the contact center in the face of a constant stream of negativity. Not all good managers can make it in the contact center environment, and vice versa, not all good contact center managers can make it elsewhere in the corporation. Successful contact center managers have a balanced mix of people skills, empathy, stress management, and tenacity. Find these people and hire them.

It is an odd paradox that the better a contact center is being managed the less is heard from it. If the sales team is having an above average quarter, everyone in the corporation knows. The engineering team has new product output as their visible triumph, while marketing thrives on visibility and exposure. Manufacturing has tangible product to manage the logistics of, and finance . . . OK, finance is like the contact center, the smoother the operation the less is heard from them. As contact center managers, it is important to be aware of this dynamic. Hunt out exposure and visibility opportunities; do not be perceived as the "bearer of bad news" all the time.

Celebrate success and do not let an opportunity to reinforce exemplary performance pass. Congratulate performance frequently and do so in front of the employee's peers. As management it is paramount to be seen in the center, to be seen that management understands what is going on in the front lines, takes calls, and is always available for escalations. Consult with the customer support representatives; get their ideas first hand and be sure to acknowledge the source once an action comes from a suggestion. Frequently show up on the graveyard shift, on Sundays, and on holidays. Be seen and heard.

## STRATEGIC ACCOUNTS

*Success depends on retaining the sanction of the strategic accounts.*

A strategic account is an account that has special status within the corporation. Typically a strategic account has impact regarding the success of a product or service. There are no industrywide criteria for an account to be granted strategic account status; each corporation has their own definition and criteria. Some of the more widely adopted criteria include:

- The account is in the Fortune/Global 1000. The fact that they use the product provides a degree of sanction and prestige. This account is particularly valuable if they agree to allow the corporation to use their name in sales and marketing brochures and during the sales cycle. Many corporations, and most of the corporations in the Fortune/Global 1000, have rules and guidelines for the use of their trademarks.

- The account is willing to act as a reference for future sales. Often during the sales cycle, prospects request a reference account, that is, an existing Customer using the product that they can talk to who is willing to give an honest appraisal of the product.

- The account is an influential industry pundit (often a television personality or in the employ of an influential publisher). There are individuals who are so widely seen and read that their opinions and insights can make or break a product. This is particularly true in the high-technology sector.

  While it is true that the first two types of strategic accounts mentioned expect preferential treatment in return for their sanction (expressed or not), the pundit, representing the best interests of the consumer, is often more interested in the product as experienced by the average consumer. The pundit, therefore, may not want to be treated as a strategic account and often, pursuant to this, may not identify themselves to contact center staff. This speaks to the idea that all Customers should be treated exceptionally well—all are strategic.

- The account is responsible for a healthy proportion of the revenue stream. Perhaps they are not members of the Fortune/Global 1000, but if they are, in effect, underwriting your checks, treat them with great respect.

- The account is an early adopter of the product and subsequently they are owed special status.

- The account may be a feeder into larger accounts, such as a subsidiary of a Fortune/Global 1000 account. Get a sale into the subsidiary, perhaps even subsidize the sale, and leverage the relationship to crack into the Fortune/Global 1000 account.

- The account may not have any revenue associated with it. Consider if the product is installed at the venture capitalist (VC) firm that is funding the corporation. To secure future investment, it would be prudent to ensure the product is performing at their site as advertised in the executive pitch made to them.

- The account may have requested and paid for preferential treatment. Consider an account that likes the product but does not like the standard services provided by the contact center. If formal support contracts are not part of the contact center business model, grant the account strategic status and draw up the a support contract within the context of an SLA.

- The account may be part of the business development program. Typically these accounts serve a similar Customer base to the one already being served.

- The account may be an alliance partner (business development). There are a number of different types of alliance partners, a few examples of which follow:

  - Technological: The partner's technology is key to the product (such as a router manufacturer to an Internet service provider).

  - Sales: The partner provides a sales channel (such as a retail music store to a manufacturer of pianos).

  - System integrator: The partner provides essential services that enable the sale of the product (such as a professional services vendor to an enterprise resource management software developer).

  - Creditability/value added: The fact that you are aligned with the partner leads credibility to the product (such as a telecommunications carrier to a wireless start-up).

There are many reasons an account demands preferential treatment. The bottom line is that strategic accounts get treated with extra special care.

Each strategic account should have an SLA in force. This ensures that the strategic account management understands the performance metrics the company will be delivering to. The downside of each strategic account having its own SLA is in the administration of the agreements. As stated in the section on SLAs, it behooves the organization to keep individual variance in SLAs to a minimum.

The key issue is determining which Customers qualify for a higher degree of care. The sales team will request (nay, demand) that all their accounts qualify as strategic accounts. Marketing will request that industry pundits, consultants, and analysts be given strategic account status. Tier 2 support will request that some accounts require strategic account status because of their high-maintenance nature. Revenue may also drive who qualifies for the strategic account status. Create, with sales and marketing, criteria for strategic account eligibility and then adhere to them; however, prepare to be flexible.

Be prepared to administer *temporary* strategic account status to any given account. The sales team may have a need to pamper a particular account for a brief period as opposed to the rest of the time. In this instance it is not feasible, nor desirable, to initiate, negotiate, and sign off on a formal SLA. Isolate the areas of exposure that are of interest to the account and deliver to their expectations. One caveat is that it is important to ensure their expectations are executable and feasible within economic constraints.[4]

# ESCALATION PATH

*The normal flow . . .*

Escalation paths are needed for all situations that cannot be contained at the level the contact originated at. Escalations can proceed on technical grounds from less technical to more technical personnel within the contact center. Escalations can cross departmental boundaries from technical contact center personnel to personnel in the quality control or engineering departments. Escalations can be effected within a team on a seniority basis from a new employee to a seasoned veteran, or, as contact center professionals receive the most flak on, from anywhere in the organization to senior management. Each escalation permutation requires guidelines and time frames.

A clear understanding of the escalation path is necessary for not only the contact center personnel, but also for sales and other departments in the organization. Each party in the escalation path must provide time frame expectations and target service levels. This is so that Customers' expectations may be established. For example, there is great power in the second tier representative being able to confidently tell the Customer, ". . . your issue has been escalated to our third tier, and I expect status from them within three hours." It is important to publish (internally and perhaps externally as well) the set of guidelines so that all personnel understand what can be expected.

Service levels are particularly important for those departments that are outside the bounds of the contact center, such as engineering, quality, and sales. If internal service levels are not established, then the contact center cannot set the Customer expectations and dissatisfaction will follow. As above, publish the guidelines and time frames so there are no surprises in the organization.

For additional information and discussion on escalations, see Figure 4.12, Data plot, escalation percentage, page 123, and review the analysis that precedes the data plot.

# ESCALATIONS, EXCEPTIONS TO THE PATH

*You do what you do and we will do what we do . . .*

There will be times when the published escalation path is undermined or short-circuited. It is in the contact center manager's best interest to keep deviations from the path to a minimum as each deviation has a number of negative effects. First, all deviations are, by their very nature, disruptive and pull resources from their scheduled activities. Second, allowing a deviation sets precedent with both the Customer and the internal champion (sales, manager, board member, and so on). Once the Customer knows they can call their champion for expedient support, they will not follow standard procedure. In addition, the internal champion learns that jumping the support queue is effective but wonders why the contact center cannot process contacts to their *other* Customers' satisfaction. In fact, the queue-jump experience undermines their confidence in the support capability of the contact center.

Contact center management must spend time educating internal departments as to how the contact center is structured. Contact center procedures and support mechanisms should be part of the orientation for, at a minimum, all Customer-facing employees and, optimally, all employees. Personnel must be taught to direct Customers to the normal support channels. All personnel that come in contact with the Customer base must be armed with a thorough understanding of the services and performance metrics by which the contact center is governed.

In the case of sales personnel, once this knowledge is imparted and internalized they can then differentiate between an egregious Customer claim and a justified Customer claim. In a negative or hostile situation, the informed employee can defuse egregious claims and direct Customers to the proper channel for resolve. In the event the hostile situation is justified, the informed employee can act as the Customer champion and bring the issue to the attention of the appropriate contact center manager (or director or VP).

*Sales must let it go . . .*

By far the most counterproductive manifestation of this dynamic is when a member of the sales team does not relinquish a Customer relationship. In this instance the

---

A particularly difficult situation to correct is when a Customer gains the ear of the CEO. CEOs can draw on and focus resources like no one else in an organization. The subsequent resolve usually delights the Customer, however, the learned behavior is that the Customer will leverage the CEO time and time again, drawing the CEO into one minor episode after another, consuming valuable time with relatively routine matters. The CEO will finally appeal to the contact center management; ". . . stop this guy from calling me!" The necessary behavior modification is not with the Customer, it is with the CEO. CEOs must be accessible, but not *too* accessible (it is a fine line they tread, and the astute CEO knows how to redirect a Customer through the normal channels).

Customer resists normal channels, the contact center, when they have issues, and they call the salesperson that courted them and made the initial sale. As this dynamic is widespread, it bears analysis and comment.

The Customer will never cease leveraging the relationship with the salesperson if they perceive the salesperson to be expediting their issue. The upside is huge for the Customer—personalized care. The downside is devastating for the sales organization— as the sales team adds more and more Customers to the roster, they find themselves spending more and more time expediting support calls and therefore less and less time securing additional sales. Worse yet for the contact center personnel is that when sales personnel walk down the hall (or telephone or e-mail) and tap directly into contact center resources, they are jumping the queue. Jumping the queue is highly disruptive to the discipline and controls that are in place. Performance metrics cannot be met if the system is continually being end-run.

The sales team must be instructed to direct the Customers to the normal support and service channels. The sales team must be armed with a thorough understanding of the services and performance metrics by which the contact center is governed. Once sales personnel have this knowledge they can then differentiate between an egregious Customer claim and a justified Customer claim. The salesperson defuses egregious claims and makes it clear to the Customer that it is in their best interest to follow the normal channel. Of course, in the event the claim is justified, the salesperson can act as the Customer champion and bring the issue to the attention of the appropriate contact center manager (or director or VP).

## ENABLING TECHNOLOGIES

*The product's success hinges upon others' performance.*

From a support perspective the optimal product is completely stand-alone—zero dependencies on technologies or environments beyond the host corporation's direct control. The Customer experience with a stand-alone product is completely under direct control. The product's success is a closed loop with the host corporation being in the advantageous position of owning all the parameters for success.

In most markets there are very few products that have zero dependencies. Using high technology as an example, there are products that are closely coupled to the host operating system (OS) layer, hardware configuration, and dependencies on the Internet. Examples abound, from software products that have hooks into the host OS to wireless handheld devices that are beholden to the wireless network carriers.

The majority of corporations have come to understand their dependencies and how to manage accordingly. A component of business development is focused on supply-chain management and dependency mitigation with all the attendant operational logistics. Unless the contact center has its own representation in the business development team, however, it is unlikely that these enabler/vendor/partner relationship dependency mitigation efforts will be seen in the contact center. Business development, product management and the legal department may have established tight working relationships with the enabling vendors/partners, but often the contact center team has been left in the cold.

It is beyond the scope of this book to delve into vendor and supply chain management best-practices and techniques. Suffice to say that close ties are needed with all vendor/partners that directly or indirectly affect the Customer experience. If the company's product is in a position where an enabling technology can have a negative impact on the user community, it is prudent to work with the vendor/partner to establish operational parameters governed by a formal SLA (see the section titled "Service Level Agreements," page 148, for additional information). In all probability, the relationship with the vendor/partner is symbiotic—your success is their success. In other words, the more units you sell (for example, pagers) the more units the vendor/partner sells (continuing the example, airtime contracts). Alternatively, you may be directly reselling the vendor/partner's product or be in a revenue pass-through relationship. (A pass-through is a business model where a transaction is processed by one entity on behalf of a silent entity. Revenue is passed-through to the silent entity untouched by the corporation processing the transaction.) Regardless of the nature of the relationship, ties and data-flow must be established between your corporate contact center and the vendor/partner's contact center. Areas to be concerned with include:

- Vendor/partner software releases or updates that may impact the product

- Vendor/partner hardware releases or updates that may impact the product

- Service disruptions including remedial maintenance (RM), preventive maintenance (PM), and corrective action (CA) events

- Pricing model changes that may impact the user community

However, and this is a *big* however, tight relations with the vendor/partner's operations teams and SLAs have little meaning when the enabling technology suffers a failure. When the Customer's device fails to operate, the Customer really does not care if the source of the problem is actually with an enabling technology partner. The Customer only desires restored operation and, perhaps, a credit for the inconvenience of the failure.

An interesting addendum to the practice of entering into SLAs to protect corporate business interests is the fact that one hopes to never have to leverage the penalties called up in such an agreement. It is best for all if the parties simply deliver the services to specification.

The remedy is to get involved in business development at the beginning of a partnership. Get into the business development mind-set and become a part of the team. Consider a business development role within the contact center.

## SUPPORT FOR ENABLING TECHNOLOGIES

*What we say and what we do.*

The last section (Enabling Technologies) established the concept that the contact center needs strong ties with vendors/partners. What actually happens in the contact center when Customers have issues with enabling technologies is often quite different from what should occur. The following three sections, "We Don't Do Windows," explore this theme.

# WE DON'T DO WINDOWS—I

*Runaway train.*

If there are enabling technologies intrinsic to the product offering, chances are very good that calls will be made into the contact center regarding these enabling technologies. The amount of aggravation these contacts present is directly related to the soft and hard costs associated with the contacts. As such:

$$AG = Qty \times T \times CPC \times LO$$

Where:

AG = Aggravation to the corporation.

Qty = Quantity or number of calls.

T = Time of day (not to be confused with duration). Contacts made during peak business hours have a higher Customer-dissatisfaction potential than contacts made during off hours.

CPC (cost per call) = The hard costs, which is another formula:

$$duration \times burden\ rate \times capital \times overhead$$

LO (lost opportunity) = While the contact center personnel are online with a Customer experiencing issues with an enabling technology, they are not available to take calls from your Customers that have issues with *your* technology. This is a "lost opportunity."

Use the formula and variables to gauge the effect of a failure on the enabling partners part. Then manage the situation so that the hard and soft costs are minimized.

The worst-case manifestation of this aggravation is when an enabling technology partner experiences endemic failures. The company supporting the product that depended on the enabling technology would experience a dramatic increase in call density during these endemic failures, which, in turn, would cause the contact center to default on their SLA, which would spawn more calls, which would further exacerbate the problem. Applying some numbers to this example:

- Trigger event—The original failure experienced by the enabler was one hour.

- The additional load—The contact center contact volume quickly rose to 250 percent above normal levels.

- Recover time—The contact center would catch up with the load queue three hours after the original failure.

- Secondary effect—The Customers generated further contacts, at a very senior level, to complain "When we needed your support *most* we could not get through for three hours!"

This is a clear example of a runaway-train dynamic driving Customer dissatisfaction to new depths. The irony is that it was not the contact center's host company's failure that put the train in motion. It was the enabler that was at the root. The recovery costs for the call volume spike are large, but the real cost in lost confidence and Customer dissatisfaction is staggering (two additional soft costs).

A similar but less concentrated scenario unfolds with software updates or the addition of dynamic link library (DLL) files or infrastructure changes at Customer sites. To be prepared for any and all contingencies, it is prudent to run a comprehensive FMEAC exercise. See appendix C, FMEAC, page 239, for details.

## WE DON'T DO WINDOWS—II

*Minimize the load.*

Continuing with the challenge of supporting a product that relies on the performance of an enabling technology, many senior managers and executives will suggest the solution is for the contact center to simply not field these calls and refer the Customer to the enabling technology company's contact center. After all, "It's not our problem," they say. As a suggestion from the ivory tower it has merit; however, it is very difficult to execute on without compromising Customer satisfaction. Customers do not want to be shuttled off to yet another CSR at another company. The contact center must be able to gracefully handle these contacts and provide the level of service the Customer base demands.

Ramping up staff to handle the call density spawned by enablers' foibles is not a viable option as it is cost-prohibitive and erodes the bottom line of the operation. Get creative. The optimal approach is to minimize external factors that affect the satisfaction of the Customer base. Consider the following:

- Owner—Assign ownership of the partner relation within the contact center. Ensure the partner also has an owner on their side. The owner is the go-to person, the person that knows the deal inside and out and can respond to a challenge in real time. Ensure the owner has backup, someone to step up when the primary owner is on vacation or otherwise indisposed.

- Communication—Work very closely with the partner and do not be caught unaware of an innovation (or simple change) on their part. Extend the idea of business development into the contact center. Keep the lines of communication well-greased and open.

- Two-way partnership—Meet regularly with the partner to talk and keep each other abreast of change. Remember, a dialogue goes two ways; treat them like a partner and give them timely notice regarding innovations that the company has planned.

- Review business drivers—Review the business drivers that drove the creation of the partnership in the first place. Ensure that the corporate objectives remain aligned. If the objectives have changed (yours or the partners), reevaluate the partnership.

- Test changes and new releases assiduously—For example, do not test just the code produced by your developers but test enablers' code as well. It is very difficult to test all code that may cohabit a machine with your code, but it is possible to test the top applications that cohabit an average host.

- As per the statement above—Attempt to arrange veto power on any changes to the enablers' infrastructure, code, and systems until the corporation's technical staff has had opportunity to vet the changes fully and completely. (Note: this is a QA or engineering function and does not strictly belong in the contact center.)

- Alpha Test team—See the section on structure, appendix F, page 253.

Next, develop a call prevention (this is sometimes known as "call avoidance") strategy to reduce the load on the contact center. See the section on call prevention, page 41.

# WE DON'T DO WINDOWS—III

*Work with your partners.*

In the event that the partnership is turning out to be unsatisfactory, with the partner refusing to act in a mutually beneficial fashion, an alternate, less altruistic course of action must be considered.

If the call density related to enablers and *their* issues is becoming an excessive burden, there are a number of strategies available to reduce the impact. Similar to managing the internal *top* x *issues* discussed earlier, it is important to focus on the main challenges that need to be resolved and to leave the secondary issues for round two. Run a root cause analysis and determine where remedies need to be applied. Stay focused.

Next, ensure there is attention on the partner's behalf at the appropriate level and that they have an appreciation of the challenge. Without visibility, no vendor/partner will take corrective action. Attempt to work through the issue with the vendor/partner in the full spirit of cooperation and mutual benefit. If a satisfactory resolution cannot be obtained, consider escalating the issue to the next level in the partner's hierarchy. Loop until a satisfactory resolution is obtained.

It is possible that the idiosyncrasy causing your organization grief is of little or no consequence to the vendor/partner; it may only need to be brought to their attention to be rectified as the issue is an unintentional and inadvertent by-product of their product/service.

Failing that, consider:

- Billing back—If corrective action is required of a vendor/partner, start sending them invoices that result from the issue. If the contacts can be traced to an issue within the vendor/partner's sphere of influence, put in place a back-to-back bill-back scheme. These usually take the form of:

  If call density exceeds $x$ within period $y$, then the company responsible will pay the contact center processing the contacts $z$ per call.

- Warm hand-off—A warm hand-off is less drastic than the bill-back technique. A warm hand-off is where the contact center hands off a Customer to the vendor/partner's contact center seamlessly. As far as the Customer is concerned, they are still on the same call and are oblivious to the fact that your staff transferred the call to another company. The benefit is that the burden has been transferred with the call; there is still a cost but it has been minimized.

  An additional value to this scheme is if your personnel have the ability to stay online while the vendor/partner's contact center deal with the call. It is both a learning opportunity and a quality assurance touch point. An added benefit is that it will reinforce relationships between the contact centers (or build them as the case may be).

- Speciality team/cross-training—Create a speciality team to become experts in the enabling technology. These cross-corporation teams are often called virtual teams (V-team). Once the enablers understand your challenges and your personnel understand their challenges, both teams will be far more effective.

  The V-team must have an executive sponsor at both companies. To nurture and support the V-team, set up regular conference calls, video links, and perhaps quarterly site visits. As with any well-run meeting there should be a solid agenda with responsibilities and time lines for these meetings. This is another reason to support contact center representation in the business development team, or, if critical mass is there, create a business development role within the contact center.

- Call overload insurance—With or without vendor/partner issues, all contact centers need a fallback mechanism (also known as *fail-over*). The fallback mechanism is to be engaged in times of higher than expected call volume and/or catastrophic infrastructure failures that render the contact center unable to meet their performance metrics. The optimal mechanism is a seamless, secondary call handling capability to be engaged on demand when the primary mechanism is overloaded. Considerations:

  ○ Technical ability—The fallback mechanism may not need the same degree of training that the primary personnel possess. In fact, all that may be needed is a warm body to answer the contact and read a script. The worse case is that it is necessary to replicate the level of expertise of the primary support mechanism (sometimes seen in mission-critical applications).

  ○ Timeliness—"On demand" has a varying sense of urgency driven by the supported product's idiosyncrasies and Customer's expectation. For example, in the event of a catastrophic failure of the contact center infrastructure, a manufacturer of screen saver software could probably last longer without the contact center than a manufacturer of cell phones.

  ○ Geographic diversity—For mission-critical support applications, geographic diversity of the fallback mechanism is mandatory. The more geographically removed the fallback is from the primary the better. Consider if the primary mechanism is based in Gander, North Dakota and the secondary mechanism is based in Dallas, Texas; it is highly unlikely that a common environmental, geological, or electrical failure will impede both operations. If an earthquake or an ice storm takes out the primary contact center, the fallback should be far enough removed to not experience the same failure. The switch-over mechanism should be automated and seamless.

○ Engage a contact center outsourcing service—There has been a rash of new contact center outsourcing facilities in the past few years. There are outsourcing services that specialize in technical support, telemarketing, order entry, special promotions, and many other areas. A retainer fee is usually required to ensure the service has staff available when it is needed. There are some services that are based on a per-transaction billing model, but as an overload mechanism that is an unlikely option. As the product matures or the business model changes, management may elect to move more services to the outsourced contact center. Use this period to get a feel for the quality of the outsourced services and use this future business potential as a carrot to help expedite the contract negotiation process (see the section on outsourcing, page 43).

○ Use internal resources—There other teams within the organization that can provide Customer support, from those that migrated from the contact center (see the contact center as a farm team, page 78) to quality assurance and developers to pre-sales to salespeople themselves. Not to suggest that Customer support is a good use of the star developer's time, but depending on the Customer need at hand, it may be the best thing for the corporation.

○ Tap into your vendor/partners—If you have established good working relationships with your vendor/partners, a mutually beneficial overload mechanism may be possible whereby, in times of overload, the contact center hot-links[5] to the vendor/partners and vice versa. Burden rate and revenue would have to be discussed, defined, and agreed upon, and a degree of cross-training would have to be anticipated. This scheme reinforces ties with the vendor/partners. Be wary that the contact dynamic of the vendor/partner does not follow similar call volume loading to the primary contract center—if you both get hammered by Customer contacts at the same time, the mechanism fails.

○ Tap into local companies—Obviously companies that you are not in direct competition with. There are always companies around that are in the same maturity point and predicament as your contact center or company. As per the mutually beneficial comments mentioned previously, it is not difficult to locate a company that is willing to assist and receive reciprocated assistance.

• Notification of service disruptions—If the product is a service or depends on the Internet, a vendor/partner, or some other mechanism to deliver value, then it is prudent to establish a notification mechanism in the event either the core service suffers a disruption or one of the enablers suffers a disruption. There are a number of effective methods for notifying the Customer base.

Some of the recipients on the notification list will want only two pieces of information: what happened and when service will be restored. Other recipients will want details. (Consider those that report to a higher authority in an enterprise supporting hundreds of copies of your product; they will not be satisfied with "It broke but now it's better.") As they are supporting your product within their organization, they need details as to precisely what happened, when service was restored, and, most importantly, how the service provider has guaranteed the failure will never occur again.

There are two poles to notification methods, passive or proactive. Passive is simply "posting" the notification in a public place (on the Internet, for instance); proactive is where the message is pushed to the user community using a method such as an automatic call protocol (telemarketing hardware used to push messages to a list of phone numbers) or an e-mail broadcast.

Which method is used to notify the Customer base is driven by a number of parameters such as:

- Mission-criticality of the product—To what degree has the user community come to count on the timeliness of the product/service (understand that the official corporate opinion of mission-criticality may differ from that of the user base)? Very carefully consider what constitutes a disruption. Poll the Customers as to what they think constitutes a disruption. For example, if delivery of the service typically takes 10 to 15 minutes, then a 15-second transparent[6] service disruption is insignificant and probably not worth issuing a notification. A 7-minute service disruption, however, is a different thing if you understand when a notification is justified and when it is not. Consider reducing the problem down to a formula or percentage, such as:

  * If the delivery window is 10–15 minutes, then the median delivery time is approximately 13 minutes or 780 seconds.

  * Therefore a 15-second disruption is 2 percent of the median.

  * Whereas a 7-minute disruption is 53 percent of the median.

  Somewhere in between the two is the acceptable notification threshold. As previously suggested, work with the Customer base to determine where the threshold should be. Document the parameters—what constitutes a notify event and what does not—and insert the parameters into the SLA template (see the section titled "Service Level Agreements," page 148).

- Technical sophistication of the user base—Posting a notification of a disruption in a place unlikely to be accessible by the user community is ineffective (and a little foolish). Ensure the notification is where the users can access it easily.

In addition, consider that not all users want or need notification of disruptions. This includes:

* Casual users—Those that only make use of your services once a month do not require daily notifications. In fact, notifications can spook casual users and scare them off the product.

* Users that are subject to centralized MIS/IT controls—If the solution is an enterprise solution then it is very likely that the host enterprise MIS/IT department is *not* going to want your corporation directly messaging the user community they are directly supporting.

    It may be necessary to administer the notification protocol and manage it based on subsets of the user community. If the protocol is proactive (push), it will be necessary to extract users from the push list.

○ Security considerations—How much information to provide regarding a disruption is an issue. In order for the notification to be of use it must be reasonably technical, however, the degree of technical detail must be tempered by the technical sophistication of the target audience, and that must be tempered by security concerns regarding your own product and/or infrastructure.

○ Commercial considerations—This is a touchy issue indeed. Consider a flat-rate billing model where the Customer prepays *x* dollars for a service. It then stands that if the service is not available, the Customer is entitled to a rebate for the time the service was unavailable. The logic is simple and the Customer base will exercise it when they have reached their saturation point on disruptions and failures. In this scenario, notifying the Customer base can be seen as supporting the right to demand rebate.

○ Frequency of disruptions and magnitude—Frequency and magnitude are intertwined with the commercial considerations bullet above. The key is understanding what the Customer's expectations are and then ensuring that the infrastructure can indeed deliver to these expectations. If there is a gap between what is *wanted* and what can be *realistically delivered* then it is imperative to recalibrate the Customer's expectations before notifications commence. Otherwise, the notifications will just serve to feed the fire burning under the product.

○ Notification litmus test. Ensure the four points of the Litmus Test for Notifications are observed in the notification protocol.

---

Customers are tolerant to a disruption or two and will not complain provided the disruptions are infrequent. There is a point, however, where the Customer tolerance threshold is breached and they demand satisfaction. Unfortunately, determining the break-point threshold is not an exact science.

## Litmus Test for Notifications

An effective notification satisfies the following:

1. Timeliness of notification—The notification should be proactive and not lag the event by an excessive period.

2. Quality of data—The notification should cover what the target audience requires to allay their concerns.

3. Veracity of data—The notification must be accurate and suited to the target audience.

4. Closing the loop—Once there is full restoration of service, alert the target audience to the fact.

Consider the following disruption notification delivery methods:

- A published but secure universal resource locator (URL) that contains the current status of the product/service. Including a history of disruptions is a very dangerous thing as it is difficult to know how the data will be interpreted, and it could very well be used against the organization by the competition.

- An Internet posting. If the user base are users of the Internet by default—that is, the product depends on the Internet to deliver services—then posting notifications on the Internet is a good fit unless the Internet service provider servicing the corporation is part of the problem, in which case an alternative notification protocol is needed.

- A voice message accessible on the corporate interactive voice response (IVR) system.

## CALL PREVENTION

*Lighten the load.*

The first order of business in a contact center is to put itself out of business. The prime operational target for the contact center is to reduce the incoming call volume to the point where the contact center is no longer needed. There are two distinct approaches that warrant consideration for reaching the target by reducing the incoming call volume:

1. Improving the product/service to the degree that Customers have no need to call for support.

2. Provide other mechanisms for Customers to use when they have issues. That is, the contact still exists but the Customer has other options besides calling the contact center.

## Improving the Product/Service

In order to improve the product/service to reduce incoming calls, the contact center requires the assistance and, more importantly, buy-in of other groups within the organization. Create cross-departmental teams with the goal of eradicating the reasons behind Customer contacts. Enlist the assistance of the following groups:

- Quality assurance—The team that validates and/or verifies the product. The team that conducts analysis exercises focused on defects,[7] functionality, ergonomics, and standards compliance is one of the contact center's most important cross-departmental affiliations. Quality assurance teams frequently have statistical analysis professionals (and tools) that can greatly enhance the ability to analyze raw contact data. The quality assurance team can serve as a third-party audit on the findings and reports coming out of the contact center. In addition, the quality assurance team has the ability to run reality checks and verify and validate recommendations for product improvements that originate in the contact center.

    *Note:* In this context do not confuse *enhancement* requests with *product improvement* requests. Enhancement requests also come into the contact center, but this section is concerned with product improvements that decrease the call volume, not Customer-spawned suggestions for improving the functionality of the product.

- Engineering/development—The programmers, the designers, and the manufacturing engineers. This is the team that can take the data gathered by the contact center and verified by quality assurance and effect changes to the product/service that will reduce, if not eliminate, the root cause of the contact.

- Sales—The sales team is out talking to the Customer base. This is the most likely source for areas to improve regarding the contact center itself. Issues such as the following typically come in via the sales team: "We should have a toll-free number," "Customers are complaining that the hold time is too long," "our staff need better training," and so on. Consider also that the sales staff should be selling the support capabilities, at minimum, as a "value-added" part of the product. The sales team must understand the support capabilities to the same degree they understand the core competencies, features, and benefits of the product itself.

- Marketing—This team is key to positioning the product as a holistic entity. Consider the product as not just programming or the silicon-and-plastics, it is more. The tangible shrink-wrapped kit is a component of the product, but so is the product packaging, the bill the Customer receives, and the post-sale support the Customer receives. Enlist marketing to assist with the productization of the services offered by the contact center. If there is a need for support (contact centers raison d'être) then the support capability of the corporation should warrant mention in the product brochures. In some instances, the contact center justifies an entire brochure of its own.

- Business development—The BizDev team is out securing new deals with new business partners, potentially under different business models than currently supported. Get involved in the business development cycle, be prepared to meet the evolving business models of tomorrow, and, more importantly, influence the direction and adoption of new business models.

## Call Prevention = Continuous Improvement

There are a number of input points that supplement the recommendations that flow from the creation of the cross-departmental teams suggested previously. As each of the points listed below is covered in greater depth elsewhere in this book, this section only outlines the benefit of each activity as it relates to call prevention.

### Input points

- Call analysis and top ten issues. Review the top issues for which the Customer base is raising contacts and initiate corrective action.

  See "Top Ten Issues," page 143, and Figure 4.21, Data plot, top failure modes, page 143, for further data.

- Customer feedback and surveys. This is a more proactive approach as compared to the first bullet. Get out and solicit input directly from the Customer base. Ascertain what their expectations are and conduct a gap analysis between what is wanted and what can be realistically deployed.

- Benchmark. This proactive tool is used to compare your corporation to other corporations in similar niches. Ascertain what services the prime competitors are providing and create a going-forward plan to ensure the Customer base views your corporate services as superior.

- Contact center personnel. Take note of what the CSRs are complaining about. Turn the complaints into suggestions for improvement. Suggestions from the trenches often have excellent payback for minimal investment.

To be most effective, the polling of the input points should be a continuous ongoing effort.

# OUTSOURCING (SUPPORT SERVICES)

*Viable providing the right selection is made under the right conditions.*

There are a number of excellent reasons to outsource support services. Many companies are focused on a central theme of "stick to the corporate core competencies." If support services are not a core competency then outsourcing may be viable, however, this must be balanced by another theme of "own your own destiny."

Contact centers exist to provide services to Customers. If the services are thought of as extensions of the product itself, it can be argued that Customer satisfaction must always be a core competency.

## Case Study—Souihorn Inc. (with Apologies to Dr. Seuss)

Consider a business where a manufacturer, Souihorns Inc., produces souihorns. The souihorns are world-class souihorns and have no competition on the open market. The souihorns themselves are robust and function well within operational parameters. Failures of souihorns are handled directly by the personnel on the manufacturing floor of the souihorn plant. The business operates under a simple and uncluttered business model that can economically and expediently sustain an entry-level company.

Much to Souihorns Inc.'s delight their souihorn is received very, very well. Orders start to roll in day and night. The manufacturing plant is running at capacity and another plant is being built to support the anticipated growth.

From a support perspective, three things occur at this point in the case study:

1. The manufacturing plant is so busy building souihorns that answering support calls from Customers has become a burden. The end result is twofold—key manufacturing personnel are being pulled off the line causing production targets to be missed, and Customers are less than satisfied with Souihorn Inc.'s ability to support its product.

2. As the number of souihorns increases, the number of Customers needing support services increases.

3. Because the manufacturing plant is at its capacity, product is being shipped that is of lower quality than the initial product (more so due to hurried and incomplete training of new hires to help with the load, but that's another parable).

Support contacts are increasing, Customer satisfaction is decreasing, product quality is decreasing, and sales are increasing. To further complicate matters a second-generation souihorn is pending. Souihorn Inc. must act and act quickly. Options are:

- Create a contact center and provide direct support to the Customer base (satisfies the need but is costly and the ramp-up time is considerable).

- Outsource support services to an existing contact center operation (satisfies the need, is cost effective, and can be up and running quickly).

The outsourcing option is selected as the superior go-forward option. An action plan is prepared and signed off and executed on.

### Action Plan

1. Hire a support manager from within or from the outside. The support manager becomes the support special project manager.

2. Manufacturing selects and releases two of the personnel who handled support calls most efficiently to the support special project team. Additional attributes that are nice for the selected personnel to have are experience with support services (help desk, contact center, and so on), project management, and training experience.

3. The support special project team defines, as best it can, the support dynamic using the guidelines from this document. See section titled "Definition Of Services," page 13.

4. The two manufacturing personnel begin an aggressive program of documenting failure modes, responses, training materials, and training presentations so that they are ready to train whatever outsource service provider is selected.

5. Using the support dynamic data as a baseline, and with assistance from two local contact center outsourcing services, a set of selection criteria is defined for the outsourced services.[8] It is understood that sales forecast information (which is a precursor to a raise in contact volume) will be a large factor in the assessment.

6. An SLA is created and appended to the selection criterion. The SLA details all pertinent performance metrics, their enforcement, and penalties if breeched.

   Because the majority of performance reports will be coming from the selected outsource service these reports are clearly defined at the proposal stage. Furthermore, a set price for changes to reports or generation of new reports is clearly documented.

   In addition, because the outsourcer is dealing directly with Souihorn's Customers, it is important to document how data will flow from the outsourcer's systems to Souihorn's marketing, engineering, and sales systems. As the data points are unknown at this juncture, flexibility must be designed into the protocol.

7. The criterion is released as a Request for Proposal (RFP) to all contact center service providers. The RFP includes sections on:

   - Pricing—Pricing options include a per contact fee, per subscriber fee, flat rate per month, flat rate per $x$ contacts, shared queue or dedicated queue, and so on.

      The optimal pricing option is driven by anticipated growth rate; compare the annual fee for options on a spreadsheet with best-case and worst-case scenarios driving a per annum cost. In the event that the Customer base has not reached critical mass, thereby allowing the bidder to present favorable pricing, highlight the anticipated growth rate as a carrot. Companies below critical Customer mass are often handled by a shared queue—the CSR may be supporting your product and a number of others—which is vastly inferior to dedicated support. However, if pricing considerations dictate that the queue is to be shared, the organization should at least have a say regarding with which companies the contracted CSR is being shared. Multilingual support is another area that can significantly inflate the pricing. If French-Canadian or Spanish support is not needed initially then opt out with an option to engage downstream.

- Preparation for growth—Can the bidder demonstrate their ability to respond to aggressive growth in the contact volume driven by Souihorn's anticipated sales curve?

  There is a science to preparing for geometric growth vis-à-vis arithmetic growth; make sure the bidders understand the issues. A question to ask is "How scaleable are the bidder's systems and protocols?"

- Employee churn—As contact centers are known as high-churn environments, can the bidder guarantee that the employees trained by Souihorn staff will be on board next quarter or next year?

  The right response to this is for the contact center to share their actual churn rate as a baseline.

- Ongoing training—Related to "employee churn," the bidder comments on their methodology for assuming product and support training of new hires to their organization.

  There are a number of points to consider regarding ongoing training. The organization does not want to bear the cost of conducting training courses ad infinitum. The bidder should be able to conduct their own training courses facilitated by the organization offering "train the trainer" sessions. Some questions to ask include "How will training on product enhancements be conducted?" and "Does the bidder have videoconferencing capability?"

- Certification and veto—Each CSR the bidder puts on the Souihorn support queue should be certified on the souihorn product. In the event that a CSR is not providing the level of support Souihorn contracted for, Souihorn has the right to have that CSR removed from the queue.

  Due process must be observed with, perhaps, a documented trail, but this veto power is mandatory. The quickest way to ascertain if the corporation's best interests are being met is to conduct a mystery-shopper[9] exercise.

- Time line—Souihorn's explosive business growth demands that the service be up within 90 days. Can the bidders provide a project plan that demonstrates that the outsourcer understands the challenges?

  Again, leverage the professional services aspect of the bidders. A thorough bidder will actually audit the organization's support needs and make recommendations. It is gratis consulting, however be wary of self-serving proposals.

- Data transfer—It is imperative that Souihorn have visibility of their Customers, therefore Souihorn must be able to mine the databases owned by the bidder.

  Without this linkage, Souihorn Inc. has effectively silenced one of the most informed voices on their success—their Customers. Own your own destiny by accessing the raw data from the outsourced service provider. A question to ask is "How open are the systems to data mining from a Customer?"

- Termination—Souihorn must have an equitable termination clause.

  Perhaps the outsourced service is not meeting expectations. Perhaps Souihorn wishes to bring the services in-house. It is preferable if the termination can be timely, transparent to the user base, and free of any penalties. A questions to ask is "How are Souihorn's best interests protected if termination is exercised?" For instance, how does Souihorn gain access to the support phone numbers, the e-mail address, URLs, and so on. Further ascertain if Souihorn can hire support personnel from the service provider.

- Stability—It is prudent to ascertain how stable any partner is.

  This is related to the "own your own destiny" comment. If the continued success of the outsource contact center is dependent on one large contract that they hold, there is a risk that the outsourcer will fail if that large contract is withdrawn. This has huge cost implications on the organization as you may have to start the process over again from the beginning.

8. Souihorn receives the bids and selects the best one (which isn't always the *cheapest*). Review very carefully, tour the facilities, and make the right decision.

9. The two manufacturing personnel train the incumbent and remain on-site at the outsourced contact center to provide direct support to the CSRs when the service goes live. The amount of time the trainers spend on-site is inversely proportional to the effectiveness of the training they provided.

10. Souihorn's support manager monitors the SLA and reviews the performance reports with the outsourced team on a monthly basis. Corrective action is applied when needed. Souihorn's support manager also ensures that Souihorn's best interests continue to be serviced by the outsourced contact center.

Done and done. Souihorn Inc. Customers are now getting the care they need.

But hold up . . . things change. Souihorn's support manager must continue to police and nurture the relationship. The support manager continues to negotiate next year's contract with the outsourced service provider, always striving for superior pricing, increased service, and additional services. The manager is also looking to the evolving business model and Customer base with the view that nothing works forever, what does Souihorn Inc. need tomorrow? Perhaps tomorrow's needs dictate a closer relationship with the Customer base; perhaps the contact center must be brought in-house to better serve marketing and sales needs. The manager needs to keep a finger on the pulse and be flexible. In fact, the support manager is well into business development territory.

### Additional Comments on the Souihorn Case Study

Relationship ownership. Perhaps the most important relationship a company has is with its Customers. In the case study, Souihorn delegated control of this important relationship to a third party. Some believe this is a catastrophic mistake made by too many corporations today. While it is true that Customer support is in a sorry state, outsourced services providers are not the cause. Some products lend themselves to outsourcing support and some do not, the line between the two being the inherent complexity of the product to be supported.

It is also true that some aspects of support are best left to an internal department. An example is strategic account support; if Souihorn Inc. became the sole supplier of souihorns to the Confederation of Southern U.S. Colleges[10] then it would certainly be in Souihorn's best interest to provide them with a direct line to a strategic support team comprised of the souihorn's top support experts.

Statistics have suggested that somewhere around half of all new products are destined to fail. (This is not a hard and fast statistic but a "guesstimate"). There are hundreds of product launches every year, and many fail. This speaks volumes to outsourcing support services; why build a support organization when the chances of success are so very slim (of course, this opinion will not play well in the corporate board room—I suggest a rewording when presenting the idea to the corporate executive). Souihorn is doing well now, but the Souihorn market is a very limited market, and once it is saturated, very few new Souihorns will be purchased. Additionally, once the infant mortality[11] failures are rectified, the contact volume will diminish rapidly. Perhaps Souihorn's best support option was to continue offering support services from the manufacturing plant. There would have been some short-term pain, but, overall, the quality of Customer support and the costs would have been optimized over the long term.

Style and playfulness. This entire section on outsourcing has a certain playfulness about it, from the invention of the Souihorn to the creation of the Confederation of Southern U.S. Colleges. Playfulness is absent in many organizations and executives wonder why morale is poor. The author contends that if the dry subject of support outsourcing can be injected with some playfulness then anything can. Go to work tomorrow and have some fun . . . play it up a bit.

## DEFINING THE STRUCTURE

*Generic and expanded organizational charts.*

This section profiles and expands on a generic organizational chart. Two organizational charts are featured. These two charts serve as entry points to the creation of a contact center to support any product/service. Each position depicted on the charts has a brief write-up in appendix B. The write-up outlines the role, reporting structure, and cross-departmental dependencies.

Every support challenge has its own needs, some of which may be unique to the product/service the contact center is providing services for. For instance, a telecommunications carrier has very different Customer support pressures than a commercial, off-the-shelf software house. A financial services house has different support pressures than a hardware manufacturer. Review the organizational charts and rename, restructure, and reposition the charts as the business model demands.

## Start-Up Environment

One of the more daunting challenges a management team can face is the high-technology chameleon known as the *start-up*. The start-up enterprise is the most exciting, dynamic, and entrepreneurial environment to work in. Clichés abound: changing the tires at 60 mph, moving at the speed of thought, and so on.

Start-ups often leverage the development team to provide support services. This has positive and negative aspects: positive because the developers get firsthand knowledge of the product's performance (no filters between the Customer and the developer), negative because the developer should be *developing,* not answering the phone.

As the start-up matures, a more formal support mechanism is introduced. This eventually leads, if the product has market momentum, to the creation of a contact center.

# DEFINITION OF ROLES, GENERIC

*Who's on first?*

This section outlines the role and responsibilities of each of the positions found on the two organizational charts: Figure 2.5, Generic contact center structure, and Figure 2.6, Expanded contact center structure. Each position is presented as a singularity, the organization's particular needs will drive how many personnel are required in each role.

To supplement the organizational charts, each department and role therein is listed and outlined in appendix B. The prime mandate for the department is discussed followed by a discussion of each role within the department. The roles are expanded upon using the following subtitles:

- Role: Description of the role focusing on prime responsibilities.

- Responsible to: The individual(s) the role is directly accountable to not only from a "reporting to" perspective but also from the perspective of those who are most affected by the individual's performance and actions.

- Key performance metrics: A list of measurable metrics to gauge success in the role. While effort has been made to recommend objective metrics, the more senior roles have a subjective bias, so guidance has been provided on the more subjective metrics. The listing is in order of priority with the first being the prime performance metric, and so on.

- Focus: This is typically "Customer-facing" or "back-office." Customer-facing is self-explanatory, back-office refers to support for the infrastructure, tools, and systems used by the contact center personnel.

- Interdepartmental dependencies: Departments within and outside of the contact center that directly or indirectly impact the potential success of the incumbent.

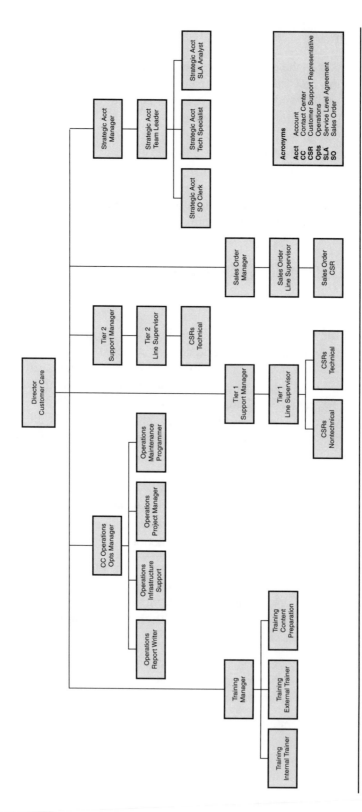

**Figure 2.5**   Generic contact center structure.

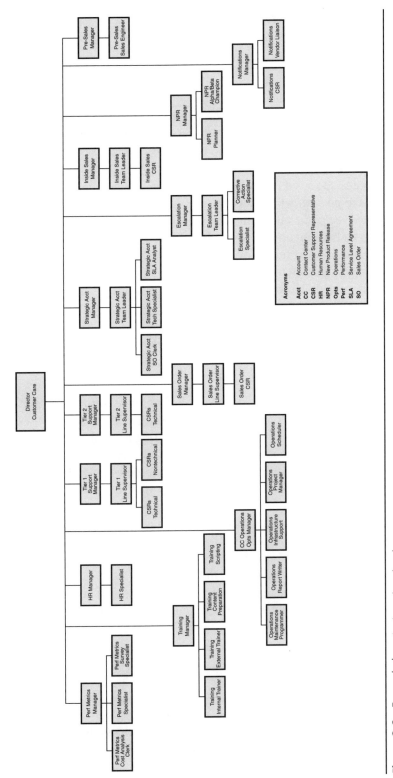

**Figure 2.6**  Expanded contact center structure.

# ROLE RIGIDITY

*Human element.*

Too much role rigidity can be counterproductive. The most effective support organizations are those that know, intrinsically, when to be flexible. This is a culture effect—if management nurtures the optimal culture then flexibility will come. Give the staff latitude and support their stepping over job and departmental boundaries and the Customers will be delighted. Rein the staff in too tightly and the Customer base will detect the rigidity and push back.

In some extreme situations it may be prudent to discard job boundaries and descriptions altogether and to go with what the Customer desires. If the Customer requests that telephone CSR Jane Doe come on out to their site and conduct on-site training, so be it (providing Jane can be brought up to speed to be effective during the sessions). The rapport between Jane and the Customer overrides the concern that Jane is not a trained trainer. The Customer is granted their wish and Jane is delighted that she is provided the opportunity to move outside her normal duties—a true win–win.

# THE BUSINESS PLAN

*From the ground up, plan, plan, and plan.*

It may be necessary to justify the design, request and compete for budget, and present a cohesive plan in regards to the contact center. The container document for these issues is the business plan. The first order of business in creating a business plan is to ensure that the company's core values and operational standards are understood; the contact center business plan must be consistent with the corporation as a whole.

In general, the best business plans are short and succinct yet contain sufficient detail to satisfy the target audience. An important attribute of a successful business plan is to have the right balance between strategic and tactical material. Each corporation has its own idea of what the optimal balance is. If at all possible, locate an existing, well-received plan and study it to get an idea of the balance. In the absence of an existing plan seek out a sponsor in the executive to guide the effort.

The business plan should be tuned for two audiences. The first audience is the executive that must sign off on the plan and give their financial support. The second audience

---

Strategic versus tactical thinking. There are many definitions of what is meant by the terms strategic and tactical. Strategic may be thought of as the vision, direction, and high-level view. Strategic thinking is characterized by possessing a strong intuition component. Tactical may be thought of as the execution, logistics, and rubber-to-the-road view. Data gathering and analysis characterize tactical thinking.

is the contact center management team—those who need to understand what they are building. The business plan becomes the blueprint for the contact center management team. The executive business plan may be a subset of a more complete business plan—develop both, but present the more succinct document to the executive.

Be careful of the paralysis-by-analysis trap of attempting to render all operational aspects "100 percent written-in-stone, this is how it will be for all time because every possible failure mode has been anticipated." Position the business plan as a dynamic document subject to revision and fine-tuning over the course of its lifecycle. If an initiative no longer bears relevance to the evolving business, do not hesitate to withdraw it. Be flexible and build-in contingency for change.

Revision control[12] of the business plan is important, particularly if the underlying business is evolving so swiftly as to demand frequent revisions to the plan. The most comprehensive system dictates that nothing is ever *deleted* from the business plan during its lifecycle; initiatives that have been abandoned remain in the plan with their justifications and with an added post-justification outlining the circumstances that caused the initiative to be abandoned. To retain the "succinct and concise" objective for the document as a whole, review the master document on a yearly basis and archive the abandoned initiatives and programs in appendixes. Doing this ensures the living document remains sharp and focused.

You should arrange to have the business plan reviewed for comment by other departments before the final submission. If at all possible, with a nondisclosure agreement in place, have the plan reviewed by a noncompetitor who manages a similar contact center. This provides an opportunity to leverage knowledge and expertise outside the immediate corporation and explore the potential for synergy between the operations. Do not ignore the more subtle forms of synergy. There may be revenue-generating business development type opportunities $(1 + 1 = 3)$, but there are also potential synergies in sharing resources, facilities, consulting services, and training. Consider both the savings and increased flexibility if the consolidated needs of two contact centers were presented to a training provider.

The business plan must link tightly to the business objectives and vision of the corporation. Ensure that every proposed initiative has a tangible benefit to the business and supports corporate goals. Build in contingencies for monetary and time line slippage to counter unforeseen circumstances beyond your direct control.

---

Note on reviewing documents: There is a shortage of effective reviewers. When passed a document for review, look first to the content as it pertains to your immediate area of expertise. Focus on the content, leave the choice of font, grammar and spelling, and other details to other reviewers that have English structure as their forte. Structure is important, but if I pass a document to the director of quality for comment, I expect to receive comment on what is written about "document control" and "quality standards," not that I mistakenly used "two" when I meant "too" or that Ariel is a friendlier font than Times Roman.

The business plan must be executable. When the executive team declares "Make it so," you had better be able to execute on the plan. Ensure that the success criteria, parameters, and time frames are realistic and can be executed. It serves no purpose to deliver a business plan that satisfies what the executive wishes to hear but cannot be realistically executed.

The business plan must factor in all variables that are to be planned and managed. Again, be creative, there is more than one way to approach a challenge. Always provide options and alternatives.

Some variables include:

- Time frame:
  - Short-term goal
  - Long-term goal
  - Phased approach (PI, PII, PIII, and so on)
  - Milestones and benchmarks
- Budget:
  - Start-up cost
  - Labor cost
  - Capital cost
  - Burn-rate cost
  - Signing authority
- Number of personnel required:
  - Skill sets needed
  - Job descriptions suitable for publication in local newspapers, headhunters, and so on
  - Local availability of staff
  - Start-up training time frame (Rome was neither built nor trained in a day)
- Physical space considerations—availability and lead time to readiness:
  - Facilities
  - Furniture
  - Access (security, lights in parking lot, shifts, and so on)
  - Parking

- Systems and tools—availability and lead time to readiness:

  - IVR, PBX, and telephony equipment including trunk capacity, available LAN bandwidth, and available Internet bandwidth

  - Desktop PCs, headsets, training tools, and so on

  - Tote boards[13]

- Operational readiness:

  - Procedures documented

  - Procedures published

Begin by creating an organizational chart based on the overall company business requirements tempered by Customer needs. Use Figure 2.5, Generic contact center structure, page 50, and Figure 2.6, Expanded contact center structure, page 51, as templates for contact center structures. Decide which positions are necessary and which are not needed to fulfill the business goals. Also, consider positions that do not appear on the generic or expanded organization charts, such as:

- A third tier for technical support may be needed.

- A videoconference manager if a large portion of business is to be conducted over video links.

- Business development manager to explore opportunities.

There are no hard and fast rules. Be creative.

## Short-Term Business Plan

It goes (almost) without saying that the optimal time to begin planning the support services is well before the product/service is commercially released. Perhaps the worst time to *begin* planning support services is when the product has already been commercially released. A short-term business plan will set the logistics in motion to realize the support services needed.

A short-term business plan has a number of characteristics, such as:

- Typically focused on just beyond the horizon.

- The level of detail contained in the plan is driven by available planning time.

- The actual duration of "short-term" is defined by where the product/service is in its maturity and adoption cycles.

Begin by outlining the immediate requirements, including:

1. Define the contact center's principle period of maintenance (PPM). In other words, the days and hours of operation. Some industry standards follow:

   1.1. Continuous support—twenty-four/seven, MTWTFSS.

   1.2. Business hour support, single time zone—0800 to 1700 Eastern Standard Time, MTWTF.

   1.3. Business hour support, North American multiple time zones—0800 to 1700 Eastern, Central, and Pacific Standard time, MTWTF.

   1.4. Holiday coverage—ascertain what holidays will need support services available. Review the following:

      1.4.1. Will the contact center be open over standard civic holidays?

      1.4.2. What services will be available on holidays (full or skeleton)?

      1.4.3. Is it only necessary to have a skeleton staff on holidays?

2. Define the after-hours contact handling mechanism. Consider the following issues, questions, and options:

   2.1. Answering service—live, machine, or voice mail—with or without provision for the Customer to leave a message. If the Customer can leave a message, a protocol is also needed to act on the message(s).

   2.2. Cut over to an outsourced service. Also define what services the outsourced service will provide by going through this entire list for the cut-over after-hours service.

   2.3. Automatic call-forwarding to pagers or cell phones. Remember to build-in compensation for those on call (such as per call, minimum hour rate, and so on). Note that there may be legislated limits as to what can and cannot be done, check with human resources.

   2.4. What is the mechanism for emergency services?

   2.5. Will the contact center support outgoing calls as well as incoming?

3. Define the basic performance metrics the contact center will have as short-term goals.

   3.1. Define the pick-up and/turnaround time duration for each method of contact. Define targets for the following metrics:

      3.1.1 Rings before a telephone contact is picked up.

      3.1.2. Maximum time a contact will be on hold.

      3.1.3. Time after receipt that an e-mail will be responded to.

3.1.4. Time after receipt that a facsimile will be responded to.

3.1.5. First-contact issue resolution.

4. Define how the targets defined in 3.1 will be measured and enforced.

5. Define the issues the contact center is to support. Consider the following:

5.1. Technical:

5.1.1. Will technical issues be a prime focus?

5.1.2. Will the contact center support outgoing technical calls and incoming?

5.1.3. What is the ratio between technical and nontechnical contacts?

5.2. Sales:

5.2.1. What portion of the total contacts will be sales?

5.2.2. Will product benefits and differentiation be a service provided by the contact center?

5.2.3. Will the contact center support incoming sales calls?

5.2.4. Will the contact center support outgoing sales calls?

5.2.5. Will the contact center support an up-sell or cross-sell capability?

5.3. Sales orders:

5.3.1. What portion of contacts will be sales order processing in nature?

5.3.2. Will the contact center process sales orders?

5.3.3. Will the contact center support outgoing order status calls?

5.3.4. Will the contact center support incoming order status calls?

5.3.5. How will credit checks work and what are the time frames associated with credit checks?

5.3.6. What methods of payment are accepted?

5.3.7. Can the current back-office systems validate and process credit cards online?

5.3.8. Can the current back-office systems expediently handle purchase order processing?

5.4. Invoicing/Billing:

5.4.1. What portion of contacts will be invoicing/billing related?

5.4.2. Will issues with invoicing/billing be a prime focus?

5.4.3. Will the contact center support outgoing invoicing/billing calls?

5.4.4. Will the contact center support incoming invoicing/billing-related calls?

5.4.5. Can the current back-office systems handle credit processing?

5.4.6. Have credit sign-off procedures been put in place?

5.5. General Contacts:

5.5.1. What portion of contacts will be general in nature?

5.5.2. Will the contact center act as a clearinghouse for all contacts coming into the company?

Now begin to correlate the data points gathered above and develop a master plan for the contact center.

6. Define how the contact center personnel will handle those contacts that do not fall into the options in subsection 5.

6.1. Define contact handoff procedure. Consider handoff to:

6.1.1. The quality assurance team for issues that require drill-down from the quality team.

6.1.2. The marketing team for issues related to analyst and press calls.

6.1.3. The finance team for issues around credit and bad debt.

6.1.4. The finance team for issues centered on investors and investment.

6.1.5. The legal team for issues where there is potential for litigation.

6.2. Define the procedure to be observed when it is necessary to escalate a contact, considering:

6.2.1. From tier to tier within the contact center.

6.2.2. Cross-departmentally.

6.2.3. To contact center management.

6.2.4. To the CEO's office.

7. Define the method-of-contact points the Customer base will use or which are desirable to direct them to. Research and understand the infrastructure and cost ramifications behind each option. Consider:

7.1. Telephones—the telephone is the easiest and most obvious first choice contact medium for the short term.

7.1.1. Is a toll-free number necessary?

7.1.2. Does the toll-free number need to be accessible internationally?

Anecdotal evidence suggests e-mail contacts actually consume more CSR time to resolve than live-voice contacts. This is particularly true if the contact center does not have systems to access and reuse responses and answers. In addition, e-mail contacts tend to request more information than Customers entering the system on voice calls. Scripting and knowledge-base systems are key to reusing existing work. Alternatively, there are e-mail based support systems available that can intelligently send an auto-response by analyzing the contents of the incoming e-mail and searching for key words.

The majority of contact centers clear e-mail contacts during slack periods such as 2:00 a.m. to 6:00 a.m. Many contact centers use these hours to get new CSRs up to speed, however, for the reasons noted previously, you need seasoned CSRs to clear and answer e-mail contacts. Have the top performers take care of the e-mails.

7.1.3. Is there adequate bandwidth available from the telecommunications provider (incoming trunk) for the anticipated call volume?

7.1.4. Is there adequate bandwidth available from the internal systems (such as the PBX) for the anticipated call volume?

7.1.5. Do the existing back-office systems support "bill-per-call" schemes?

7.1.6. Do the existing back-office systems support "bill-per-time" schemes?

7.2. Facsimile—somewhat old-school and not a desirable contact mode to support, however, facsimile remains a popular entry channel for sales orders and documentation that requires a signature, as electronic signatures do not enjoy universal acceptance as of yet. Define the handling of facsimiles:

7.2.1. Does the anticipated facsimile volume indicate that the contact center should have dedicated facsimile capability? In other words, does the anticipated facsimile volume dictate a facsimile system dedicated to the contact center?

7.2.2. Consider a facsimile server. Documents within limitations are never lost or misplaced on a facsimile server. When a Customer transmits to the right facsimile number the resulting e-document is always available online to the contact center.

7.2.3. Is there adequate bandwidth available for the telecommunications link serving the facsimile?

7.3. E-mail—an excellent medium to provide support services. E-mail contacts have a relaxed sense of urgency. The issue itself may be critical to the Customer, but in choosing e-mail as the contact method, the Customer has shown some latitude in when they expect a resolution. Consider:

7.3.1. Does the existing e-mail system support automatic responses when the server receives e-mail?

7.3.2. Define the response turnaround time (and declare it in the auto-response message).

7.3.3 Can the existing e-mail system differentiate requests for support e-mail from the standard business e-mail stream?

7.3.4. Does the existing e-mail system support time-based, threshold-driven alarms to ensure that nothing falls through the cracks?

7.4. Web-based, chat mode—does the Customer base lean toward a Web-based chat mode (ICQ, instant messenger, and so on)?

7.4.1. Can existing back-office systems tie in to the relatively transient world of chat mode where a single CSR may be hosting a number of simultaneous dialogs?

7.5. Is wireless support necessary—is there a need to direct support services to wireless devices?

7.6. Web-based, Customer self-service—does the sophistication of the target niche indicate that Web-based self-service is viable?

7.6.1. Are there resources available to populate a knowledge base (the back end of a Customer self-service engine)?

7.6.2. Is the technical expertise in-house to deploy a system of this complexity?

7.7. VoIP (Voice over Internet Protocol)—if and when a Customer gets frustrated with online tools, is VoIP viable?

7.7.1. Can the existing infrastructure scale to support VoIP?

7.7.2. Can the telephony infrastructure scale to handle the anticipated contact volume?

7.8. Walk-in (over the counter)—does the Customer base or the product demand a walk-in service?

7.8.1. Can the existing back-office systems track walk-in (service tickets, track and trace mechanisms, return processing, and so on)?

8. Create a short-term organizational chart outlining the personnel that are mandatory. Temper the organizational chart with the time frame and the local talent pool available to the corporation.

9. Using the organizational chart created in step 8 as a reference point, begin the hiring process in concert with the human resources team. As a general rule of thumb, hire the management layer first and work down from there. The more managers and supervisors established, the better the interviewing workload can be distributed.

An added benefit of this approach is that the management and supervisor level are actively involved in the hiring of their teams. The style and mood is set for the employees, and the managers and supervisors do not find themselves in the unenviable position of having their teams pre-hired and defined.

10.  Once the management layer hiring effort is underway, the next hiring priority is to ramp up the training team. Ensure that the personnel comprising the training team are the best talent available as they are key to the effectiveness of the contact center in general.

11.  As a matter of priority, have the newly hired training team (or training *individual* as the case may be) create a training plan. Training, like all programs, will take time to fine-tune, but it is imperative to get the training team operational as soon as possible.

12.  Map out the systems needed for the contact center. Use subsections 2, 5, and 7 as references. Include:

12.1.  Telephony infrastructure.

12.1.1.  Is there an existing private branch exchange (PBX) system? Is it scalable?

12.1.2.  If so, what tracking and tracing functions does it support (call metrics, and so on)?

12.1.3.  What bandwidth is available?

12.1.4.  How many communication sets can it support?

12.1.5.  Is there a headset option instead of the standard handset?

12.1.6.  What are the associated costs to upgrade the PBX to an operational state?

12.2.  Telecommunication links. How many simultaneous incoming contacts can the telecommunications trunk into the contact center support? Include all modes of contact in this analysis: telephone, facsimile, Internet, VoIP, and so on.

12.3.  Does the organization have an existing help desk system? If not, what can be deployed in the short-term until a purpose-built system is operational (for example; a small operation could use Microsoft's Access database system until a full system is deployed).

12.4.  How will the sales staff obtain visibility on Customer issues handled by the contact center?

12.4.1.  Is there an existing module in the system the sales force use? (Many sales force automation and customer relationship management systems have integral support modules.)

12.5. Knowledge base.

    12.5.1. Is there an established knowledge base system? (Often the quality team has a knowledge base system).

    12.5.2. How many entries does it have?

    12.5.3. Is it up to date?

    12.5.4. Is there a formal update protocol established?

    12.5.5 Is the authoring protocol established?

13. Map out the MIS/IT support required for the systems defined in subsection 12. For example, if the contact center is operational twenty-four/seven, the support team for the systems used by the contact center must also have provisions for twenty-four/seven support.

14. Services billing.

    14.1. Are there existing systems in place to allow the contact center to bill for services rendered?

    14.2. Are the billing and invoicing models the contact center wishes to leverage supported by the existing billing system (per contact, per minute, per second, recurring annual contracts, and so on)?

    14.3. Are financial reports available to track and analyze contact center revenue? (To ease the transition into the long-term plan, design the contact center on a P&L (profit and loss) basis from the start).

    14.4. Is there a protocol established between accounts receivable (AR) and the contact center? For example, if a Customer has been negligent in paying for a service, the service should be discontinued and flags set on the systems that the contact center personnel use.

Once these parameters are defined, written-up, and reviewed, the short-term business plan is ready for presentation. Present the short-term plan to the executive for budgetary approval. Ensure it is clearly understood that this phase is short-term only and that a long-term plan is pending. Make adjustments per the comments and suggestions and resubmit until all are satisfied with the plan.

Now the hard part—execute on the short-term plan and segue into the creation of a long-term plan.

---

One hardware manufacturer had a product that was so well designed that it practically never failed. Calculations based on the deployed population showed a mean time between failure of approximately thirteen years! In fact, a single bench technician supported thousands of installed devices.

## Long-Term Business Plan

The long-term plan will build on the short-term plan. Compromises made in the short-term plan due to economic or time-frame challenges will be rectified in the long-term plan. The duration implied by long-term is, like short-term, a variable. If the short-term plan was bursting with compromises then it is imperative to execute on the long-term plan sooner rather than later. Do not risk compromising the satisfaction of the Customer base because of inadequate planning and preparation or there may never be an opportunity to execute the long-term plan. Alternatively, if the short-term plan has yielded an effective operation, secured Customer satisfaction, and is sustainable, then there is some latitude on executing on the long-term. Alternatively, perhaps the product is not meeting the sales objectives, the anticipated market acceptance is low, or the product is so well engineered that support services are unnecessary; there is the luxury of time to fine-tune the long-term plan.

Create a long-term organizational chart outlining where the contact center must grow to meet the long-term requirements. Plan for the overlap the long-term plan shares with the short-term plan. Manage the transition to minimize disruption to the operation and to the Customer base. In addition, keep the contact center personnel abreast of the plan and its progress. Otherwise, the rumor mill will be churning at an unmanageable rate, undermining both the morale and the transition effort itself.

It is an excellent idea to also keep the Customer base appraised of the transition effort. In doing so, the contact center can count on some latitude from the Customer base if disruptions to the service are experienced. Present the plan to the executive and obtain budgetary approval. Then . . . execute.

# ANALYZING EXISTING STRUCTURE

*A contact center exists, but what is it?*

This section deals with joining an up and running contact center. The relevance of the section depends largely on the seniority and reach of the role the reader finds they have accepted in the operational contact center. The parable of the five blind men and the elephant springs to mind. To minimize the blind man syndrome, the astute new manager in an existing contact center conducts an audit. The sequence is:

1. Ascertain what the corporation needs from the contact center. Solicit input from the existing contact center management layer; the business development, sales, marketing, quality, and finance teams; and the executive layer. Understand and document what the individual requirements are. Be receptive and open as it may be found that the needs are mutually excusive of one another.

2. Ascertain what the Customer base desires. First obtain the sanction of the sales team, then go to the Customer base and survey them by whatever means is most appropriate (live conversation, telephone conversation, hard copy survey, whatever).

There are five blind wise men. They are asked by the villagers to identify an animal that has appeared in the village square. Because none of the blind men can access the entirety of the animal, an elephant, they each feel and grope only a portion of the beast and then hold forth on what they believe the beast to be. The blind man examining the trunk concludes that the animal has remarkable similarities to the snake and therefore is a member of that species. The blind sage examining the ears concludes that a beast with such wings certainly must fly and therefore is a bird. And so on.

If the sales team was asked what the salient issues are with the contact center, they may tell you that "Customer wait time" is killing the business. Finance would suggest that costs are out of control and need to be reined in, "It's killing the business." Engineering would tell you the quality of data coming from the contact center is so poor they can't ascertain where the problems are. And so on.

3. Ascertain what the competition is offering. The key is to analyze how others are managing the market, not to become a "me-too" enterprise, but to exceed and be viewed as the thought leader. Obtain a support-centric benchmark study related to the market niche the corporation is engaged in. Survey prospects that are known to use the competition's products/services (the sales team will be able to supply a list of prospects that use the competition's product).

4. Correlate. Correlate data from steps 1 and 2 and define the middle ground acceptable to corporate pressures (1) and Customer's requirements (2). Temper that with what was learned from the competition (3) and fine-tune until balance is achieved.

At this juncture a vision is established of what the contact center should be.

5. Ascertain what services the contact center is currently providing. If there is an existing contact center business plan, obtain a copy and study it. Obtain empirical performance metrics and talk to the contact center personnel to glean what is possible, what is right, what is wrong, and where improvement is needed or desired.

6. Review the tools the contact center has, then conduct an audit of the tools:

   - Are the software tools the right tools?

   - Are staff actually using the tools?

   - Is the information provided by the tools meaningful (timely and accurate)?

   - Is the staff adequately trained to utilize the tools to their full potential?

7. Gap analysis. Conduct a gap analysis between points 4 and 5.

8. Document and plan. Document all the data gathered in previous steps. The act of documenting the data points will serve to bring the issues into focus. Concentrate on the gap analysis in step 7. Detail the gap then outline the remedy. Include budget, time frame, milestones, and benchmarks.

Extend the interviews beyond the management layer. Frequently, superior improvement ideas and certainly the most accurate assessment of what is and what is not working is found by talking to the personnel in the trenches. Those on the phones every day know the score and often how to improve it. To find the most knowledgeable personnel, ask the CSRs to nominate a spokesperson. If they do you probably have the right individual. However, if a spokesperson cannot be nominated (due to apathy, infighting, or whatever) then the contact center has far greater problems than benchmarks and performance metrics.

9. Presentation and approval. Present the entire report to the executive. Solicit approval to move forward with the plan. Upon acceptance, copy all stakeholders so that there is no confusion as to where the contact center was and what it is becoming.

Shop the newly sanctioned plan around the organization. Obtain consensus and buy-in, and make sure the contact center personnel understand what the future is and where they are going as a whole. Finally, celebrate the achievement with all who contributed.

# CORPORATE CULTURE

*The human element.*

The steps listed for analyzing an existing control center conveniently ignore the real-world factors that serve to complicate an audit and execution on an improvement plan. The most global, real-world impediment is the culture of the organization and the egos of peers. Perhaps the worst-case scenario is joining a cynical and insidious management team—beware the ides of March. Be sensitive to your perspective of your peers, in understanding them it is possible to counter and obtain their sanction.

Expect to encounter the following personality profiles:

*The creator*—This is the individual responsible for the current state of the contact center. They often have a primary focus elsewhere in the organization (more often than not engineering or sales). The contact center grew under their care due to proximity (engineering) or need (sales). Perhaps your role was created to take the contact center to the next level and to allow the ad hoc creator to concentrate on their primary mandate.

Creators usually have strong motherhood feelings about the personnel, structure, and procedures they built. A less-than-optimal position is if the creator views you as an interloper, which is to suggest they do not want to relinquish control of the contact center. As it is important to secure this individual's buy-in to smoothly transition the contact center, get them on your side as quickly as possible. Speak to their success and the mechanisms that are working, but focus them on what is needed for tomorrow.

*The manipulator*—This is an individual who has a hidden agenda to champion. Political in nature, the manipulator is a corporate animal to keep your eye on. Typically, manipulators are self-centered and concerned more with their needs and aspirations then what may be best for the corporation. Be careful of what is shared with the manipulator, as it may be used in a fashion not anticipated. Probe and ascertain what the individual's key drivers are. Understand what their hidden agenda is. Proceed with caution.

*The malcontent*—The malcontent refuses to acknowledge the merit in anything. To the malcontent, the entire corporation is dysfunctional. The irony of the malcontent is that they often provide gems of great insight; the challenge is to strip the veneer of negativity surrounding the insight. Malcontents often wrap themselves in the protective guise of "devil's advocate." The fact is if the astute contact center manager has done a thorough analysis then they have already acted as their own devil's advocate and will have a ready reason/answer for the action under scrutiny. One of the most effective counters to the malcontent is to adopt Dr. Edward de Bono's Six Thinking Hat paradigm. See appendix I, page 265, for further data.

## Consider Also the Overall Culture of the Organization

Culture, like many other aspects of corporate life, is not one-dimensional. Larger organizations can have venerable strata of cultures stacked upon one another. Finance may be an ultraconservative paper-driven department whereas marketing might be marked by a rebellious, youthful playfulness. Engineering may be completely dominated by their code-source-store technology, and sales may appear to be cowboys on the last technological frontier. These are hybrid organizations, and cultural behavior, within hybrids is often by design. Successful organizations need both the risk-taking entrepreneurs and the staunch button-down bean counters. They balance each other and perform their individual (or departmental) tasks with aplomb.

*Revolutionary vis-à-vis evolutionary*—The revolutionary organization thrives on upheaval and is designed to weather change well. Evolutionary organizations are more apt to let change occur slowly, almost organically. Thought-leading organizations are, by definition, revolutionary, and it follows that "me too" organizations are evolutionary in nature.

The epitome of a revolutionary organization is the high-technology start-up where decisions for massive change can be made readily. Execution is still complicated, but as organizational buy-in is usually assured, change can be effected very rapidly. That is not to suggest, however, that a revolutionary approach does not have a place in larger and/or mature organizations. On occasion, market-driven circumstances may force a revolutionary change—the proverbial turn-on-a-dime dynamic. As with the majority of the techniques discussed in this book, this is just one more tool in the belt to be deployed when appropriate.

Evolutionary organizations are distinguished by management by consensus and steering committees, and characterized by slow and managed change. Some evolutionary organizations are found in the high-technology sector also, but they are more frequently encountered in blue-chip industries and large organizations. Evolutionary organizations tend to make fewer mistakes than revolutionary organizations, but they are hardly ever on the cutting edge of innovation—and there's nothing wrong with that.

*Aggressively progressive*—The aggressively progressive organization is characterized by innovation for the sake of innovation, usually marked by a revolutionary style accompanied by a high-technology focus. The visionaries making the decisions at aggressively progressive businesses see or hear of a new development (fad in this context) and wish to deploy it as quickly as possible.

The telling signs of an aggressively progressive organization are quick changes, numerous projects that have run out of steam, and a rather cynical project management team. The most time-consuming aspect of this style of culture is the frequent new management paradigms that are forced upon the unsuspecting management layer. These organizations are often quite structured with one-, two- or three-year plans, however, the plans are often set aside when the excitement of a new innovation surfaces. The magic is to be aggressively progressive when necessary; balance is key.

*Conservative*—The conservative organization is always evolutionary in style. While there may be pockets of revolutionary thought and style, the modus operandi is to get initiatives formally approved. The conservative organization follows structure and procedure, which is fine, providing the following is with eyes wide open and not blind. These organizations are very structured. There are three-year plans in place and any deviation from the plan is thoroughly analyzed before moving forward.

*Chaos*—The chaos culture is an organization that is often championed by the engineering department. Marked by the precept that the organization must encourage creative thought, these organizations are generally quite enjoyable to work in and with. However, the discipline needed in a contact center is often at loggerheads with the chaos model. It is important to calibrate the lords of chaos to the difference in approach demanded by the Customer base and contact centers in general.

These organizations are somewhere between the conservative and aggressively progressive styles. It is very possible to find a great deal of structure within a chaos model, but the propensity for, and ease of, abandoning a plan is very high. Many high-technology start-ups (and some mature organizations as well) are based on the chaos style. Some organizations plan just beyond the event horizon, often no more than three months into the future. Revolutionary change is the standard (which, curiously enough, renders it nonrevolutionary).

# HIRING STAFF

*Hire the best and the rest will follow.*

Attract and retain the best talent and the contact center will prosper. This section details the attributes and mechanisms for maximizing the hiring cycle. For each position listed in the organizational charts (see Figure 2.5, Generic contract center structure, page 50, and Figure 2.6, Expanded contact center structure, page 51), there are basic success criteria. These criteria help define the skill set required to be effective and successful in the position. Standardized tests are an excellent tool to ascertain if an interviewee is an adequate fit or an excellent fit.

## Criteria

The list that follows outlines some of the basic criteria around which standardized tests may be developed.

Both hard and soft skills are outlined as well as a number of personal qualities. Hard skills are those skills that lend themselves to testing and typically have an academic basis. Hard skills include computer literacy and technical skills. Soft skills do not lend themselves to testing and are much harder to isolate. Soft skills include demeanor and stress management skills. Personal qualities are also difficult to test for, and the line between a soft skill and a personal quality is often grey.

Ironically it is the soft skills that are in highest demand in a contact center and the most difficult to determine proficiency in. Soft skills are typically not easy to teach; the incumbent develops the attribute over time. The hard skills, such as technology, can be learned provided the attitude and aptitude is present. Therefore, hire individuals that have *personality* (soft skill) with a penchant to learn and absorb technical information (hard skill).

In practice, the key criteria list should be reviewed and a weighting applied to each bulleted item. The weighting is determined by assessing how important the attribute is in relation to the role in supporting the target product/service. Then, in concert with human resources, develop a set of questions to exercise those items with the highest weighting. Give each candidate the test and mark and grade accordingly for suitability to the position and operation. Hire the top scoring incumbents, they should be the "best fit."[14]

### Key Criteria Examples

*Writing skills (hard skill)*—If the support model includes e-mail responses then the ability to write clearly is paramount. Consider also the ability to generate reports and memorandums. Writing skills that are clear, concise, succinct, and tuned to the audience are desired.

*Verbal skills (soft skill)*—Very important for telephone-based CSRs. Test for articulation and clarity of message. The live interview process itself provides opportunity to converse with the candidate. An excellent technique is to ask the interviewee to chat about a hobby or favorite activity. General demeanor indicators will also surface during the chat test.

*Probing skills (soft skill)*—Frequently, the Customer inadvertently puts up a smoke screen of unrelated data, opinion, and conjecture. The successful CSR can navigate through the chaff to find the real issue. This skill is linked to the ability to listen and analyze data points in real time.

*Computer literacy (hard skill)*—Test to ascertain if the candidate possesses the degree of computer knowledge required for the role. This may range from needing only to be able to use the telephone system (minimal computer literacy) to requiring an industry certification (such as a Microsoft Certified System Engineer or Cisco certification). If the position is to be tied to a help desk or customer relationship management system, consider the interviewee's keyboarding (typing speed and accuracy) skills, the driver being how fast and accurate they can get information into the system.

*Technical skills (hard skill)*—What degree of technical knowledge is needed? Be sure to also consider the background technical knowledge that may be required. For example, if the prime product is a print driver, it would be very beneficial for the CSRs to be conversant on the industry-leading printer manufactures (HP, Epson, and so on) and have a knowledge of the basic print technologies (laser, ink jet, dye sublimation, and so on).

*Stress management (soft skill/quality)*—The interviewee must have experience and knowledge of how to deal with their own stress. The key attribute to look for is the ability to perform under difficult and often hostile conditions.

*Learning aptitude (soft skill/quality)*—The speed at which the interviewee can embrace and understand a new concept. This is driven by the tempo at which the target product/service is evolving as well as by the sophistication of contacts the contact center is clearing. It is related to the ability to think clearly and logically given, potentially, a number of variables and to the individual's own ability to respond to change. A leading indicator of an interviewee with an aptitude for learning is to inquire as to what skills they have acquired and honed on their own initiative.

*Perseverance (soft skill/quality)*—The degree of focus and determination the interviewee can, and will, apply to the resolve of a challenge. A CSR with this quality will assiduously research the resolution to an issue. Alternatively, a CSR devoid of this quality will pass the contact off to another CSR, avoid the issue, or, worst of all, throw up a barrage of technobabble to get the Customer off the line.

*Demeanour (quality)*—The optimal demeanor, be it verbal, written, or even within one's body language, is positive, crisp, snappy, and generally upbeat. Consider tone of voice, degree of natural courtesy, and people skills.

*Team player (soft skill)*—The explanation and value of a team player is obvious, but rather difficult to test for. The interviewee's *team-playerness* will surface after a few weeks on the team.

---

The other side of this issue is the expense of coming to an equitable resolution. One particularly focused CSR, in the spirit of perseverance, expended almost an entire week of her time calling a number of meetings and writing a small dissertation on the Customer's issue. The Customer, however, had only posted a query, they had not experienced a failure nor been inconvenienced in any way. The cost of the resolution to the query was far out of proportion to the Customer satisfaction value. Plato once mused, "do not be more precise than the subject warrants."

*Administrative/organizational skills (quality)*—Will the interviewee be a good corporate citizen? Will the individual be timely when it comes to time sheets, expense reports, vacation requests, and the other myriad forms that must be filled out to be a good corporate citizen? Or will the supervisor/manager layer spend an inordinate amount of time nagging the individual for these administrative duties?

Once the hiring criteria is established, weighted, and documented, the execution takes place—interviewing.

## Interviewing

Interviewing is similar to training; almost everyone thinks they do it well. The fact is, not many can for a number of reasons. The following list outlines some of the more undesirable behaviors observed in interviewers:

- The rambler—This interviewer talks continually. They flesh out the question to ridiculous detail. The interviewee hardly has an opportunity to answer the questions asked.

- The genius—This interviewer is so enamored with their accomplishments and triumphs that they dominate conversation with anecdotes based on their own achievements. Like the rambler, the interviewee gets little opportunity to talk and strut their own skills.

- The bushwhacker—They spend the interview deviously trying to trap the interviewee. The bushwhacker leaves the interviewee with a sense of paranoia and little opportunity to speak to their positive attributes.

- The technical guru—These beasts abound in high technology. In a hardly-veiled effort to display how superior and clever they are, they like to question the interviewee about arcane technological facts. The technical guru can be spotted by their propensity to use an acronym whenever possible. The interviewee is made to feel insignificant and deflated.

- The pitcher—Often from the sales team. This individual sells the interviewee on the product. While being sold on the company is a good thing, there is little value in selling the product to the interviewee (they wouldn't be there if they did not want the opportunity). These interviews are enjoyable for most interviewees as there is little pressure put on them, they only need to nod positively to keep the pitcher's momentum up.

- The non-conversationalist—The most difficult style to encounter when one is the interviewee. The non-conversationalist limits their responses to monosyllables. It is very difficult to get an interviewee to open up and show their potential when the non-conversationalist is conducting the interview.

- The optimist—The ever positive. The optimist often has some valuable feedback on an interviewee, however, being that all the feedback is positive, the optimist's opinion is compromised.

Not one of the interview styles listed here delivers meaningful data on whether or not to bring an interviewee on staff, which supports the suspicion that not all personnel make effective interviewers. The fact is, some personnel who may be exemplary performers should never be given the lead in the interview process.

Find those staff members that are inclined and motivated to conduct effective interviews. The first phase in weeding out the least effective interviewers is to ascertain who does not wish to conduct interviews; those who are not motivated and inclined are unlikely to perform well. That is fine, excuse them from the exercise.

The second phase is to conduct test interviews with existing personnel. These trial interviews should be observed by a panel including those who were excused in the first round (just because they do not wish to be frontline interviewers does not mean their opinions are invalid). Identify who are the most proficient interviewers, make recommendations on how to further improve their skills, and go to it.

There is an alternative to doing the interviewing with internal staff. The entire hiring process can be outsourced. The upside is that there is no resource hit on the existing personnel and professionals will conduct the interviews. The downside is that in order for the process to succeed, the documentation still needs to be created by the contact center. It is only the actual interview time that is saved. In addition, the contact center personnel will receive the new hires far easier if they had an active hand in the hiring process.

## Group Hiring—the Job Fair

When ramping up a new team, or when sales are undergoing a geometric growth period, there may be need to hire en masse. An effective approach is to play host to a job fair. The advertisement campaign is the same as when searching for individuals except the advertisement invites the prospect to a group session.

See Figure 2.7, Job fair hiring sequence, for a graphic outlining of the sequence of events pursuant to a successful job fair.

# SAME OLD SAME OLD

*Dissenters dance to their own drummer.*

There is an axiom in Human Resource circles that states "like hires like." Most managers tend to court and hire individuals that share their outlooks, attributes, and experiences. This inclination towards sameness can limit effectiveness. If all team members think alike and share common backgrounds then innovation is hamstrung. It may not be possible to curtail hiring biases but being aware of the dynamic may inspire some to hire outside the box, or even to hire the dissenter personality.

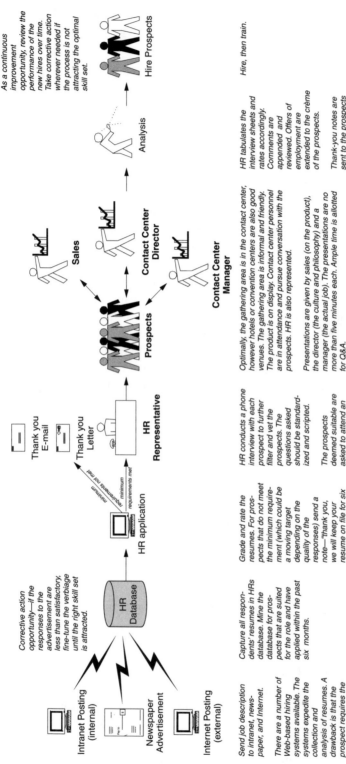

**Figure 2.7** Job fair hiring sequence.

Dissenters are those that question the status quo. Dissenters are an excellent source for disruptive innovations that can serve to springboard an operation to greater achievements. The downside of the dissenter personality is if they gravitate too frequently to the devil's advocate role. Like everything else in life, it is balance that is needed. Hire a dissenter or two and consult them frequently.

> Groupthink is that insidious dynamic where a team, executives included, sits about the corporate boardroom praising the product and each other. Not a modicum of dissent is tolerated in these sessions. This behavior is entrenched in more corporations than not.

It is also beneficial to stimulate cross-pollination. Stir the contact center teams often, froth them up, encourage innovation, disruptive and otherwise. Be on the lookout for groupthink and stamp it out immediately where it has taken root. Bring dissenters on board—be careful not to confuse healthy dissention with the *cynical malcontent*—listen to their insights and skim off the cream.

## Probation

Probation is a given, what is discussed in this section is timing and the term. The contact center management must work closely with human resources, the experts on personnel issues. There may be local or federal laws that restrict what can and cannot be instigated regarding probation periods and termination. That said, even in the more lax jurisdictions it is an excellent idea to assiduously document probation proceedings and any grievances.

The first thing to consider in the contact center environment is that it presents special challenges to both the personnel on the contact line and the management layer. There are few other positions in an organization where so much latitude is granted to an entry-level employee under so few tangible (enforceable) guidelines.

Most other corporate positions are isolated from direct contact with the Customer base by the contact center and, furthermore, by time. Support provided by the contact center is real-time. What other teams operate in real time? To illustrate: outside of the contact center, ramifications of an action on the part of an individual employee are mitigated; a junior software engineer's work is thoroughly exercised and tested before a Customer gets the product, or low-impact tasks are assigned until proven. Contact center personnel are real-time and on the front lines. These circumstances justify special probation schemes for the contact center personnel.

There are two periods that present an excellent opportunity to review a hiring decision—during the training period and directly after. The industry standard for probation is three months, but that is not sufficient time to vet the employee in a contact center environment. The recommendation is to extend the probation to six months in the contact center—three during training and ramp-up, and three once the employee has graduated.

Consider an employee who has all the necessary skills but they are somewhat introverted. They, of course, fail the probation period on the front line due to their introverted nature. It is not smart or necessary, however, to terminate an employee because they cannot handle the stress of real-time Customer interaction. The corporation has already invested the training and orientation effort into the employee, and it would be foolish to squander this investment. The employee may be better suited in either an off-line role or elsewhere in the corporation. If the employee has shown merit, hold on to them, retrain, and reposition.

# STAFF RETENTION

*Controlling churn is important.*

There are few people who envision tenure in a contact center as a final career objective. There are some who enjoy working through Customer issues six hours a day, day after day after day. There are some who aspire to managerial positions within the contact center, but the operation only requires so many supervisors and managers.

The contact center is an entry point into the workforce in general. Many new hires in the contact center join the team with the strategy that once their foot is in the door, they can move elsewhere in the organization. This is fine, the organization needs good people with initiative and focus. The challenge for the hopefully less transient contact management team is providing quality Customer care in a revolving-door environment.

The star contact center personnel will move out of the contact center quickest. Their abilities will be recognized and they will move on within the organization. This is a good thing for all parties. A not-so-good scenario is where an employee completes the training provided and funded by the contact center, and takes their newfound skill set to another organization. This is a hole that needs attention.

The longer an individual is retained within the organization, the higher the return on the investment made in that individual. There is incredible value in the tacit knowledge that is contained in the grey matter of those employees who have been with the organization the longest. Keep these employees engaged and motivated and the tacit knowledge pool will increase. The effectiveness and efficiency of the employees will increase in tandem with the tacit knowledge pool.

> Tacit knowledge is implicit knowledge—the knowledge that is nearly impossible to conduct training on and only comes from being in the same organization for a reasonable period (knowing the names of the movers and shakers in all departments, for example).

A staff retention program should be put in place to keep the star performers in the company. For the program to have optimal effect, the program itself must be sold to the employees as a value-added aspect to working at the corporation. The training team in tandem with the human resources team must get the good word out so that the employees:

1. Realize what a great place the corporation is to work

2. Recognize their personal potential

There is value is writing success stories based on those team members that move through the contact center and the organization in general. The desired effect is to inspire the members of the contact center to realize their full potential—a win/win proposition for all.

## EXIT INTERVIEW

*You win some you lose some.*

The exit interview is an opportunity to garner data about the day-to-day operation of the contact center from an informed source. As the exiting employee no longer has any vested interest in the contact center, the comments they put forth are always candid. There is need to be on guard, however, regarding potential personal vendettas and undeserved hostility in the exiting employee's comments.

It is preferable if the interviewer is not the exiting employee's direct supervisor, but their supervisor's supervisor. This allows management to get an understanding of how well their reports are functioning. Some of the data points that should be discussed in the exit interview are:

1. The specific reason(s) for leaving.

2. Open the discussion to suggestions for improvement. Do not limit the discussion to tools; include comments on environment, personnel, product, and so on.

3. Ascertain what the operation would need to improve to entice the employee to stay (assuming that the exit is fait accompli and efforts to retain the employee have failed).

4. Ask for opinions on their supervisor's performance. This data can be used during the supervisor's review, as fodder for continuous improvement, and, in extreme cases, immediate corrective action.

In addition, the exit interview affords an opportunity to impress upon the departing employee the rules regarding what they can and cannot share with their future employer and other interested parties. A brief review of the noncompete and confidentiality agreement should be conducted. See the section titled "Noncompete/Confidentiality," page 162, for further details.

## COMPENSATION

*One gets what is paid for.*

Figure 2.8, Relative compensation level, generic contact center, is a guideline to compensation levels in a contact center. The graphic outlines the relative salary level for each position depicted in Figure 2.5, Generic contact center structure, page 50.

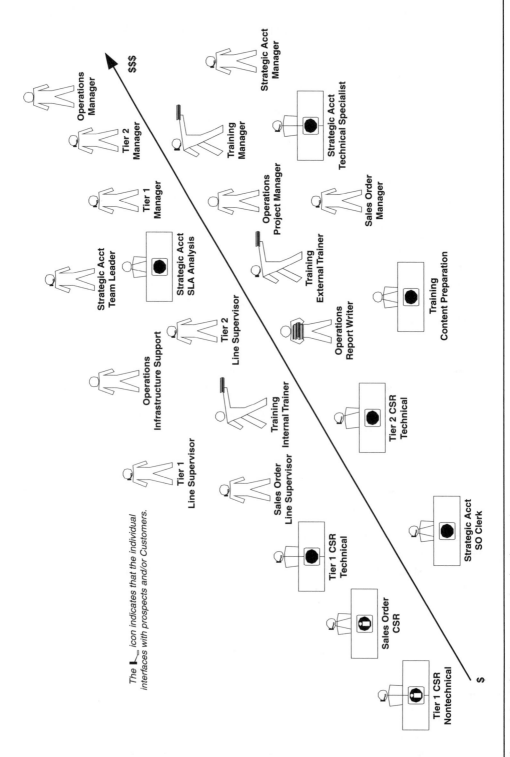

The **I**⌐ icon indicates that the individual interfaces with prospects and/or Customers.

**Figure 2.8**  Relative compensation level, generic contact center.

The issue of graduated compensation (a pay raise at the end of the probation period) is to be avoided. It sets precedent that a pay raise is to be expected when milestones are reached. This is an administration burden as not only does the system need to be tracked, it also needs to be created (for instance, what are the milestones). A superior approach is to base salary adjustments on merit, not milestones. Introduce structured pay ranges for each function but leave latitude for managers to reward star performers.

As the compensation scheme is reviewed, bear in mind that there are no hard rules when it comes to recognizing and rewarding performance. It is not uncommon to have an individual reporting to a manager that actually makes more money than the manager. The star players may deserve revisiting the compensation standards in the contact center as it pays to keep the best. Special arrangements may have to be considered to retain the top performers, such as:

*Additional vacation time*—Time offered above the vacation time agreed to when the employee came on board. Employees respect the value of additional vacation time very much.

*Stock options*—Employees are granted the right to purchase a limited amount of stocks at the strike price established by the market (if the corporation is public) or at an estimated fair market value (if the corporation is pre–initial public offering [IPO]). One caveat is that the stock option can actually become a disincentive if the market value of the stock dips below the strike price an employee is offered. If the stock dip is long-term, a companywide correction, subject to market rules, may need to be executed.

*Bonuses*—Performance-based bonuses have been popular in the past, however, there is some question as to the effectiveness of bonuses over the long term. The administrative costs and ill will generated (those who do not reap bonuses often feel ill done by) by a bonus plan completely eradicates any positive momentum. Proceed with caution.

*Flextime*—Employees are given the option of when they put their hours in. If 11:00 a.m. to 7:00 p.m. is a better fit to an employee's domestic responsibility, then flextime provides the latitude to act. It is highly recommended, however, that core hours be established when all employees must be in attendance if for nothing else than team meetings. Flextime adds an extra dimension to time reporting, there is an administrative cost to supporting flextime.

*Job sharing*—This is where two employees share a single role and prorate the (single) salary and benefits. There may be some disparity between the performance of each half of the pair, but in a contact center environment this should not cause too much grief provided the disparity is manageable.

*Telecommuting*—This provides the employees with the ability to work from their home. The employees reap flexibility and it is a real boon to employee satisfaction; however, telecommuting has a number of pitfalls and traps. Enter into a telecommuting option very carefully. Isolate and document the performance measures and selection criteria (that is, who may or may not qualify for telecommuting). If telecommuting is extended to CSRs, and support personnel, ensure the telephony system can handle transparent call forwarding to outside lines.

*Day care facilities/subsidization*—This is, perhaps, more of a perk than a compensation model idea. Providing a day care service expands the available employee pool significantly, however, only the largest contact centers have the critical mass to justify an in-house day care program. The creative manager can outsource local day care facilities and assist with the costs.

*Business/family balance program*—A formalized employee program to ensure that there is balance between the individual's work life and their personal life. Many of the other bullets in this section could be categorized under a business/family balance program and probably would be if the program came first. This program requires buy-in and assistance from human resources—in fact, the program should totally belong to human resources. Before proceeding with a business/family initiative, ascertain if it will be well received by the contact center personnel; if the average age in the contact center is 35, the program will receive far greater acceptance than if the average age is 22.

*Corporate concierge*—The provision of a concierge to take the burden of daily "run-around" tasks off the employees is an interesting concept that has surfaced of late. Suitability to a contact center environment is questionable, but with controls and rules in place it may be viable. Restricting access to the services of the concierge to the management layer has been executed with success, but may sow seeds of discontent among the non-elite.

## ADVANCEMENT POTENTIAL

*Contact center personnel as a farm team.*

One of the most effective methods used to manage and reduce churn is to have a career advancement program in place. A new employee can envision their career from entry level to management. An employee can gain entry at the contact center and, with the human resources team, map out their entire career within the corporation. The obvious advancement path within the contact center is depicted in Figure 2.9. Advancement path I.

A less obvious path is for the employee to cross-pollinate within the contact center as depicted in Figure 2.10, Advancement path II.

Customer Support         Team Leader         Supervisor         Manager
Representative

**Figure 2.9**   Advancement path I.

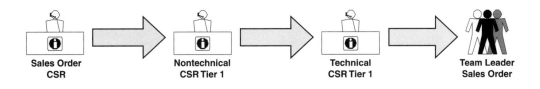

**Figure 2.10**   Advancement path II.

As the employee touches teams within the contact center their knowledge horizon is increased. This is highly beneficial as interdepartmental conflicts are minimized when personnel understand the challenges and issues faced by their colleagues. In addition, procedural changes made by managers and line supervisors are unlikely to compromise other teams if management understands their roles from the inside out.

In an optimal organization the entire management team will have experience at all levels within the contact center. This is a worthy goal but not realistic as there is little chance a nontechnical individual could perform in the second tier technical support role. Cross-pollinate when at all possible, including having the technical personnel spend time at the less technical positions.

To be optimally effective for both the individual and corporation, advancement should not be limited to the contact center but should have links to other departments in the organization. Figure 2.11, Advancement path III, depicts a generalized set of options for career advancement.

Some of the more apt and popular teams contact center personnel migrate to include:

- Quality assurance/control—Technical CSRs quickly amass an understanding of the Customer's mind-set and what they are looking for in a product. Their troubleshooting experience provides an excellent background for some of the detective work quality professionals perform. On the downside, the regimentation of the quality team may be difficult for a hotshot troubleshooter to adjust to.

- Sales—The contact center is an excellent farm team for the technical side of the sales team. Many products are complicated enough to demand pre-sales support within the sales team. The optimal fit for this position are those CSRs that have excellent technical product knowledge and have well-developed interpersonal relationship skills. The four-legged[15] sales model pairs a just-out-of-the-contact center technical whip with a seasoned sales representative.

- Product management—Similar to the comments regarding the quality team, former contact center personnel have their finger on the pulse of the Customer. They know the wants and requirements as they have been dealing with Customers on a daily basis. The former contact center employee also brings a stable of Customers with them who they have built a rapport with over time—invaluable to a product management team searching for informed and friendly data sources.

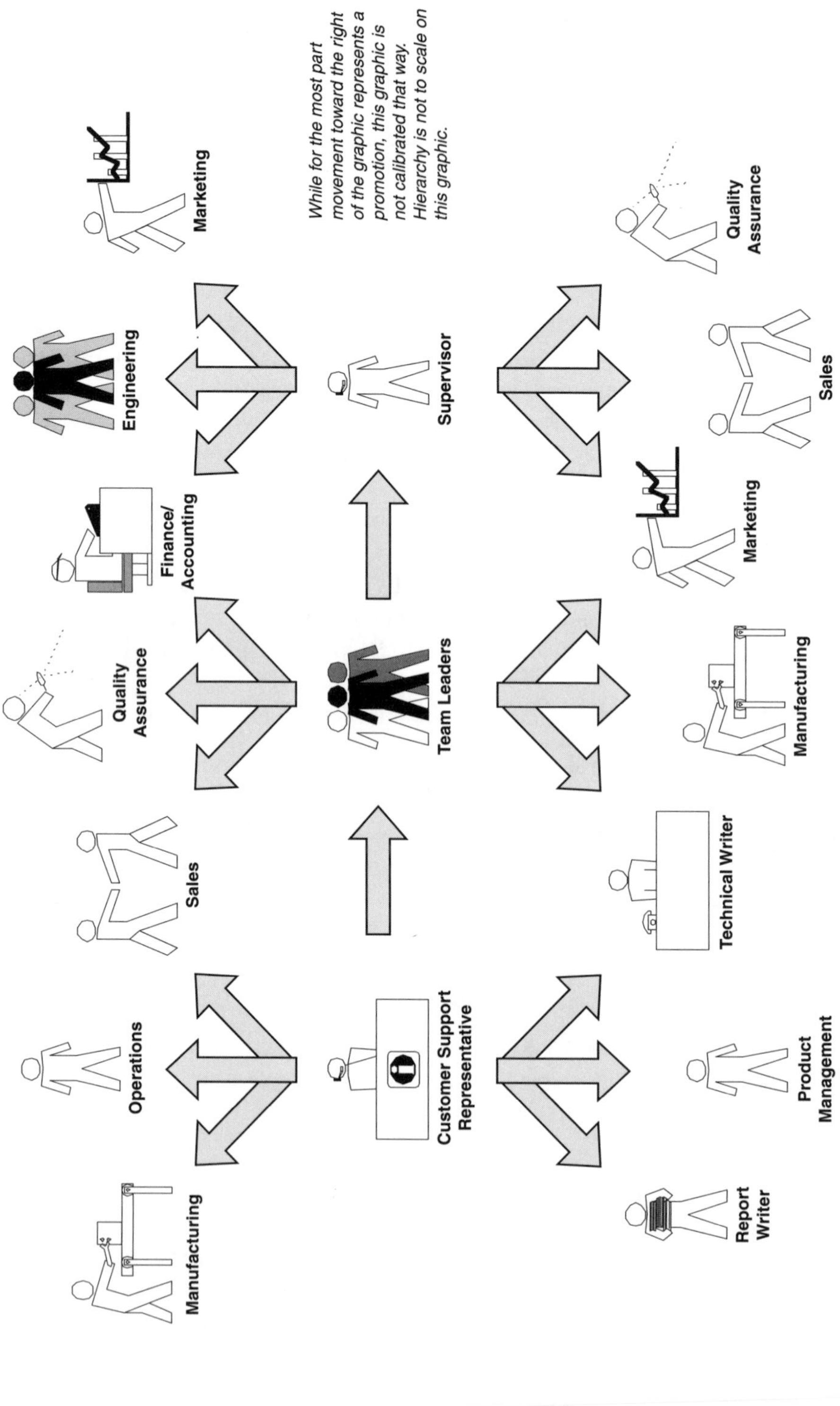
Manufacturing
Operations
Sales
Quality Assurance
Finance/ Accounting
Engineering
Marketing
Customer Support Representative
Team Leaders
Supervisor
While for the most part movement toward the right of the graphic represents a promotion, this graphic is not calibrated that way. Hierarchy is not to scale on this graphic.
Report Writer
Product Management
Technical Writer
Manufacturing
Marketing
Sales
Quality Assurance

**Figure 2.11** Advancement path III.

- Human resources—As the contact center is a formidable human resources challenge, contact center personnel tend to transition smoothly into human resources roles. A former contact center representative in human resources is invaluable for those organizations that are experiencing personnel problems within the contact center; the contact center personnel recognize an informed advocate in the human resources team. That can be very powerful in restoring order to a contact center undergoing a churn crisis.

## ENVIRONMENT AND CULTURE

*Positive vibe spawns positive energy.*

For the purposes of this section the definition of "culture" is limited to environmental components such as the facility, furniture, and creature comfort factors. Management style has a huge impact on the *culture,* but it is too complicated and broad a topic for this book. It will suffice to suggest that the attitudes, actions, and communication style of the management layer define and drive the culture of the contact center.

The environment must be conducive to providing a positive Customer experience. Put yourself in the CSR's position, answering the phone for hours at time and dealing with a continuous stream of hostile Customers. The stress these CSRs sustain each and every day is considerable. In addition, consider that many of these same people are some of the most junior staff members in any given company, and do not discount the monotony that they face. Consider if there is an endemic failure of the product, the contact center staff would be inundated with Customers asking the same question (Customer self-service mechanism aside for the moment), it is not easy.

It stands to reason that the contact center personnel must be comfortable and surrounded by positive images. Design the workplace to meet employees' functional requirements in a comfortable and pleasant fashion. The physical environment must be in harmony with corporate goals and image. The walls should be painted bright colors to surround the CSRs in a positive, uplifting environment. Provide areas where stressed CSRs can go to freshen their perspective and recharge their energy. Figure 2.12, Conceptual floor plan, presents just that. The following introduces some ideas to enhance the effectiveness and comfort of the CSRs:

- Relaxation lounge. An area with subdued lighting furnished with couches and comfortable chairs. High-quality commercial carpeting is desirable for sound suppression and ease on the feet. Design it with more of a living room ambiance than a business area. Consider if the area should be a "management free" area as well. Use of the lounge should be unrestricted and free of management surveillance.

   A foosball table and/or a billiard table are good additions to the lounge area. Computers with Internet surfing and gaming ability have huge currency with personnel. Tread carefully with the introduction of a stereo sound system as it is unlikely that any grouping of individuals can agree on what constitutes suitable

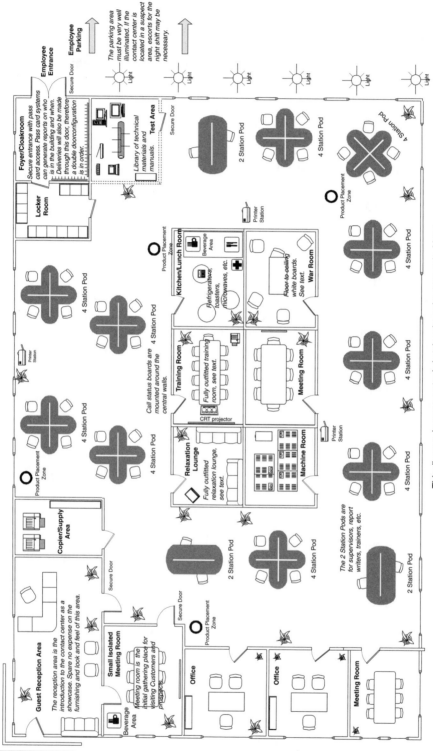

**Figure 2.12** Conceptual floor plan.

music. With that last comment in mind, supply headphones for the personal computers in the lounge area. A number of telephones ostensibly placed in the lounge for personal calls deliver a positive trust message to personnel.

- War room. An area to brainstorm issues and hold conference calls and team meetings. It should be designed to be less comfortable than the lounge but still comfortable. Consider floor to ceiling white boards for capturing notes and ideas. If the budget allows, procure one of the electronic white boards that can capture the information written on it digitally—an excellent technology that facilitates retrieval and distribution of important data points. Keep areas of the white board reserved for ongoing challenges. There is great benefit in coming to the war room and having yesterday's or last week's notes posted. The next meeting starts where the team left off as opposed to consuming the first half of the meeting in recapping and summarizing last meeting's issues.

  The war room is also a great place to post key metrics that the contact center is tracking. As the white board acts as a collective "memory," trends can be tracked and understood.

- Training center. As stated elsewhere in this book, training is a continuous activity. Training services apply to internal employees (not necessarily limited to contact center personnel) and external individuals such as Customers, partners/vendors, resellers, and so on. Therefore, it is prudent to create a permanent professional training center within the contact center. The training area should feature as permanent fixtures all the equipment needed to effectively transfer knowledge. The more self-sufficient the training center is, the more effective the training team can be. Consider the following tools and fixtures (the list is presented from most important to have to least important to have):

  - Presentation projector (personal computer VGA interface and overhead projector)—A projector is an excellent tool to facilitate presentations to large groups. The fact that the projector is driven from a personal computer allows the trainers to tweak presentations in near real time. Overhead projectors are not recommended as they are outdated, have a high consumables cost in transparencies and foils, and are not update friendly.

  - Hardware/software—Equip the training center with the same hardware and software as found in production in the contact center. The training area should preferably be on its own LAN segment physically isolated from the main production system. The isolated LAN insures that the trainees will not adversely affect the production system or introduce spurious data onto the live system.

  - Ancillary hardware/software—If the training program includes hands-on laboratory sessions, and it should, all the hardware and software needed should be a permanent fixture in the training center. The trainer should verify, in concert with the MIS/IT team, that all needed components are up and running well before the scheduled start time of the session.

The author observed one training session where half the allotted training time was consumed by the trainer leaving the room to get a missing disk, followed by a minor installation routine, followed by a hunt for a small Ethernet hub, followed by . . . . Not a very effective session, and the fee certainly was not justified.

- Printers—The training area should have its own printing resources for both materials and laboratory sessions. Color printers are preferred as they send a quality message and allow for a more expressive and polished hard copy of presentation materials and handouts.

- Electronic white board—An excellent tool that allows any notes the trainer may post on the white board to be scanned and taken away by the trainees or recalled for future sessions.

- Partitions—The number of trainees the training center can accommodate simultaneously is driven by the size of the contact center, the size of the sessions directed to external personnel, the frequency of the training sessions, and the scheduling thereof. To get the most out of the training area consider one large room that can be partitioned into smaller areas. Soundproofing between the areas is mandatory. As per earlier comments on isolated systems, each of the partitioned areas should be self-sufficient and isolated from each other as well as the production system(s).

- Beverage center—To keep disruptions to a minimum, a coffee machine and perhaps a small refrigerator dedicated to the training area goes a very long way. Try to anticipate all the trainees' comfort needs so that the trainees have no reason to exit the training area.

- Washrooms—If at all possible, position the training room close to washrooms.

- Telephones—To be used for outgoing calls only. There is nothing more disrupting then the trainees taking calls while they are on training. The only thing more frustrating is the trainer taking support calls during the course of a session. It is also a good idea to disconnect the public address system in the training area (providing no local bylaws are compromised in doing this).

- Copier—Again on the self-sufficient theme, a small copier in the training area reduces disruption potential. Color copiers send a quality message and result in a more professional look than black-and-white-only copiers.

- Video link/conferencing—Training sessions are one of the best uses of videoconferencing capability. Full training and update sessions can be broadcast to remote offices.

- Video capture—A less expensive alternative to a live video link is to record sessions. Economical technologies are available to record and edit live sessions and distribute on videotape (for example, VHS tapes) or digital (for example, DVD discs). There will be some post-production work needed in regards to editing, insertion of titles, noise reduction, and other sundry video production activities. In lieu of professional editing two options are available: there are often personnel in the MIS/IT department or the contact center itself that have an interest in video postproduction work, post a notice and see if a body comes forward; or, contact a local college that offers a video production program, they may be happy to do it as a real-world application for the program. There are risks in the level of quality of the final product, but it only has to be functional, not a contender for an academy award.

- Cafeteria/lunch room. If the contact center is large enough to justify a fully operational cafeteria, then consider outsourcing this service to a professional food services organization. This speaks to the idea that the contact center should stick to its core competencies. If the critical mass is not there to justify a full cafeteria, an area is needed for personnel to store, consume, and dispose of their lunches, dinners, and snacks. Position the lunchroom so that it is away from the production floor; it should be a sanctuary of sorts. Consider the following fixtures (the list is presented from most important to have to least important to have):

  - First aid kit—Most often found in the lunchroom. Minimal advice on the contents is presented here as local bylaws will drive what you can and cannot make available and administer to the personnel.

  - Coffee machine—Self-explanatory. Do not skimp on the coffee machine. The $39.99 big box store special is fine for use at home but not for the rigorous environment of a contact center. Procure a commercial model supported by a commercial service.

  - Tea, hot chocolate service—Some commercial coffee machines also boil water for tea or hot chocolate. The hot chocolate and tea should be available on a similar basis as the coffee (that is, if coffee is free, the other beverages should be as well).

  - Refrigerator(s)—For food and beverages. Commercial models with glass doors are the best units, however a standard noncommercial unit will suffice in smaller operations. Cleaning and upkeep is greatly simplified with the commercial models.

  - Microwave(s)—For food and beverages. As was the case for the refrigerator, a commercial grade model is desirable.

  - Dishwasher—Self-explanatory. Again, a commercial model is the best option.

  - Toaster—A nice touch.

One organization redeployed the obsolete printers from the engineering department into the contact center. These printers were so old that they did not support the printing of graphics. Management had figured that the contact center printed e-mails and schedules for the most part and, hence, graphics were a nonissue. It did not take long for the denizens of the contact center to figure out that while they couldn't print a simple Gantt chart, the engineers were printing the latest Web pages in glorious full color. Two things happened: contact center personnel started printing most of their documentation on the engineering printers, thus wasting the walk-down time and the additional chat time with the engineering personnel, *and* the contact center personnel got the meta-message that they were second-class corporate citizens. The fix was simple: don't treat the contact center as a dumping ground.

- Cutlery, plates, cups, glasses—Nothing fancy, in fact, keep it as plain as possible to reduce the potential for pilfering.

- Telephone—Place a telephone in the lunchroom for personal calls.

- Crisis management manual—Post a hard copy of the crisis management manual.[16]

- PC equipment and tools. Equip the personnel with the most appropriate tools to do their jobs. A number of organizations (albeit small organizations) often use their contact centers as a dumping ground for obsolete hardware and software. It is often the old machines from the engineering/development group that find themselves redeployed in the contact center. Frequently, the "lemons" are also dumped into the contact center.

  That is not to say it doesn't make good economic sense to redeploy assets; it certainly does. It is true that the engineering/development department has the greatest need for cutting edge technologies to perform their jobs, but be cognizant of the message dumping sends to the personnel working in the redeployment areas. If the redeployment strategy is mismanaged at the employee-perception level, then the message received by the contact center personnel is that they are second-class corporate citizens. This is a key culture driver and can be demoralizing when mismanaged.

- Headsets. In many contact centers, the CSRs are on the phone the majority of their day. Headsets are a simple way to make the CSRs more comfortable and effective. Wireless headsets are recommended if the budget allows. The wireless headsets allow the CSR to move around the contact center freely. Free movement facilitates a number of things:

  - The CSR can comfortably stand up and move around. This is mandatory for support calls that stretch into hours. Simply standing up provides the CSR with a change in environment, and although it seems minor, it is still a change and has a positive effect. The CSR can stretch and refresh without interrupting the conversation flow.

- The CSR is provided with freedom of movement. In fact, they can pace if they so desire.

- The CSR is free to move to an area where samples are set up or where test environments are up and running. They are free to use their hands to open packages, documentation, type in commands, assume control of the Customer's machine, and so on.

- The CSR is free to move to another, perhaps senior, CSR for support or advice. This is far superior to handing the call off to another CSR, interrupting the rapport already established and annoying the Customer.

- Pods and furniture. A number of companies market furniture specifically designed for contact center environments. One of the more effective arrangements is to migrate away from the standard cubicle-based furniture to a work-team or pod arrangement. In a pod system, CSRs are placed in small teams of four to eight individuals. Each Customer CSR sits facing into the middle of the pod. The pods have low walls between the individual desktops to encourage interaction.

  Pod teams can be structured in any number of ways. An excellent approach is to mix junior, intermediate, and senior CSRs in the same pod; somewhat like a built-in training, education, and escalation team.

  Another excellent approach is to have multidisciplinary pods where first tier, second tier, sales order entry, and invoicing representatives are all within the pod. The majority of incoming Customer issues can be contained within the multidisciplinary pod as there is broad expertise for each individual CSR to draw from. Consider setting up healthy competition between the pods. Base the competition's success criteria on Customer satisfaction metrics. Move personnel around to cross-pollinate and correct weak areas.

- Hoteling. Not recommended. Hoteling is a strategy marked by a nomad dynamic. In hoteling, each CSR does not have a permanent pod or desk that they are assigned to. When the CSR arrives for their shift they find an open pod.

  If hoteling has a place in the contact center it may be with those staff members who travel more than 50 percent of the time. As they are on the road the majority of the time, it is hardly economical to set aside a space and expend the capital to outfit the workspace (furniture, desktop computer, phone set, and so on).

---

One pod is the same as the next with the same telephone set, computer, and software. What does differentiate prime pods from less desirable ones are soft advantages such as proximity to windows, distance from the managers' area, and small comfort factors. In the twenty-some years the author has been in the workforce, "hoteling" has surfaced as all the rage three times—each time hoteling surfaces as a model (fad) it just as quickly falls back to its slumbering place.

- Lockers. Each CSR should have access to a locker for personal effects. This is particularly true if each shift reuses the same pods/cubicles and desks as the previous shift. If each CSR has their own desk, however, one locking drawer in the desk will suffice instead of lockers. On the other end of the spectrum, if hoteling has been introduced, lockers are a must. Most often the lockers are found in the cloakroom. It is a good idea to design the locker area so that it is secure.

   It is preferable if management supplies the locks, as the look of the area will then be uniform. Some personnel, however, may wish to supply their own lock. The lockers do not have to be the floor to ceiling style as found in high schools, half- or third-size is sufficient.

- Foyer/cloakroom. Staff will need an area to store their outerwear. Depending on the geographic location of the contact center and the resulting climate, the cloakroom options run from a simple small room with hooks and hangers to something more elaborate to accommodate heavy outerwear (like a parka), boots, slush, and snow drain-off and removal.

- Lighting. Natural lighting is preferable, with as many windows and skylights as possible. Minimize seating strife and gripes by positioning the pods and desks to the natural light so that all seats are equally close to the windows. This suggests a floor layout where the meeting rooms, training areas, equipment room, and other general purpose areas are clustered in the center of the floor with CSRs on the outside of the core by the windows.

   A twenty-four/seven operation requires artificial lighting. Row upon row of large, circa 1960s-style fluorescent lights are not conducive to a friendly working environment. Subdue the lighting, and if the pod style is chosen, consider lighting at pods and at each work area so that the employee can turn on or off or perhaps even dim the lighting in their personal work area.

- Carpets. Carpets are excellent for damping the ambient noise level and making the environment kinder. If there are test labs in the contact center or areas where computer equipment is to be disassembled, opt for anti-static carpet to keep electrostatic discharge (ESD) issues to a minimum.

- Ambient noise. Contact centers are inherently noisy environments. There is the normal machine noise found in all computer-based organizations compounded by each and every telephone contact going on at any given moment. There are two systems to combat the ambient noise in common use today:

   ○ White noise—The oldest and simplest ambient noise mitigation technology is white noise generation. The white noise management system works by introducing a soothing constant board frequency noise. Somewhat like the noise of a waterfall but at very low volume so that to hear it you have to search it out. It works for some yet others find it intrusive.

○ Phase cancellation—Another system analyzes ambient noise and introduces an equal but 180° out-of-phase noise thereby cancelling out the offending noise. These systems work best when machines (computers in this case, unless the contact center is close to a manufacturing floor) generate the majority of the noise. Machine noise tends to be static (unchanging) in nature as opposed to the constant pitch and amplitude shifts generated during telephone conversation.

- Personal computers for recreational use such as Internet surfing and games. These personal computers can be placed in the employee lounge. The purpose is to provide access to computer programs and activities typically not sanctioned by the organizations. Recommend multimedia capable machines (speakers, fast display, maybe even joysticks) to enhance the relaxation potential of the personal computers. Set up an employee-to-management electronic mailbox to act as an anonymous suggestion box mechanism. On the downside, some rules will have to be established on the use of the common personal computers. Consider restricting access to pornographic sites, hogging of the resource, downloading of content, anonymous-source spamming (employee uses a general access computer to send untraceable messages), and so on.

- Product examples. This is a very easy idea to execute on but often overlooked. The contact center should have access to the same product that the Customers receive. That is, exactly the same so that a CSR can feel and look at the exact same packaging the Customer is viewing. Include everything in these examples— waybills, invoices, errata sheets, and manuals.

- Gratis, or subsidized, beverages and snacks. A number of corporations have set precedent by providing free soft drinks, juice, and mineral water to their employees. Some corporations have gone so far as to introduce free snacks such as popcorn. This practice is hardly businesslike in the traditional sense, but if free snacks are de rigueur in the area the corporation is drawing personnel from, then go with the precedent. At minimum, a water-dispensing machine should be provided.

  Many corporations allow outside vendors to place and maintain vending machines in corporate lunch areas. Maintenance of the equipment, pricing, and product choice is the vendors' responsibility.

  A middle ground between "free" and the vendor approach is to subsidize the pricing of products found in vending machines in the corporation's lunchroom and cafeterias. The employee purchases the products at cost from the vending machine, the corporation then pays the profit margin out to the vendor to justify the deployment of the machines.

  Be sensitive to disparity in services between departments or groups within the corporation. If the engineering department has access to free soft drinks and the contact center personnel do not, there exists a tempest in a teapot. This is not necessarily wrong, there may be very good reasons why engineers need free soft drinks, just be sensitive to the disparity.

One important aspect of all of these schemes that should not be overlooked is the administrative burden. Even if an outside vendor is maintaining the vending machines, someone must let them in the door, issue security badges, and track their movements. In large organizations, consider hiring a full time go-fer, someone to take responsibility for these necessary tasks.

- Day care facilities/subsidization—The provision of an on-site day care service is a real boon to the entry-level personnel contact centers attract.

## TWENTY-FOUR/SEVEN OPERATION

*Rain nor snow nor holidays nor . . .*

A twenty-four/seven operation presents a number of unique challenges to businesses. The twenty-four/seven operation discussed in this section is not of the international variety in which the supported product enjoys continuous use as the sun circles the earth, rendering the call density static (based on population pockets), nor does this section deal with the wherefores and whys supporting the reasons for establishing a twenty-four/seven operation. For data points on why an operation may need to be twenty-four/seven, review the section titled "Understand the Business Model," page 9. This section details more of a national operation where the Customer base has demanded twenty-four/seven support and the call density falls off sharply outside of standard coast-to-coast business hours.

Some of the considerations that need to be managed in a twenty-four/seven operation include:

- Compensation—Many operations pay a premium to those who do shift work. There is no universal rate for the shift premium, and the range varies wildly from company to company and sector to sector.

- Hiring—The fact that the operation is twenty-four/seven may be a deterrent to hiring top performers. There are not many young people (the prime demographic profile for contact centers) who are motivated to work shifts and weekends, and hiring may be even more difficult if there is a glut of jobs for young people in the surrounding area. Advertisements for staff should clearly state that the operation is twenty-four/seven, and if the operation is not currently twenty-four/seven but there are plans to move to twenty-four/seven, start hiring with full disclosure of the intent to move to twenty-four/seven;[17] it will save management much grief downstream.

- Graveyard shift—Management, particularly those most concerned with the financials, are always concerned about the spectre of "staff sitting about with their thumbs up their whatever." The personnel on-site during the graveyard shift (midnight to 8:00 a.m.) do not have to be underutilized. The graveyard crew can be kept busy by having them champion:

- ○ E-mail—Relegate the answering of incoming e-mails to the lax periods in the evening and morning.

- ○ Training—Provide self-study and computer based training (CBT) modules so the employees can upgrade their skills.

- ○ Projects—General projects (from data analysis and research to procedure documentation) can be carried out during the lax periods. If the graveyard shift is positioned as a stepping-stone to a more fulfilling role within the operation, many personnel will jump at the opportunity.

- Security—In addition to building security is the personal security of personnel moving in and out of a business late at night. Depending on the location of the contact center (some operations are in less than desirable neighborhoods), security guards may have to be engaged to escort employees to and from parking and, potentially, (all-night) restaurants. The optimal arrangement is for night staff to have access to secure underground parking in the same building as the contact center. Daytime Saturdays and Sundays present similar challenges.

- Staffing to the Customers' best interests—There are a number underlying attributes consistent with those who perform best on the graveyard shift: they work the shifts as a personal preference, they are self-motivated, they require little management, and they have seniority. If all four attributes surface in one individual, management can sleep soundly; otherwise, pick and choose carefully. The worst-case scenario is when the late shift becomes viewed by employees as an opportunity to stand down. Keep the staff motivated and busy on all shifts.

> Do not shy away from putting star performers on the graveyard shift. The Customers who call will definitely appreciate it and management is assured that the tasks assigned are performed well.

- Management—There is no question that management is required on all shifts, however, the full management contingent is probably not required on all shifts. One manager, who has a good grasp of all the contact center functions (see cross-pollination), should be able to manage the late-night and graveyard shifts.

- Scheduling—Personnel scheduling is a logistics challenge in any operation. In a twenty-four/seven environment, the task is Herculean. In a contact center of any size, a scheduling manager in the operations team (see Operations, Scheduling Manager in appendix B, page 237, for an outline of this role) is mandatory. It may be feasible in smaller operations to piggyback the scheduling manager role onto another management staff member, however, as the contact center grows, the scheduling task will consume more and more time.

    At the inception of a small twenty-four/seven operation, management may allow personnel to trade shifts among themselves and otherwise tamper with the official master schedule. Once the operation hits critical mass, however, rules need to be established; employees may still swap shifts but only via official channels.

# ENDNOTES

1. Alternatively, there are senior managers who exhibit very dangerous behavior when faced with negative data. Some have a motherhood posture regarding the product and tolerate no negative vibe on their offspring. Reports that are negative are often met with contempt or scorn. The message to get through is "don't shoot the messenger."

2. A *one-off* is a singularity. The creation of one single unit. The negative connotation of one-offs is that "one" of anything is very expensive to manufacture.

3. Hard-coding usually refers to values being programmed into a system at the application software layer. In this example *hard-code* means that, from the users' perspective, they cannot change the threshold value or the behavior of the rules. Superior business rule–based systems allow the administrator to soft-code rules and values using scripts or a simple graphical user interface (GUI). It is only the legacy systems that require knowledge of an arcane programming language (for example, Cobol) to change or modify a rule.

4. Be prepared to have the occasional disagreement with the sales team as your definition of what is feasible and economical and theirs are often worlds apart. It is difficult to elegantly scale to the situation where there are "standard Customers," a number of strategic accounts with SLAs, and "special handling needed" Customers. You should attempt to reign in the number of strategic accounts and "special handling" cases as too many unique support arrangements quickly become unmanageable. The exception to this rule of thumb is when the Customer is totally funding their special handling, in which case the contact center can hire dedicated Customer managers to manage the accounts.

5. Hot-link is a mechanism whereby a CSR has the ability to hand off a contact to another corporation's contact center directly through the PBX. That is, the host contact center and the target contact center are linked at the PBX level—there is no need to dial the full phone number, enter a queue, and wait for a representative.

6. "Transparent" meaning the user is not in any other way affected by the 15-second service disruption. It is only a delay of 15 seconds; no user intervention is needed to recover from the glitch (the user need not reattach, reinitialize, reboot, and so on). If the user must reboot to recover from your 15-second glitch, then you must add the reboot time to the disruption time, in which case 15 seconds quickly blooms into 15 minutes.

7. Smaller organizations or organizations at the start of their growth do not always have a fully developed quality assurance department. If this is the case, the contact center can be the quality champion and introduce and nurture this key function within the contact center until a better reporting fit is claimed. For more on quality assurance, see ISO 9004:2000.

8. Using the services of the potential outsourcers allows your organization to leverage their expertise as a professional services component, usually gratis.

9. A mystery-shopper program allows an organization to benchmark their services. The mystery shopper is in the employ of the service being benchmarked or is an independent third party. In this case the mystery shoppers are head-office employees who call the outsourced contact center. Optimal mystery-shopper exercises provide prepared and scripted questions and a grading system.

10. The author made this organization up. However, if they and souihorns both existed, then it is probable that the marching bands of the South would use Souihorn brand souihorns.

11. The infant mortality dynamic is best illustrated by the Weibull curve (bathtub curve)—in this context, the Weibull curve plots failure rate against the lifecycle of the product under study.

12. Revision control is a science unto itself. The quality professionals in the development team may already have a system in place for software, hardware, and documentation revision control. For a significant cost saving try to piggyback the contact center documentation set on the existing system. There should be few objections as the incremental cost is low and one documentation standard for the corporation is simply good management.

13. Tote boards are displays seen in contact centers that continuously display pertinent metrics such as: number of Customers in queue, on-hold time in seconds, and general SLA data points.

14. Hiring reduced to a formula looks good on paper, but in practical use often fails. Like in all procedures, respond to stimuli, fine-tune when needed, and eventually the formula will stand up to practical use.

15. Four-legged sales—a team comprised of two people, one a technical whip and one a deal-closer.

16. Chapter 3 offers guidelines on creating a crisis management manual. *ISO 14001 Emergency Preparedness and Response* is an excellent source for additional reading.

17. Introducing twenty-four/seven to an operation is highly disruptive. If you are in a position where the transition is needed, engage a change management professional to assist with the transition planning and to manage the existing personnel.

# 3

# Standard Operating Procedures

## OBJECTIVE

*What may be learned in this chapter.*

Small operations can function with a minimum of published procedures, however, as operations grow and procedural critical mass is reached, there is a need to formalize (write down) and publish (post) a set of standard operating procedures (SOPs). This chapter guides the reader through definition and generation of SOPs.

This chapter covers the following topics:

- The importance of a published set of SOPs

- Creation and maintenance of SOPs

- Process audits and their applicability

- Crisis management

- Lists of questions that will assist contact center management in focusing and understanding the challenges discussed

## DOCUMENTATION

*Document and document and document . . .*

Documenting the processes and procedures the contact center personnel are to follow is a daunting, but necessary, task. The resulting documentation set is typically referred to as the standard operating procedure (SOP) guidelines. The level of granularity of each documented procedure is driven by the size and scope of the contact center being disciplined. All contact center personnel should have access to online and hard copy versions of the SOP documentation set.

# SOP CREATION GUIDELINES

*Size and scope.*

As a general rule of thumb, it is preferable to keep the SOP documentation to a minimum. Brevity should be foremost in the minds of those that are participating in the documentation effort, which suggests that all procedures do not demand documentation. It is nigh impossible to fully document procedures that require a degree of subjective reasoning. In these cases, management must trust the individual employee's maturity and discretion.

The first step is to develop a standard template to be used by all personnel participating in the process documentation stage. Impress upon the participants to work within usability guidelines such as:

- Graphic versus written—Flowcharts are generally easier to comprehend and action then the written word. Establish guidelines for the use of flowchart shapes and conventions to ensure commonality in the final documentation set.[1]

- Guideline versus minutiae—Impress upon the personnel writing the draft procedures that some latitude should be exercised; not every single action in a process must be documented.

- Single page versus the tome—Break down long and complex procedures into their component parts. Label the broken-down procedures as subprocedures to the master complex procedure. Endeavor to encapsulate every procedure or subprocedure on a single page. Reuse recurring procedures; branch off from any given flowchart to a recurring procedure.

- Difficult versus simple comprehension—Respect the reading and comprehension abilities of the target audience. A reasonable baseline for contact center personnel is to write to a grade eight reading level. Limit the use of academic style and esoteric words (such as "minutiae").

Bring it together by:

- Consistent versus unfocused—Leverage the professional writers on the training team to collate the drafts and begin to assemble the SOP document set. Impress upon the line supervisors and others contributing to the document to not dwell on grammar and punctuation but to focus on the accuracy of the content. Leave the grammar and punctuation to the professional writers on the training team.

- Usable versus unusable—The finished SOP document set is a reference guide. Personnel must be able to easily access, search, and navigate the procedures.

- Publish electronically versus hard copy—One of the best applications of a corporate intranet is to publish the SOP document in HTML/XML (hypertext markup language and extended markup language) format. Hard-copy versions placed in strategic locations about the contact center are necessary in the event that the computer system(s) fail.

It is important to note that the SOP is a reference document and that personnel are not expected to "memorize" its contents. Each member of the contact center should know their own procedural areas inside and out and only have to resort to the SOP when filling in for a position or performing a procedure outside their own immediate area of expertise.

If the contact center is subject to an audit, be it Customer-driven or an ISO 9000 audit, the important thing for the personnel to have internalized is where they can locate the procedure, not to have memorized every process. The correct answer to an auditor's question on a procedure outside an individual's area of expertise is, "I don't know off the top of my head, but I can find the procedure in the SOP guide right here on the corporate intranet."

## MAKING IT HAPPEN

*Distribute the load.*

Writing the SOP is a daunting documentation challenge, but like any other large task divided into manageable pieces, it is doable. Following are some recommendations for proceeding:

1. Hire or nominate a project manager for the SOP document from internal prospects. This project manager owns the document and its administration. Initially, this will be a full-time job and may continue to be so depending on how volatile the procedures are within the organization. In a less-volatile organization, the project manager can take on additional projects once the document is created and is in maintenance mode. A dedicated resource must be assigned to the project or it will fail.

2. Begin with the organizational chart. Map out the first-level *vital* activities that each group represented on the organizational chart performs.

3. Delegate the first-pass documentation of the procedures to the line supervisors. Impress upon them that the initial pass is to document what the personnel are actually doing and *not* what the line supervisor thinks they should be doing. (See the following section entitled "Process Improvement Audit.")

4. Negotiate and establish reasonable time frames for each participant to submit their procedures in draft form.

5. Gather the draft input and assign the editing to one of the professional writers on the training team.

6. Go back to step two, but now map out the second-level *vital* activities for each team. Loop again until all procedures are captured. (Note that some supervisors will have fewer loop cycles than others.)

7. Once all procedures are captured, review, approve, compile, and publish the document.

8. Now run a process improvement audit.

# PROCESS IMPROVEMENT AUDIT

*Continuous improvement, kaizen, just make it better...*

One of the most beneficial aspects of the documentation process is that a full review of the existing, often ad hoc, procedures is facilitated. As each supervisor documents the existing procedures for their respective teams, they have the opportunity to question every stage to see if the following criteria are met:

- Does the procedure or subprocedure serve a valid[2] purpose? Many operations blindly run procedural sequences that no longer serve a purpose. A good example of this is the collection of tax data to satisfy a tax law that has, in fact, changed, or the collection of Customer data for a program that marketing terminated months ago.

- Is there an easier/faster/more economical/more expedient way to achieve the same end? The personnel who use a procedure every day are an excellent source of ideas and suggestions on how to improve the procedure or process.

- Can/should the back-office system(s) undergo changes to better serve the procedure and users? Too frequently, users feel they are being held hostage by antiquated systems or procedures. Question everything. The *systems* are supposed to serve the contact center personnel, not the other way around.

> Ripple effect—like a stone thrown in calm water. One seemingly innocuous change made in a front-end procedure rippled all the way down to accounts receivable and stripped all of the shipping charges from deliveries, resulting in a four-digit write-down at the end of the quarter. Before anything is changed, run a risk assessment and understand the ramifications.

As stated previously, the time to change the procedure is not during the documentation phase, unless the change is easy enough to implement without risk or ripple effects. Create a separate database to track recommended changes. Fold the recommendations into the larger process.

Gather the stakeholders together and conduct a procedure audit using the newly created SOP draft document. The project manager should be prepared to take notes on all the recommended changes. If this is the first time the contact center has documented procedures, anticipate abundant recommendations.

The next stage is to prioritize the procedural change recommendations. Run the recommendations through a priority filter to help focus on which changes should actually be implemented and in what order. Suggested priority filters are:

1. Is there an immediate benefit to the Customer?

2. Are the risks inherent in the change understood?

3. Have other departments that may be affected by the change had an opportunity to comment on the change?

4. What are the cost implications?

5. What are the training implications?

The final step in the audit process is to do it again . . . and again . . . and again.

# CRISIS MANAGEMENT

*Plan for everything . . . within reason.*

Managing system and technology failures are dealt with elsewhere in this book.[3] The crises referred to in this section are external to the contact center, yet have an impact on the contact center.

The SOP document covers systems usage and day-to-day activities, however, a fully prepared contact center anticipates and prepares their personnel for extraordinary situations. Extraordinary, in this instance, refers to a circumstance outside the focus of the contact center (which is Customer service and satisfaction). One caveat to observe is to be sure to respect local laws regarding what, as a corporation, you can and cannot do. One of the potential crises that may befall an organization is the failure of the corporate computer systems. The crisis management document should be printed and posted at accessible places around the contact center.

The crisis management document could contain sections on how to respond to the list of extraordinary situations below. As per the SOP:

1. A template format is highly desirable so that there is consistency among the crisis-handling recommendations.

2. Each situation-handling recommendation should fit on a single page—brevity is key to usability.

3. As the crisis management document will be used during extraordinary situations, panic may be a factor; keep it concise and to the point.

Include for each situation:

1. Instructions on how to proceed with the employees' safety. For example: in the case of a fire, evacuation should be the first order of business; in a medical emergency, a listing of staff members who are certified to perform basic emergency services is useful, and so on. Employees' safety is the prime driver.

2. Phone numbers for the emergency service most apt to assist with the situation.

3. Notification procedures so that the management is officially aware of the situation.

4. Fallback procedures if necessary. In the case of a full evacuation it will be management's decision to initiate the fallback mechanism. For example: fallback may divert all contacts to a partner or outsource service.

5. Designated employee to act as the emergency lead hand. The designated employee should receive specialized training. Every designated employee should have a backup designate in the event that they are unavailable. Twenty-four/seven operations will need a number of designates for each emergency type on each shift.

Recommended sections for the crisis management document include:

- Bomb threat—police and fire station contacts, contact information for the designated lead hand for bomb threat emergency procedures, and clearly defined evacuation procedures.

- Chemical handling—fire station contact, medical services contact, and contact information for the designated lead hand for chemical handling emergency procedures.

- Earthquake—police and fire station contacts (they will undoubtedly already be aware that there has been an earthquake, the contacts are to be used only if needed), contact information for the designated lead hand for earthquake emergency procedures, guidelines to ascertain severity and subsequent action based on observed damage and earthquake magnitude data from news services, and clearly defined evacuation procedures.

- Fire—fire station contacts, contact information for the designated lead hand for fire threat emergency procedures, guidelines to ascertain severity and subsequent action based on potential damage, and clearly defined evacuation procedures.

- Heart attack—fire station/paramedic contacts, contact information for the designated lead hand for medical emergency procedures, guidelines to ascertain severity and subsequent action based on potential damage, and clearly defined evacuation procedures.

- Inclement weather (an ice storm, for instance)—contact information for the designated lead hand for weather issues, guidelines to ascertain severity and subsequent action based on that severity, and clearly defined escalation procedures.

- Theft/robbery—contact information for the designated lead hand for theft issues, guidelines to ascertain action based on severity of the alleged crime, and clearly defined escalation procedures.

- Extraordinary circumstances: shooting threat—police contacts, medical service contacts, contact information for the designated lead hand for extraordinary circumstances, guidelines to ascertain action based on severity of the alleged threat, and clearly defined escalation procedures.

- Extraordinary circumstances: suicide threat—police contacts, medical service contacts, contact information for the designated lead hand for extraordinary circumstances, guidelines to ascertain action based on severity of the alleged threat, and clearly defined escalation procedures.

# ENDNOTES

1. Programs like Visio and CorelDraw have icon use guidelines built into the templates—it may be easiest to simply adopt these.
2. A "valid" purpose either serves the Customer's best interest or a business interest.
3. *ISO 14001 Emergency Preparedness and Response* is an excellent reference guide for crisis management in general.

# 4

# Metrics

## OBJECTIVE

*What may be learned in this chapter.*

Whatever can be measured can be managed. Metrics drive business, metrics drive sports teams, and metrics drive performance. Metrics can bring into focus areas that need attention and areas that have improved. Metrics, over time, provide management with a barometer for progress. Well-defined metrics (and there is some study required to get to the right metrics) are the leading indicators of the health of the contact center.

This chapter covers the following topics:

- The importance of measuring performance and defining meaningful metrics

- Continuous improvement cycles and their applicability

- Reports and their applicability

- Performance, support, financial, and product metrics

- SLAs and their applicability

- Lists of questions that will assist contact center management in focusing on, and understanding, the challenges discussed

## CUSTOMER PERCEPTION

*Look to those whom you serve . . .*

Some readers may think it peculiar that a chapter on performance metrics has "Customer Perception" as its first section. As it is the Customer that the contact center is serving, it stands to reason that the Customer should be, nay must be, the central figure

> Invite industry experts to review and comment on the operation. Solicit comment based on areas that are suspected of needing attention or, better yet, give the expert carte blanche to evaluate and comment on the operation. Arrange a management-swap program with other contact center professionals, and share ideas and innovations. Build bridges with other contact center professionals (true business development).

in the definition of acceptable performance metrics. Metrics should always be thought of in the context of the Customer's perception.

The concept of Customer as the prime driver is fundamental; embrace the idea and act upon it, and the corporation will prosper. Open the corporate kimono a touch and survey the Customers, talk to the Customers, listen to the Customers, and act on their suggestions. Before proceeding, review Figure 4.1, Customer-centric continuous improvement cycle.

Once the analysis of Customer input is complete and corrective action has been effected, run the process again, and again, and again. Do not assume the future will bear any resemblance to the present or the past. The Customer expectation bar is being raised everyday. It is far superior to be among the corporations that are helping move the bar than to be in the me-too/catch-up crowd.

Benchmarking studies[1] are a valuable additional source of contact center performance metrics data. Locate the benchmark study that most closely matches your industry profile and demographics and compare it with your corporation's targets and goals. Temper the Customer wishes and comments you have solicited with the benchmarking data. For example, the time a Customer spends in the limbo known as "on-hold" could be reconciled in the following scenario:

- Data gathering phase:

  1. In a survey of Customer concerns, issues, and wishes, it is apparent that Customers never wish to be put on hold. In other words, the Customers want an on-hold time of zero seconds.

  2. Benchmarking data indicate that, in a poll of 300 companies with similar demographics, technologies, and profile to the corporation, the on-hold time median (mid-point) is 30 seconds with a deviation of ± 15 seconds.

  3. Analysis of current capabilities indicates that, during peak periods, the on-hold time frequently exceeds six minutes (360 seconds).

- Analysis phase:

  4. A gap analysis is conducted and the conclusion is made that budgetary constraints prohibit an on-hold time of zero seconds. It is cost-prohibitive to have a fully-trained CSR available 100 percent of the time unless the Customer bears the entire cost. The gap analysis further indicates that in order to meet the industry benchmark of 30 seconds:

     a. Additional training is required.

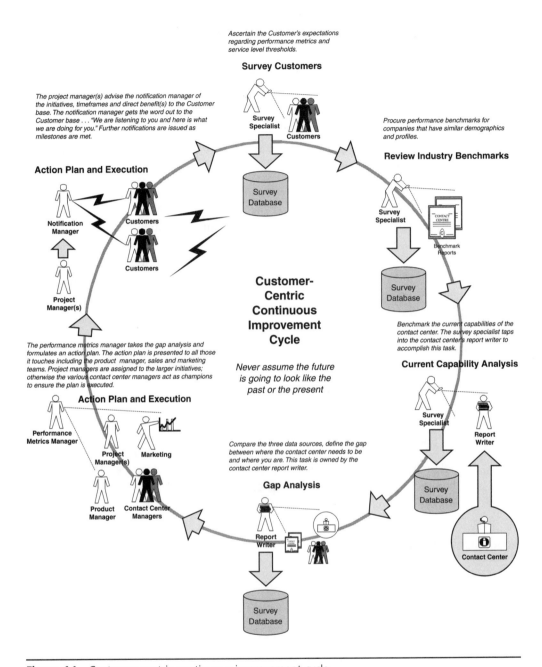

**Figure 4.1** Customer-centric continuous improvement cycle.

b. Additional staff at peak periods is required.

c. A friendlier graphical user interface (GUI) to the in-house knowledge base system must be designed and implemented as the CSRs expend an inordinate amount of time navigating the knowledge base.

Deployment time frame analysis indicates that, even if the three initiatives are run concurrently, 26 person-months of effort are needed over twelve calendar months.

- Execution phase:

  5. Develop and execute an action plan to meet the benchmark of 30 seconds.

  6. Develop and execute an action plan to offer, for a fee, a "zero seconds on-hold" premium service support option.

  7. Send a message to the Customer base advising them of the actions and the time frames. It is paramount that the Customers be aware of the initiatives taken to render conducting business with the corporation streamlined and easier for them. In addition, all Customers that took part in the survey exercise should be provided with the results and the responses to their concerns and comments. As milestones are met, send out status updates to the Customers so that they are informed and feel part of the initiative.

- Review phase:

  8. Monitor the "meet the benchmark" initiative of 30 seconds and, once met, formulate an additional plan to exceed the benchmark standard *and* reduce costs at the same time.

  9. Go back to step 1 and run the sequence again.

Abort-and-try-again comment. Some readers may have seen the error in the scenario from the very start, which is that the Customer's request is unreasonable. While no one enjoys on-hold time, it is a reality of conducting business via the telephone. The corrective action is in the wording of the survey. The Customer should not have been given an option of "zero time," but should have been directed to a more realistic and reasonable option.

## Analysis Radar Tool

It is often difficult to know which aspect of any given challenge requires attention, that is, where should attention be focused? The answer may be obvious in some situations, but when the challenge is multifaceted, it is often difficult to arrive at the optimal solution.

As an example of a multifaceted dynamic, consider the challenge of defining to which Customers you should market a gold service plan. Sales, marketing, business development, finance, and the support personnel in the contact center all have different mandates. A number of these mandates are mutually exclusive or simply in conflict with one another. The contact center may want a Customer on the gold service plan because they are a very high-maintenance account and should be paying a premium for the service they are receiving. Sales may view an account as worthy of gold status because the up-sell and cross-sell potential is very high. Marketing may want the community of influential industry analysts to be added to gold status, and they probably will want the status extended gratis. Finance is concerned with minimizing the costs associated with supporting the user community, and gratis gold status is in conflict with minimizing costs. In order to reconcile these criteria and yield the optimal focus, they could be entered into a spreadsheet, assigned a weighting, and those Customers with the highest scores would be the target accounts.

Once the criteria are agreed upon and weighting is assigned, a survey may be conducted of the Customer segment at which the program is directed. In this situation, the survey itself is internal as the data points are owned and known by marketing, sales, business development, or the contact center.

Figure 4.3, Customer segmentation analysis, depicts the result of a survey. The sample size is ridiculously small (six Customers), but it illustrates the technique. Column H (W Sum) is the weighted sum, which is figured as follows:

Weighted sum = the value ascribed to the reference (ref) criteria × its weight.

In arithmetic terms:

$$H1 = (A1 \times 5) + (B1 \times 10) + (C1 \times 8) + (D1 \times 5) + (E1 \times 10) + (F1 \times 5) + (G1 \times 10)$$

$$H2 = (A2 \times 5) + (B2 \times 10) + (C2 \times 8) + (D2 \times 5) + (E2 \times 10) + (F2 \times 5) + (G2 \times 10)$$

And so on for H3, H4, H5, and H6.

| Ref | Description | Source | Weight (110) |
|---|---|---|---|
| 1 | Strategic alliance | Marketing | 5 |
| 2 | Market leader/influencer | Marketing | 10 |
| 3 | Market maker | Marketing | 8 |
| 4 | High maintenance | Contact center | 5 |
| 5 | Reference site | Sales | 10 |
| 6 | Up-sell probability | Sales | 5 |
| 7 | Relationship | Sales | 10 |

**Figure 4.2** Program analysis.

| Customer | A Ref 1 | B Ref 2 | C Ref 3 | D Ref 4 | E Ref 5 | F Ref 6 | G Ref 7 | H W Sum |
|---|---|---|---|---|---|---|---|---|
| 1 | 0 | 7 | 7 | 4 | 9 | 8 | 10 | 379 |
| 2 | 0 | 8 | 2 | 10 | 9 | 3 | 7 | 324 |
| 3 | 0 | 8 | 4 | 5 | 9 | 5 | 7 | 325 |
| 4 | 8 | 10 | 8 | 10 | 0 | 2 | 3 | 276 |
| 5 | 8 | 2 | 2 | 0 | 0 | 2 | 3 | 116 |
| 6 | 4 | 10 | 9 | 8 | 10 | 8 | 9 | 459 |

**Figure 4.3** Customer segmentation analysis.

The analysis indicates that Customers 6, 1, and 3 are the optimal picks to engage in the gold service initiative.

The power of this analysis technique is that the weightings may be adjusted in any number of ways to refocus the analysis. For instance, if management wished to view the final analysis without the influence of the marketing team (the soft sciences), the marketing weighting could be zeroed out and a different conclusion could be leveraged very quickly.

An effective management tool is the ability to use the radar technique to graphically depict complex relationships.[2] Figure 4.4, Radar maps, depicts the data found in

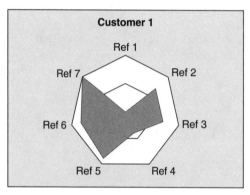
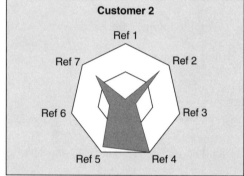
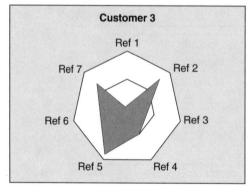
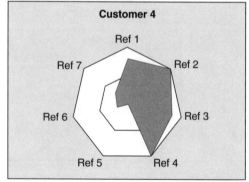
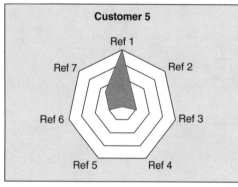
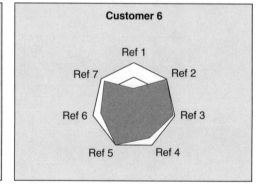

**Figure 4.4** Radar maps.

Figure 4.3, graphically. An optimal radar map is one where the shaded segment completely eclipses the underlying radar web (meaning the entity being analysed is fully maximized on all axes). Customer 6 in Figure 4.4 is the closest to a perfect fit.

The radar maps can also be used to quickly assess where the weaknesses may lie in the data sample. For example, review Figure 4.5, Grouping by department. The issues are grouped by the department at the source of the issue. Marketing's issues are references (Ref) one, two, and three; sales are five, six, and seven; and the contact center issues fall in between as reference four. Apply this sectional grouping knowledge to the review of Figure 4.4, and the data plot can be reviewed on a whole other level.

## Causality

Perception is tricky business. Whenever dealing with perception, always consider cause-and-effect (causality). Economics experts measure causality in terms of elasticity. Elasticity describes a nonlinear relationship whereby a small rise in one variable has a large effect on other variables. It is elasticity that accounts for a disproportionate Customer response to phenomena that are deemed (by the management team) to be of little consequence.

Consider that 32 percent of the call volume is centered on one question, "Where is the nearest repair depot for the product?" The fix is economical and expedient—place an info sheet in the product box detailing the contact information for regional repair depots. This suggestion should result in a dramatic decrease in the call volume for this issue, but what were not considered were the corporate accounts who have their own

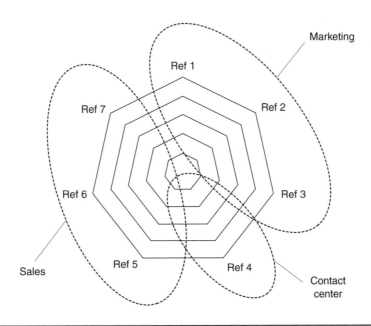

**Figure 4.5**  Grouping by department.

internal repair protocols with negotiated price breaks on spare units, repairs, and turn-around times. The end result is a very angry major account who wants to know:

1. Who made the decision to put the info sheets in the boxes

2. Why he wasn't personally notified of the change to the product packaging as he orders hundreds of units a month

3. How the corporation is going to help remedy the situation in which his user community is calling the wrong number for service, creating additional costs, and confusing everyone

A small, seemingly innocuous change yields a large problem. The remedy is to be preventive, be sure all the ramifications of a change are explored. Ensure a protocol is in place so that all stakeholders affected by a change have input into its deployment. The protocol need not be exhaustive, sign-off need not be required at all levels, and tacit approval is probably the superior approach for those lightly touched by any given change. Consider publishing upcoming product changes on the Internet well in advance of the change; this should provide ample time to voice and allay concerns.

## ANATOMY OF A TELEPHONE CONTACT

*What it is.*

As the telephone is the most popular medium for Customers to initiate contact, it will serve as the baseline for a road map of the pertinent performance metrics and indices. The other contact modes available to the Customer base can be mapped to components within the telephone contact model.

A breakdown of the components which comprise a telephone contact are diagrammed in Figure 4.6, Anatomy of a telephone contact. The contact outlined is typical of a medium- to high-difficultly call within a high-technology support context. Medium- to high-difficulty was chosen as the baseline because it is important to illustrate a callback contingency in which the Customer's issue is not closed on the first contact. The total duration of the depicted call is two hours and 38 minutes, but two hours and 24 minutes (91 percent of the total time) were consumed in the *off-line research* phase. In a commercial market, such as support for a consumer microwave oven, calls of this duration should make up a very small percentage of the total. Alternatively, in a speciality market such as financial services, two hours plus may be the norm.

Each component of the sequence depicted in Figure 4.6 has been provided with a number of descriptors:

- Name—A label that has general usage among contact center professionals. Many of the labels and terminology used in a contact center serve as a *lingua franca* between the contact center and the quality, engineering, and development departments. While some of the terms have set and agreed-upon definitions such as mean time between failures (MTBF), there is always variation in interpretation.

*The size of each segment is proportionate to that activity's duration*

Time →

| Time to Pickup | Time On-Hold (in Queue) | Contact Duration | Off-Line Research | Outgoing Call Contact Duration | Contact Closure |
|---|---|---|---|---|---|
| **Unit of measure:** Seconds | **Unit of measure:** Seconds | **Unit of measure:** Minutes | **Unit of measure:** Hours | **Unit of measure:** Minutes | **Unit of measure:** Minutes |
| **Example:** 16 seconds | **Example:** 45 seconds | **Example:** 8.2 seconds | **Example:** 2.4 hours | **Example:** 3 minutes | **Example:** 2.8 minutes |
| **Criticality:** High | **Criticality:** High | **Criticality:** Medium | **Criticality:** Low | **Criticality:** Low | **Criticality:** Low |
| **Comment:** Measured from the first ring on the contact center telephone system to the time the call is picked up by either an IVR system or a receptionist. Customers are very sensitive to this time. | **Comment:** Measured from when the call is picked up by either an IVR system or a receptionist to the time that the appropriate CSR picks up the call. Customers are very sensitive to this time. | **Comment:** This is time the CSR is on the call with the Customer. Provided the CSR knows the subject matter, the Customer is not overly sensitive to this period as the Customer simply wants resolution. | **Comment:** Any time during which the CSR has to research the challenge in order to resolve it. Customers are not sensitive to this time provided the CSR has discussed a mutually agreed-upon time frame *and* the CSR adheres to it. | **Comment:** This is the time for the CSR to call back a Customer with the solution. Very expensive. | **Comment:** Administration time, close off the trouble ticket, update the knowledge base, and so on. |
| **Common issues:** Most common complaint is the time waiting. Be careful of exaggeration when dealing with escalations regarding the duration. | **Common issues:** This period is the most complained about and is the number one cause for nontechnical escalations. Again, be careful of exaggeration when dealing with escalations regarding the duration. | **Common issues:** Most common complaints made about this period are directed at the CSR and their (perceived or otherwise) lack of product/problem knowledge. Complaints regarding "re-explaining the problem to everyone I spoke to" are also abundant. | **Common issues:** Complaints typically are in regards to the CSR not following up and/or not delivering the solution on time. The fact that the call could not be resolved during the first contact is first a Customer satisfaction issue, and second, very costly for the contact center. | **Common issues:** Typically a clean activity provided the resolution is what the Customer was looking for. | **Common issues:** Internal issues abound with CSRs not adequately documenting fixes and resolutions, which denies a continuous improvement opportunity. |

**Figure 4.6** Anatomy of a telephone contact.

Even an industry standard like MTBF is subject to confusion as the "B" in MTBF can designate *before* or *between*. "Before" and "between" describe very different dynamics.

As a rule of thumb, all reports and documents should provide a glossary of the terms used, how they were derived, and must be consistent from report to report, month to month, and year to year.

• Suggested unit of measure (seconds, minutes, hours, and so on)—Standard time-duration units for each component are provided. These suggestions are not universal as each product/service has its own baseline of acceptable time frames. The units chosen apply to a contact center clearing calls on a commercial product that is both mature and has well-known failure modes.

• Example—Self-explanatory. The example time frames provided were derived from a contact center providing support on a commercial software product. The examples are not intended to be used as targets for an actual contact center but only as a barometer based on real-world observations.

• Criticality assessment (high, medium, or low)—Assessment of the criticality of the phase as seen from the Customer's perspective and its impact on their satisfaction. This is an important concept that needs to be internalized and understood. Customers are more or less sensitive to time depending on the activity and the visibility they have. Perhaps the most infuriating period for Customers is the time they are waiting, either put on hold or in a queue.

• Comment—An explanation of the phase.

• Common issues—Guidance on some of the common issues, complaints, and challenges for the phase.

## REPORTS

*One can only improve that which can be measured.*

Reports are a very important aspect of a performance-driven organization. In fact, it could be postulated that it is the accuracy and utility of the reports that make or break an organization. The frequency of issuing performance reports is driven by the need. Monthly performance reports are recommended as a minimum, daily performance reports as a maximum. The options are:

• Real time—Real-time reports, by definition, are not hard-copy reports. They are typically online tools accessible from any computer with access rights to the performance tools. The real-time tool interrogates the target system and returns status on key criteria (as set by the user). The best real-time tools are graphical, allowing the reviewer to quickly access the status of the entity being monitored. In addition to delivering status to authorized users, real-time tools are often the engine behind the tote board.

> One of the best metaphors for real-time reports is the car "dashboard." The utility of the car dashboard is such that the vast majority of drivers can sit in the driver's seat of a car they have never seen and discern the status of all the critical systems intrinsic to the running of the internal combustion engine. The dashboard is a management tool that is simple to use and interpret in real time—therein lies the magic.

Real-time tools are called up as needed so there is little need to automate. Thresholds can be set, however, that, when exceeded, cause a message to be flashed on the user's screen or forwarded to the appropriate manager's e-mail or pager. Some systems support streaming banners that can be unobtrusively placed on the user's computer desktop.

- Daily—These micro performance metrics are for use by the contact center in promoting continuous improvement and isolating hot issues. They're also used by product and project managers in gauging the impact of a particular program or initiative. Automate these reports as much as possible. Publish them on the intranet (secure) so that all who care to review them may do so.

- Weekly—These medium performance metrics are to be used for the same purpose as the micro performance metrics. Provide rollup and summary reports on each and every metric found on the daily report. Automate and publish these reports as you do with the daily reports.

- Monthly—These macro performance metrics are for use by contact center personnel to provide a big-picture view of the performance of the contact center. Provide rollup and summary reports on all tracked metrics using data from the weekly reports. Monthly reports are often provided to Customers with SLAs. Keep in mind that any data shared with the Customer is sensitive and should be cloaked in a nondisclosure agreement. In addition, Customer reports should only contain data points that are related to the Customer in question and not data from other accounts. The reports delivered to the Customer should be either hard copy or in a protected electronic file format such as Adobe's .pdf format.

    Automate where possible. Publish the general results on the intranet, only provide access to Customer-specific reports to the relevant account managers and sales personnel.

- Quarterly—These macro performance metrics are tempered by financial data. Provide rollup and summary reports on all tracked metrics using data from the monthly reports. Senior management is the audience, and the purpose is to secure financial justification and to track Customer satisfaction indices. Automate as much as possible. Publish all rollup and summary reports but do not provide general access to the financial data. For the greatest impact, arrange for full hard-copy reports for senior management. Use high-quality paper and color charts and have the report properly bound.

- Semiannually—These macro performance metrics are used in the same fashion as the quarterly reports. Publish as suggested by the comments regarding quarterly reports.

- Annually—These big-picture performance metrics are, again, used as per the quarterly reports but with an onus on overall return on investment (ROI) and Customer satisfaction indices. Publish as suggested by the comments regarding quarterly reports.

- On-demand—These are typically precise and focused reports based on particular issues or dynamics that require analysis. On-demand reports are often one-shot requests or timed to coincide with short-duration marketing or sales programs.

## Custom Reports

Custom reports may be required for a number of audiences. There are Customers that have SLAs in place that demand, in addition to their monthly performance and status reports, custom reports for particular periods or focused on a particular issue. Product management may make a request for a report detailing contacts over a particular time period related to a particular failure mode. The financial department, under the guise of "our continuing efforts to minimize costs," have a need for reports justifying capital expenditures. Finally, on occasion, the odd vice president will demand an immediate report on call density on Tuesdays when a full moon was forecast. Whatever the driver, ensure that the performance systems support a high degree of custom report generation and that the staff are trained to leverage the report engine.

Custom reports are usually facilitated by one of two methods: the system vendor provides an integral report-writing capability or a commercial off-the-shelf (COTS) report engine is utilized.[3] The key issue that differentiates the two approaches is the training burden created by using the report engine. When attempting to hire a report writer, a COTS solution is vastly superior compared to a proprietary engine, however, the proprietary software manufacture would counter that the proprietary approach is fine-tuned for the environment and the needs of the contact center industry.

The least advantageous situation is where the software vendor supplies all custom report requests. Not only must each custom report be paid for, but the operation is at the whim of the vendor's sense of urgency and time frame.

# STANDARD METRICS

*De facto metrics.*

There is a de facto set of performance metrics for contact centers so there is little reason to invent a custom set for any given contact center. An excellent information source for the de facto metrics can be found on the Help Desk Institute Web page (see appendix E).

The majority of systems designed for contact centers and help desk environments come bundled with a standard report set. All that is needed to start using the system is to

When at all possible, draw a picture and leave the raw data dumps to those that have time to pore over hundreds of pages of numbers and figures. It is far easier to interpret trends and performance criteria by reviewing a simple graphic vis-à-vis column after column of numerical data.

build up the sample size; a clear picture of the performance will emerge. An excellent source for current best practice(s) and metrics for help desks and contact centers can be found on the Help Desk Institute Web page as well.

The examples that follow are descriptions and/or graphic plots of contact center performance data points. The graphics are representative of the axiom "a picture tells a thousand words," which is particularly applicable in this age of data overload.

The examples are to be used as a catalyst for stimulating contact center managers to work out how to best measure and report the key drivers within their realm of influence. The tool used to generate the graphs and plots found in this section was a standard version of Excel.

The section is divided into four types of metrics:

- Performance metrics—These are time-related metrics concentrated on how well the contact center is meeting the SLA targets and goals.

- Support metrics—These function-related metrics concentrate on the route any given contact follows to resolution.

- Financial metrics—These financial metrics depict the cost of resolving a contact and the costs associated with operating the contact center in general.

- Product metrics—These metrics are to be shared and analyzed by the quality and engineering teams. Product metrics address the questions: How is the product performing? and What are the top failure modes the development team should focus on?

Each of the examples has the following descriptors:

1. Descriptive name—Self-explanatory.

2. Definition—Self-explanatory.

3. Unit of measure—The recommendation for the baseline metric: seconds, minutes, dollars, or volume. These suggestions are not universal as each product/service has its own baseline of acceptable time frames. The examples chosen apply to a contact center clearing calls on a commercial product that is both mature and has well-known failure modes.

4. Criticality—The majority are assessments of the criticality of the metric as seen from the Customer's perspective regarding its impact on their satisfaction. The remaining, non-Customer-centric metrics assessments are from the perspective of the target audience for the metric (that is, finance or the executive).

5. Contributing factors—Those factors that directly or indirectly impact the ability to realize the target.

6. Application—Suggestions on interpretation of the data and suggestions on the most likely corrective action(s).

7. General comment—Additional comments on the example.

## Performance Metrics

Performance metrics are time-related metrics related to SLA targets and goals. Performance metrics are measures of the contact center's ability to respond to a contact in basic terms of how fast, how many, and how long. An intelligent, software-driven private branch exchange (PBX) system provides a wealth of performance reports. The PBX metrics software is functional right out of the box but is unlikely to be optimized for the organization and structure.

The PBX software must be configured with identifying codes and handoff triggers, and the CSRs must be trained on how and when to use the codes. This task is paramount in a new contact center; set the best people on the task and understand that it is not a trivial undertaking.

The following bulleted list outlines universal metrics supported by the majority of PBX systems:

- Pickup time. (See Figure 4.7, Data plot, pickup time, for an example graphic plot of this metric.)

  ○ Definition—A measure of the time the Customer waits on the telephone line before their call is picked up by a CSR or an automated interactive voice response (IVR) system.

    The example depicts the average wait time over the course of a 24-hour weekday using sample data from a PBX system over the period of June 1, 2002 to June 8, 2002. The SLA target is included on the graphic as a "red-line" threshold. An equally useful plot depicts the same data over a longer period, such as a month or a quarter (three months). The SLA threshold itself bears comment in that it is a flat line. This indicates that the target is the same regardless of the hour of day. Many Customers in many niches care only about business hours, or alternatively, non-business hours. This allows the contact center management to get creative with targets as they do not have to be linear but rather can relax at non-peak periods and tighten during peak periods.

  ○ Unit of measure—Rings translated to seconds. Note that the standard time between rings, in North America, is six seconds.

  ○ Criticality—High.

  ○ Contributing factors—Contact volume may overwhelm personnel, the incoming telephone trunk bandwidth, or the back-office systems.

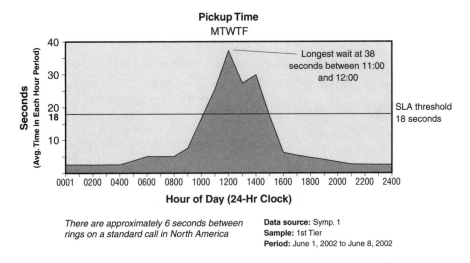

**Figure 4.7**   Data plot, pickup time.

- ○ Application—Tracking and plotting this time will assist in resource and system-loading planning activities. The graphic clearly indicates that the contact center is in violation of the SLA target between the hours of 1100 and 1200. A root cause analysis should be conducted to ascertain exactly which contributing factor is causing the violation condition and to drive the appropriate corrective action.

- ○ General comment—Customers are very sensitive to this particular period of waiting time. The shorter the wait-time, the less likely the Customer base will become dissatisfied. A reasonable target is between two to three rings (12–18 seconds) and a reasonable target before a CSR picks up the call is less than 30 seconds or five rings.

- Time duration between automated voice system pickup and CSR pickup. No example plot has been provided as the plot is very similar to Figure 4.7.

- ○ Definition—Self-explanatory.

- ○ Unit of measure—Seconds.

- ○ Criticality—Same as for Figure 4.7.

- ○ Contributing factors—Personnel resource loading may be too high.

- ○ Application—Use to plan resource deployment over time. For example, if there are periods where the wait time is beyond the SLA target, hire additional personnel for those periods.

- Incoming call duration at each tier. (See Figure 4.8, Data plot, contact duration by function.)

  ○ Definition—A measure of the average total time for each contact stratified by support tier.

  ○ Unit of measure—Minutes, in most cases.

  ○ Criticality—Medium.

  ○ Contributing factors—Lack of product knowledge (both the Customer's and the CSR's), product overhang,[4] and training.

  ○ Application—Staffing levels, tier stratification, and training decisions are driven by contact duration. As an example: in the graphic plot it can be seen that the third tier is online with the Customer for the longest duration. As the third tier is comprised of the most expensive personnel fielding contacts, it makes sense to reduce the duration. Conduct a root cause analysis to determine the nature of the contacts the third tier is fielding. If the duration is as long as it is because the issues are complex (hence not resolved by the first or second tier) then all is in order providing the volume of contacts is low. However, if the duration of the contact is being increased by the third tier being obligated to start the call from square one, then the duration may be reduced by having a better handoff protocol between the second and third tiers.

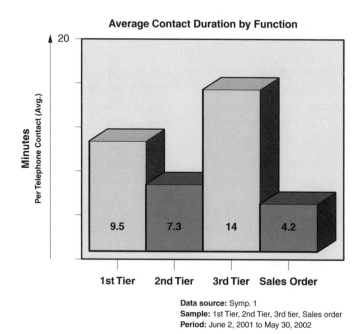

**Figure 4.8**    Data plot, contact duration by function.

- Incoming call volume over time. (See Figure 4.9, Data plot, calls over time.)

  - Definition—A measure of the average contact volume over a defined period. Special events and sales programs are typically normalized out of this plot as it is steady-state contacts that are being measured, not event-related spikes (which are equally important to measure and understand). The plot may be as granular as the needs dictate, however the standard periods to plot are daily, weekly, and monthly.

  - Unit of measure—Average number of contacts.

  - Criticality—Low.

  - Contributing factors—There are many contributing factors that are unique to the business niche and the subsequent user demographics the contact center is supporting. For example, support for a software gaming program aimed at teenagers will be skewed to non-business (actually non-school) hours with potential spikes during holiday periods and long plateaus during the summer holidays, whereas support for a quality management system software suite aimed at hardware manufacturers in the Fortune 100 would be skewed to business hours with an even distribution throughout the period (non-business-hours spikes are likely to be linked to upgrade or overhaul events).

  - Application—Resource planning. Plotting calls or contacts over time drives staffing and hours of operation decisions. As per the example set forth in contributing factors, the plot can be used as a lagging indictor of when to apply resources. A daily plot (see Figure 4.9) indicates that the principle period of maintenance (PPM) shows a strong relationship to North American coast-to-coast

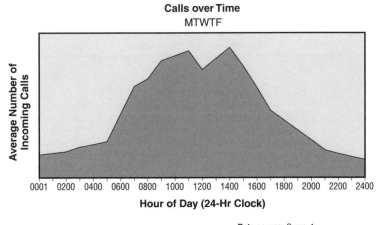

**Figure 4.9**  Data plot, calls over time.

business hours. Based on Figure 4.9, a case could be made to do away with twenty-four/seven support.

Plots based on a monthly time frame may indicate additional contact dynamics. For example, a software house specializing in small-office backup software may identify huge contact upswings at the end of any given month. To manage the upswing, additional staff are required at the end of each month. The number of additional resources required can also be ascertained by reviewing Figure 4.9.

Plots based on a yearly time frame may indicate that the contact volume is diminishing yet sales continue to be strong and are trending upward. Further analysis is required to identify the root cause for this positive trend, but something changed for the better in the product. Perhaps the quality initiative to eradicate the top five contact reasons is paying off, or the deployment of a Customer self-service (CSS) tool has resulted in fewer direct hits on the contact center.

- Abandoned call ratio. (See Figure 4.10, Data plot, abandoned call ratio.)

  ○ Definition—A measure of how many telephone contacts are terminated before the issue is resolved. Usually the Customer initiated disconnect while they were on hold or otherwise waiting for a CSR to pick up.

  ○ Unit of measure—Average number expressed as a percentage of total calls.[5]

  ○ Criticality—Very high.

  ○ Contributing factors—Call volume, training, and the personality profile inherent in the user base all contribute to the abandoned call ratio. The user personality profile may account for an inordinate abandoned call rate. Consider a software house specializing in games for teenagers. Teenagers, for all the leisure time

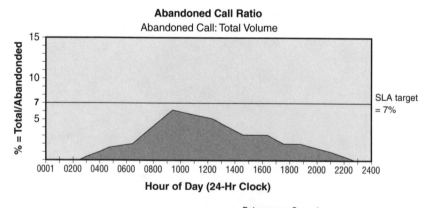

**Figure 4.10**    Data plot, abandoned call ratio.

they actually have at their disposal, have zero tolerance for being put on hold; presumably, they have better uses for their valuable time such as eating or sleeping. Now compare the personality profile of an MIS/IT professional; they are in the support business themselves and are, as a result, more patient. Understand the personality of the user base when presenting abandonment rates.

- ○ Application—Used to drive decisions regarding resource planning and CSS introduction and/or enhancement. (Note: a target of zero abandoned calls is admirable but unrealistic.) In the event that the ratio is higher than the target, a root cause analysis must be conducted to isolate the contributing factors and to produce an actionable remedy. Perhaps the best course of action is to conduct a survey to ascertain why Customers terminate calls. If the PBX or help desk system captures incoming contact information, instigate a program to call the Customer back to ascertain why.

    The abandonment ratio often tracks the average on-hold time very closely (see Figure 4.11, Data plot, average on-hold time). As the on-hold time increases so will the abandoned call ratio.

- ○ General comment—This ratio should be one of the first on the astute contact center manager's fix-it list. Figure 4.10 depicts a contact center working within their SLA targets. In the continuing effort to enhance Customer satisfaction, it may be time to lower the threshold on this particular operation to five percent.

- Average on-hold time. (See Figure 4.11.)

    - ○ Definition—The time the Customer is waiting in an "on-hold" state.

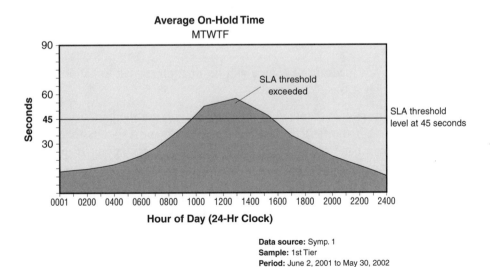

**Figure 4.11**   Data plot, average on-hold time.

○ Unit of measure—Seconds to minutes.

○ Criticality—Very high.

○ Contributing factors—Resource loading in relation to contact volume and training of the CSRs are the two main contributing factors.

　　The performance of enabling technologies and the contact center's links with the enabler's systems is an additional factor that can impact the on-hold time. Consider a contact center supporting a J2ME (Java 2 Micro Edition) Java–based CRM application designed to run, or piggyback, on a cellular telephone. CSRs may have visibility into the status of their own operations center, but do they have visibility into the various carriers that administer the networks that the cellular telephone is dependent on? The CRM cellular interface users may call the contact center if and when any component in the chain fails. As the Customers are paying a fee to use the CRM on cellular service, they may expect the CSRs to be ubiquitous. Hence, on-hold time increases as personnel scramble to find answers regarding the status of some other corporation's technology.

○ Application—Staffing level, resource planning, training validation, and deployment of Customer self-service tool decisions are driven by the on-hold time.

○ General comment—Figure 4.11 indicates that the contact center is in violation of their SLA target. The threshold is exceeded for a good portion of the business day, 0945 to 1400. The on-hold time maximum is in a 33 percent overrun state (60 seconds over 45 seconds is 15/45), but that may only mean Customers terminate the call, in frustration, after 15 seconds. The source data for this graph and the source data for Figure 4.10 must be correlated to understand exactly where corrective action is needed.

• Average call handoff frequency (escalation). (See Figure 4.12, Data plot, escalation percentage.)

○ Definition—A measure of source and destination related to handoffs between contact center teams.

○ Unit of measure—Percentage of total call volume for the handoff source team. For instance, if the first tier technical support team responds to 2500 calls a day, and they hand off 400 calls, their handoff percentage is 16 percent. The subsequent order of analysis is to ascertain the destination team for the 16 percent handoff statistic (that is, to whom is the contact being handed off?).

○ Criticality—Low from the Customer perspective unless the internal handoffs are so frequent that the Customer feels they are always being shuffled around. However, from the contact center manager's perspective, handoffs are of very high importance as not only are they a source of Customer dissatisfaction, they are very costly.

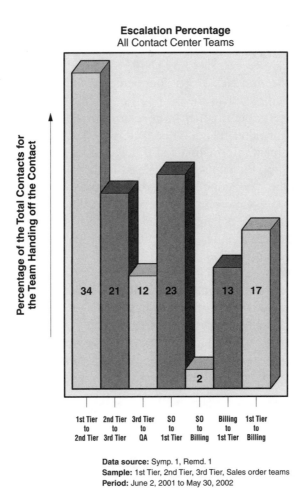

**Figure 4.12**   Data plot, escalation percentage.

○ Contributing factors—Escalations typically have two prime sources to consider: poor training is a major cause and/or Customers cannot navigate the IVR system to get them to the team that is best suited to assist them with their challenge.

○ Application—It is important that controls and systems are in place to ensure that Customers get to the right team as expediently as possible. Note that the data plot does not take mis-escalation into account. (Mis-escalation is when an escalation is directed to the wrong team, such as when a billing issue is erroneously sent to the second tier technical support team instead of the billing team.)

○ General comment—The contact center under the microscope in Figure 4.12, has a number of serious "handoff" issues. The following dissertation is a root cause analysis examining each bar on the data plot in detail.

## Root Cause Analysis of Figure 4.12, Data Plot, Escalation Percentage

*Bar 1: First Tier to Second Tier.* Thirty-four percent of all the contacts coming into the first tier team are redirected to the second tier team. This may not be a negative dynamic, for example, if the first tier team is structured as *technical* triage to the second tier team, then a handoff rate of 34 percent is by design and can be expected. The first tier gathers pertinent information and if they can resolve the issue they do so and close the contact. If not, the contact is escalated to the second tier team who immediately benefits from the work completed by the first tier in that all the preliminary data has been captured and entered into the system. This allows the second tier to concentrate solely on the technical challenge at hand. This model may be characterized by suggesting that the higher the technical skills of the individual taking the call, the less time they should be performing data entry functions.

If technical triage is not the model for the Contact Center in question, however, a 34 percent handoff rate indicates there is a problem. There are a number of root causes that may lie at the core. Perhaps the first tier personnel are poorly trained, the IVR system is making it difficult for Customers to navigate to the second tier, or the first tier team is so overburdened with contacts that they pass the overflow to the second tier. Perhaps the knowledge base does not have adequate depth, or perhaps it is unwieldy to navigate. An examination of each of these potential root causes follows.

*Training.* The Customer is connecting with the correct team for a resolution to the issue at hand, however, the first tier team lacks the training and/or expertise to resolve the contact without resorting to escalation to the second tier. The situation is further complicated by the churn rate, which is to suggest that the training is effective but the CSRs do not have adequate experience. They are trained properly but move on to other functions within the operation before they can effectively apply the training they have received. The remedy is to ascertain the first order root cause(s) and respond accordingly by supplementing the training, stemming the churn the rate, and/or introducing a disincentive for CSRs who escalate too readily.

*Interactive Voice Response System.* As noted elsewhere in this guide, the mapping (the sequence to get to where you want to be using the numbers on a touch-tone telephone) and setup of IVR systems is a challenge.[6] The mapping must be easily navigated so that the Customer gets to where they want/need to be in as few keystrokes as possible. If the root cause analysis concludes that Customers searching for second tier services inevitably end up in the first tier queue then review the mapping and correct the misrouting. Table 4.1 shows some of the more popular glitches in IVR mapping.

*Overflow/Overload.* Similar to the triage model discussed previously. Escalations due to overflow or overload may be by design. If the second tier has the bandwidth, it is reasonable to direct overflow from the first tier during contact volume surges, however, 34 percent seems to be a rather high run rate. The remedy is to review resource allocation at the first tier during the escalation spikes.

*Knowledge Base.* The knowledge base may not include the data the first tier requires to resolve Customer issues. The remedy is to ensure the second tier contributes to the knowledge base and to ensure that for every unique escalation to the second tier, an entry is made into the knowledge base. This way the knowledge base grows with the experience of the team. Ensure that the knowledge base itself is useable. It must be easy to navigate in real time, intuitive, fast, and have the right data in the correct context.

The root cause analysis used to determine why the run rate is at 34 percent seldom draws conclusions as well-defined as found in the previous definitions. More likely than not there will be elements of all the causes contributing to the 34 percent. The remedy is to prioritize and deal with the highest-impact (Customer satisfaction being the guide) elements first and then work down to the lower levels. A Pareto analysis would assist in focusing the priorities.

***Bar 2: Second Tier to Third Tier.*** Twenty-one percent of all the contacts entering via the second tier team are redirected to the third tier team. Much of what was written in regards to first to second tier escalations applies here as well and will not be repeated.

A run rate of 21 percent is too high, particularly if the third tier is, as it is in many organizations, comprised of engineers and developers who have their primary tasks to perform. Every time an engineer or developer is pulled from their primary task, new product developments and features will suffer delays.

Assume the product is sound and robust. Typical root causes for this dynamic are shown in Table 4.2.

**Table 4.1**  IVR mapping challenges.

| Problem | Remedy |
| --- | --- |
| Ambiguous options | Simplify |
| Too many words | Simplify |
| Infinite loops | Test thoroughly (and after every change to the system) |
| "0" does NOT bring the Customer to a warm body | Use standards, such as "0" always connects to the receptionist |
| Too many levels | Simplify. A target of no more than three levels reduces the labyrinth vibe. |

**Table 4.2**  Escalation root cause (cursory only).

| Problem | Remedy |
| --- | --- |
| Inadequate training on the more technical challenges with the product | Revisit training program and adjust |
| Hiring practices | The second tier skill set must be better defined and the applicants must be vetted |
| The knowledge base does not include the data the second tier needs to perform | Ensure the third tier contributes to the knowledge base and ensure that for every unique escalation an entry is made into the knowledge base |

There is the possibility that the second tier is not directly responsible for the high escalation run rate and therefore is incapable of directly providing the remedy. It may be that the product itself is causing the high run rate, or that the product may simply not be ready for commercial release. Leading indicators of this condition include:

- Failure modes that are not anticipated.

- Failure modes that are more complex than anticipated.

- A high rate of interaction between the product being directly supported and the supporting/enabling technologies.

- The product is not robust enough for the target user base (in other words, it fails frequently).

The remedy is for the contact center to provide the data points to the product manager, the quality team, and the engineering/development teams so that the product specifications can be revisited and corrective action initiated.

The root cause analysis used to determine why the run rate is at 21 percent seldom draws conclusions as well-defined as found in the definitions mentioned here. More likely than not there will be elements of all the causes contributing to the 21 percent. The remedy is to prioritize and deal with the highest-impact (Customer satisfaction being the guide) elements first and then work down to the lower level. A Pareto analysis will assist in focusing the priorities.

An additional data plot that may be of interest is the portion of calls that are escalated from first to second to third tier. That is, situations where the Customer is escalated or handed off two or more times.

***Bar 3: Third Tier to QA (Quality Assurance).*** Twelve percent of the contacts escalated to the third tier (assuming that the third tier does not take contacts directly) are redirected to the quality team. A run rate of 12 percent is not problematic, no analysis is required.

Note on third tier and QA: The escalation model depicted is a standard model found in many support centers, however, an equally valid model stipulates that the second tier escalates to the Quality team. The Quality team verifies and validates the failure mode and may gather additional data points regarding the failure. If the Quality team cannot effect a remedy, then and only then is the issue escalated to the third tier.

***Bar 4: SO to First Tier.*** The sales order team escalates 23 percent of the contacts to the first tier. This is usually a leading indicator that the Customer base does not know who to call when they experience problems. Subsequently, the Customer contacts the group or individual that took their order. The corrective action in this scenario is to convince the sales team to let go. The sales team must relinquish control of the Customer relationship. The Customer may resist normal channels when they have issues and call the salesperson that courted them and made the initial sale. As this problem is widespread, it bears comment.

The Customer will never stop leveraging the relationship with the salesperson if they perceive the salesperson is expediting their issue to the *proper* authority. The upside is huge for the Customer, personalized care; the downside is devastating for the sales organization. As the sales team adds more and more Customers to the roster, they find themselves spending more and more time expediting support calls and therefore having less and less time to close additional sales. This dynamic is at play in many organizations. Inevitably, the root cause analysis reveals that the sales personnel perceive that the support organization is dysfunctional. Further analysis reveals that the sales personnel formulate the "dysfunctional" belief based on what their Customers tell them, and further analysis yet reveals that the Customer has learned that to get exemplary support they only have to make a couple of claims about the support organization's lack of attention to move the salesperson to expedite (the cliché "pushing the right buttons" comes to mind).

This is not to suggest that there aren't dysfunctional support organizations out there, there most certainly are and it is those organizations that need this book most. But, the sales team must understand the performance metrics under which the contact center is operating and sell that capability to the user base. This dynamic is most pronounced with junior sales team members; seasoned sales personnel know better.

Even more disruptive for the contact center personnel is when sales personnel walk down the hall (or telephone or e-mail) and tap directly into contact center resources. They are jumping the queue! Queue-jumping is highly disruptive to the discipline, systems, and controls that are in place.

The sales team must be taught to direct the Customers to the normal channels. The sales team must be armed with a thorough understanding of the services and performance metrics the contact center is governed by. Once sales has this knowledge they can differentiate between an egregious Customer claim and a justified Customer claim. The salesperson can then defuse the egregious claims and make it clear to the Customer that it is in their best interest to follow the normal channel. Of course, in the event the claim is justified, the salesperson can act as the Customer champion and bring the issue to the attention of the appropriate contact center manager (or director or VP).

***Bar 5: SO to Billing.*** Two percent of the contacts coming into the sales order team are escalated to the billing team. This is an excellent run rate.

It indicates that the vast majority of Customers know whom to call and can navigate successfully when they have billing issues. There is only a small percentage that enters the system via the sales channel for billing issues.

***Bar 6: Billing to First Tier.*** Thirteen percent escalated to the first tier. This is not a problematic run rate. Root cause analysis would probably undercover that Customers contact the billing team because they do indeed have a billing issue. Once the billing issue is resolved, the Customer then surfaces a technical issue that the billing team dutifully escalates to the first tier.

An additional point of interest in this scenario is that the Customer's technical issue alone did not warrant a call to support. The technical failure mode was of a low enough impact that the Customer could live with it. To validate and verify this hypothesis one only has to drill down to the core technical issues in the 13 percent that were escalated.

***First Tier to Billing.*** Seventeen percent of contacts coming into the first tier are escalated to the billing team. Some of these escalations would be the reverse dynamic to that noted above under "billing to first tier," that is, there was indeed a technical issue and, once resolved, the Customer wished to deal with a less severe billing issue. The remaining escalations can usually be attributed to the fact that no matter how clearly the IVR mapping is published, Customers will go to the first support option (often the first tier).

***Additional Analysis.*** By summing the bars in the data plot based on the source for the escalations, it is evident that:

- Tier 1 escalates 51 percent of the contacts coming to them. Over half the contacts are escalated! It begs the question "is Tier 1 just a telephone switchboard?" Further analysis of the data points is required.

- The sales order team escalates 25 percent of the contacts coming to them. One quarter! How many more sales orders could be processed if these escalations were reduced?

  - Alternative 1—If the number of escalations were reduced, could the head count be lowered?

  - Alternative 2—What is the lost opportunity cost? How many more outgoing sales calls or up-sell opportunities are being missed?

- Further analysis is required. The first data point to capture and analyze is the average "time" the escalation calls consume. See Figure 4.13, Data plot, time before escalation, and note that the sales order team consumes about 2.3 minutes before passing the contact on. 2.3 minutes represents the average time it takes to open a contact in the contact center customer relationship management system and initiate a lookup on a Customer record. How much of a problem this represents is unique to each contact center.

## More Performance Metrics

- Average time before calls are escalated. (See Figure 4.13)

  - Definition—A measure of the average time a contact is held at one tier before being escalated to the next tier.

  - Unit of measure—Minutes.

  - Criticality—Medium. Customers are generally tolerant of time spent with any given tier provided progress is being made.

  - Contributing factors—Training is typically the key factor in escalation management. If the training is inadequate then the CSRs may spend an inordinate period of time before realizing that another team in the contact center is better positioned to deliver a resolution.

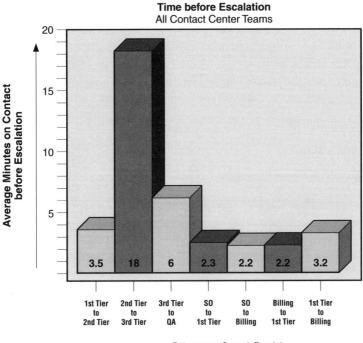

**Figure 4.13**  Data plot, time before escalation.

○ Application—This data plot is essentially a measure of how quickly the CSRs can assess a situation and determine that they are not the optimal level (tier or team) to deliver the resolution. If the determination time is excessive then the training program should be revisited.

○ General comment—Assume first that the examples given are driven by a CRM system that has an established Customer lookup time of 2.3 minutes (138 seconds). That is, it takes an average of 2.3 minutes to initiate and locate any given Customer data record. Therefore, one can expect that all the first tier, sales order, and billing team plots will be 2.3 minutes or greater. The fact that Figure 4.13 indicates that both the sales order and billing teams can escalate a contact before 2.3 minutes underscores one of the many inconsistencies that can surface when using averages and data from multiple sources. The potential reason the sales order and billing teams can accomplish the seemingly impossible task of escalating before the Customer record has been located is because the 2.3 minute average was established by averaging data from all teams. But the first and second tiers are technical personnel whereas the sales order and billing teams have a more clerical background. Simply stated, the sales order and billing teams are much faster keyboardists compared to the first and second tier teams.

The point is, know from whence the data comprising the reports originated, understand the constants, the inconsistencies, and their roots.

Figure 4.13 illustrates only one area that may be of concern: second tier to third tier escalations average 18 minutes. This can be rationalized by analyzing the activities the second tier CSRs are performing in those 18 minutes. The activities include:

* Data gathering

* Troubleshooting

* Knowledge base searches

* Recommending a few solutions

* Collaborating with their immediate peers

Being that the source product driving the data plots is reasonably complicated, 18 minutes is within expected operational parameters. No further analysis is warranted.

- Outgoing call duration (no example plot).

  ○ Definition—A measure of the average time a CSR spends as the call originator.

  ○ Unit of measure—Minutes.

  ○ Criticality—Low from the Customer's perspective, high from the contact center management perspective as CSR initiated calls are very expensive in labor, lost opportunity, and telephony costs. The cost of a callback is always high and therefore should be minimized.

  ○ Contributing factors—Situations that force outgoing calls appear in Table 4.3.

**Table 4.3**   Outgoing call drivers.

| Problem | Remedy |
|---|---|
| A satisfactory remedy could not be obtained without research. | May indicate additional training is needed. |
|  | May indicate the knowledge base is not up to date (or effective). |
| Customer's left a request for a callback | Often this means the Customer is calling for a specific CSR as opposed to the far more desirable calling into the CSR pool. The Customer needs to be instructed that the pool of CSRs better serves them. |
| Follow-up call | Not strictly a problem if well managed and the follow-ups are, on average, just validating a suggested remedy. |
| Courtesy call | Not a problem, however, the contact center management must decide if the return on courtesy calls is worth the expense. |

○ Application—This plot (considered in tandem with Figure 4.14, Data plot, outgoing calls over time, and Figure 4.23, Data plot, call volume by event type, page 147) is an industry standard indicator of contact center effectiveness and efficiency. Due to the cost and obvious inefficiency of CSR-initiated calls, the majority of management teams are mandated to drive the internally initiated call volume to zero. The only exception to this rule is in the case of the follow-up call, which is driven more by proactive Customer satisfaction than issue resolution.

• Outgoing call volume over time. (See Figure 4.14.)

○ Definition—A measure of average number of outgoing calls made by contact center personnel in a given period.

○ Unit of measure—Number of calls. May also be expressed as the percentage of total calls.

○ Criticality—High. Courtesy calls put aside, the fact that a callback is needed is a clear indication that the contact center is not resolving issues on first contact.

○ Contributing factors—Training is one of the key drivers; also review staffing levels.

○ Application—The plot is useful in determining periods that demand additional staff to field calls. The plot will also underscore if the support burden is seasonal or cyclical in nature, which may impact product management decisions. This plot, analyzed in tandem with Figure 4.23, page 147, will tell the astute contact center manager a great deal about what they can expect in the future and how to plan resources accordingly.

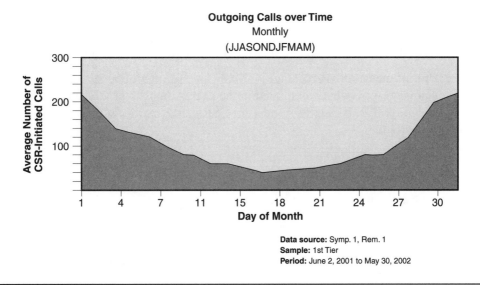

**Figure 4.14** Data plot, outgoing calls over time.

○ General comment—The time line period chosen in which to plot the data is important. Figure 4.14 has a period of one representative/average month and clearly shows an upswing in contacts at month-beginnings and -ends. This type of call behavior is to be expected if the contact center is supporting a product that is cyclical in nature (such as an enterprise backup software product as backups are often run at month-end). However, if there were peaks elsewhere during the period, root cause analysis is needed to determine why. Once the root cause is known, corrective measures may be implemented to attempt to evenly distribute the call load over the period.

For example: using support for an enterprise backup software utility as a possible remedy to even out the contact distribution is to embark on a marketing program to convince the user community's MIS/IT professionals that there is no technical reason to schedule enterprise backups/updates/tests for the end-of-month period. If the program suggested picking the second or third week of the month, and 25 percent of the user base adopted the idea, then the contact upswing would be flattened and, in turn, staffing levels would be more consistent and, in turn, easier to manage.

## Support Metrics

Support metrics focus attention on how contacts move through the contact center to resolution. Support metrics include measures of how CSRs actually use the working time available. Support metrics are derived from data found in the help desk system used by the CSRs, supplemented by the data available from the PBX system. The help desk software must be configured with identifying action and event codes, and the CSRs must be trained on how and when to use these codes.

The following list outlines a number of useful reports and graphic plots.

- CSR Time per Function. (See Figure 4.15, Data plot, time per function.)

   ○ Definition—A comparative measure of how the CSRs spend their time.

   ○ Unit of measure—Percentage of total time. The granularity of the activities, that is, exactly what is included in the plot, is important. For the metric to be meaningful, it is best to divide the CSR's actions into no more then five or six activities.

   ○ Criticality—Medium.

   ○ Contributing factors—Systems, resources, and interdepartmental interaction contribute to the ratios and their proportions.

   ○ Application—Time per function is a direct indicator of how well contact center personnel use their time. It is an indirect indicator of the efficiency and usability of the back-office systems the CSRs use on a daily basis.

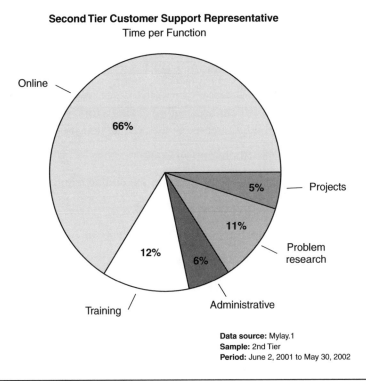

**Figure 4.15**   Data plot, time per function.

○ General comment—Figure 4.15 depicts a healthy mix of activities for the second tier CSR team. Sixty-six percent of the time, the second tier CSRs are prepared to field contacts. This is very good.

Twelve percent for training (and retraining) is a reasonable percentage for a high-technology environment, considering the rate at which technology evolves. Lower percentages can be expected for less volatile industries. An additional plot of interest would be to ascertain how much of the 12 percent is spent "just keeping up" and how much is spent on career development.

Six percent of the time is expended on administrative chores. This is excellent. It is in an indirect indicator that submitting time sheets, expense reports, and other sundry administrative functions are streamlined and efficient. Percentages hovering around 30 percent are not rare, particularly for those organizations that are more paper-driven than online.

• Contact Density over Time. No example plot is provided as the plot is very similar to Figure 4.9, Calls over time, page 119, only differing in the extension of the time base.

○ Definition—Contact density over time is an excellent modeling and trend analysis tool. It is a lagging indicator of contact density—it will clearly show if contacts are on the increase or decrease.

- Unit of measure—Average number of contacts.

- Criticality—Minimal direct impact on the Customer, however, the Customer will be affected if the manager does not learn from historical data and deploy resources accordingly.

- Contributing factors—There are a number of factors, direct and indirect, that impact the density trend. Increases in the contact density could be attributed to:

  * An increase in sales (more customers)

  * Additional responsibilities assigned to the contact center

  * Upgrades to the product being supported

  * Increase in the complexity of the core product

  * Customers demanding enhanced services

  * A marked decrease in product quality

  Conversely, a decrease in the contact density could be attributed to:

  * Elimination of prime failure modes (root cause analysis and corrective action have been effective)

  * Deployment of enhanced Customer self-help tools (for example, improvements to the embedded help file)

  * Better documentation for self-diagnosing and -healing applications

  * Increased product quality

  * Increased upgrade stability

  * Internal or external knowledge base tool deployment

  * Frequently asked questions system delivery enhancement

- Application—Use the density over time to assess the impact of new product, sales, and marketing programs based on historical data.

- General comment—This plot and subsequent report contains sensitive material and should have a limited distribution.

- Contact stratification by contact mode. (See Figure 4.16, Data plot, contact method.)

  - Definition—A comparative measure of the methods Customers choose to use to access the contact center. All contacts are summed and then delineated by the mode of contact the Customer used.

  - Unit of measure—Percentage of overall contact volume.

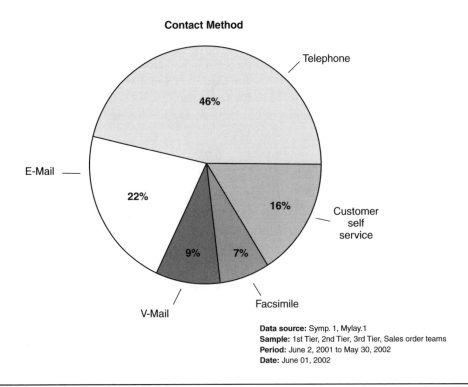

**Contact Method**

Telephone

46%

E-Mail

22%

16%

Customer self service

9%      7%

V-Mail

Facsimile

**Data source:** Symp. 1, Mylay.1
**Sample:** 1st Tier, 2nd Tier, 3rd Tier, Sales order teams
**Period:** June 2, 2001 to May 30, 2002
**Date:** June 01, 2002

**Figure 4.16**   Data plot, contact method.

- Criticality—High. An understanding of the contact stratification is very important in ascertaining if existing channels are effective. The plot is also used as a
  resource-planning tool.

- Contributing factors—Ease of access is the salient contributing factor. The
  Customers will migrate to the mode of contact that is easiest for them tempered
  by their success in receiving a resolution.

- Application—The data plot is used to ascertain if the contact modes and service
  channels the contact center provides are being utilized as expected. The data
  can be used to draw attention to service channels that are not being optimally
  utilized. Assessment of any service channel usually distills to one factor—cost
  of the channel. Analyze the contact stratification data plot together with Figure
  4.19, Data plot, cost per support contact by mode, page 139. Using data from
  the two plots, management can define which channels are cost-effective and
  then initiate programs to direct the Customer base to the preferred contact
  modes. One additional data point that is needed to complete the picture drawn
  by the data plot is the Customer's opinion of how they wish to contact the organization. It is prudent to survey the user base to ascertain how they wish to
  interface with the contact center.

○ General comment—Customers are using the CSS capability only 16 percent of the time. Considering the high costs of deploying CSS engines, this service channel is underutilized. The remedy is to evaluate the capability itself and ask, Is it user-friendly?[7] Then review the Customer's access preferences and ask, Do the Customers, as a whole, have Internet access? Lastly, review the introduction program for the CSS application and ask, Do Customers know about the tool and how to access it?

Facsimile contacts are running at seven percent. Unless there is a compelling underlying reason to retain facsimile as a service channel, it would probably be best to phase the facsimile channel out if for no other reason than the fact that facsimiles have been rendered obsolete by e-mail and instant messaging technologies.

V-mail at nine percent is interesting. As suggested previously, one needs to understand the cost of each support channel. As v-mail usually assumes and forces a callback with the attendant long distance charges, telephone tag matches, and on-hold time, it is best to induce a disincentive to v-mail. Additionally, few v-mail systems are linked to the help desk system, which means a v-mail contact can get lost, thereby spawning a dissatisfaction event. Finally, v-mails are usually left for individuals; individuals take vacations, go to training sessions, and move on, in or out of organizations. It is preferable to direct the Customer base to the contact center as a pool of resources and to set up disincentives to Customers' calling "individuals." Unless there is a compelling reason to retain v-mail as a service channel, *and* unless v-mails are captured by the help desk system, it is probably in the contact center's best interest to phase out v-mail as a service channel.

## Financial Metrics

Financial metrics detail the costs involved in supporting the product/service. Financial metrics draw attention to the true lifecycle cost of making a sale. Financial metrics temper the data available from the help desk and PBX software systems with monetary values. The finance or accounting departments are the source for the monetary values supplied to contact center management. All financial reports contain sensitive material and should be of limited distribution.

There was one, allegedly mature, low-margin product that suffered no fewer than three failures during the course of its warranty period. The failures were catastrophic, hard failures that necessitated the return of the product to the repair depot. The company from which the author's company purchased the product lock, stock, and barrel did not include support costs in the financial assessment of the product because "support is simply a cost of doing business." As it turned out, once the financials were worked into the product lifecycle cost, it was more economical to stop selling the product and bury it under the parking lot instead.

- Cost per Incoming Contact by Team (salary, capital, overhead, and so on). (See Figure 4.17, Data plot, cost per contact by function.)

  ○ Definition—A measure of the average loaded cost for each contact delineated by the team who resolved and closed the contact. The spreadsheet that drove the data plot is also included as Figure 4.18, Spreadsheet, cost per contact.

  ○ Unit of measure—Dollars.

  ○ Criticality—High. This data plot is a leading indicator of the financial viability and general effectiveness of the contact center.

  ○ Contributing factors—There are a number of factors that contribute to the total average cost of a contact. These include: system usability, burden rate, salary, capital, overhead, to name a few.

  ○ Application—The data plot can be used to isolate areas that cause the most financial concern. If further drill-down is deemed necessary to understand the contributing costs, the data can be isolated and analyzed.

  ○ General comment—For the most part it is the loaded salary level that is driving the costs in Figure 4.17. The first and second tier teams are running at near parity and field the majority of the contacts. The third tier has the highest

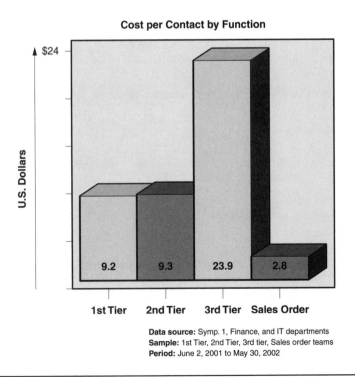

**Figure 4.17**   Data plot, cost per contact by function.

**Cost per Call**
**June 1, 2002**

| Team | Avg. Per Call (Minute) | Salary Cost per Call | Loaded Cost per Call[3] | Capital Cost per Call | Total Cost per Call |
|---|---|---|---|---|---|
| First Tier | 9.5 | $3.63 | $ 7.98 | $1.24 | $ 9.23 |
| Second Tier | 7.3 | $3.58 | $ 7.89 | $1.43 | $ 9.32 |
| Third Tier | 14 | $9.47 | $20.84 | $3.06 | $23.89 |
| SO | 4.2 | $1.05 | $ 2.32 | $0.46 | $ 2.78 |

**Salary/Capital Calculations**

| Team | Avg. Salary (June 2001) | Hourly Wage[1] | Salary per Minute | Avg. Capital Cost +IT Support (per Yr.)[2] | Capital Cost per Hour | Capital per Minute |
|---|---|---|---|---|---|---|
| First Tier | $35,000 | $22.91 | $0.38 | $12,000 | $ 7.86 | $0.13 |
| Second Tier | $45,000 | $29.46 | $0.49 | $18,000 | $11.78 | $0.20 |
| Third Tier | $62,000 | $40.59 | $0.68 | $20,000 | $13.09 | $0.22 |
| SO | $23,000 | $15.06 | $0.25 | $10,000 | $ 6.55 | $0.11 |

[1]**Assumptions**

235 productive working **days** in a year[4]

6.5 productive working **hours** in a day

[2]**Assumptions**

Capital costs from IT. Includes: systems, desktop, support, infrastructure, and so on.

[3]**Assumptions**

2.2 Loading factor from finance. Includes benefits, facility, training, development costs, and so on.

[4]**Assumptions**

Productive days in a year based on the following:

| Days/Yr. | Vacation | Sick | Civic Holiday | Weekends | Remaining Productive Days |
|---|---|---|---|---|---|
| 365 | 10 | 10 | 8 | 102 | 235 |

**Figure 4.18** Spreadsheet, cost per contact.

dollar run rate due to engineering-level salaries but, typically, also fields the fewest calls. The sales order team costs are very low for two reasons: relatively low salaries and the short duration of a sales order contact (the lowest of the four teams).

Figure 4.18 is the worksheet that drives the numbers found in Figure 4.17. The worksheet contains the raw data points and any assumptions made and carried through to Figure 4.17. All financial reports contain sensitive material and should receive limited distribution only.

- Cost per Incoming Contact by Contact Mode. (See Figure 4.19, Data plot, cost per support contact by mode.)

  - Definition—A measure of the loaded costs for contacts delineated by the mode of contact the Customer chose.

  - Unit of measure—Dollars.

  - Criticality—High. This data plot is a leading indicator of the financial viability of the contact center based on the service channels supported.

  - Contributing factors—There are a number of factors that contribute to the total average cost of a contact delineated by the contact mode including: system usability, burden rate, salary, capital, overhead, and so on.

  - Application—This is an excellent tool for ascertaining where the contact center's budget is being expended and, more importantly, which are the optimal service channels. For example, it may be concluded from Figure 4.19 that the CSS support channel is by far the most cost-effective contact mode. As with the other data plots, however, this plot cannot be assessed in isolation, more analysis is

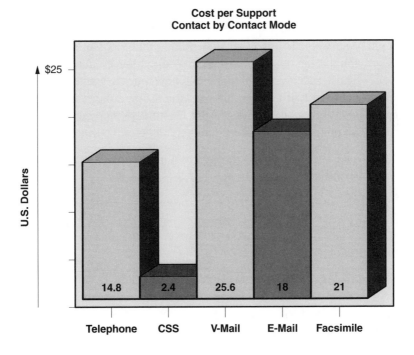

Figure 4.19    Data plot, cost per support contact by mode.

needed. This data plot should, at a minimum, be cross-referenced to Figure 4.16 and should also be tempered by the Customer's opinion of what service channels provide optimal satisfaction.

○ General comment—The first inclination is to do away with the two most expensive and least effective service channels: v-mail and facsimile. Tempering the data from Figure 4.19 with data found in Figure 4.16, it is apparent that facsimile contacts account for seven percent and v-mail accounts for nine percent of all contacts. That is 16 percent of the total contact volume.

It is evident that the best place to redirect the v-mail and facsimile contacts is to the underutilized and comparatively cost-effective CSS channel. As CSS is running at 16 percent of total contacts, adding an additional 16 percent, even though that's doubling the volume, should not tax the infrastructure or CSS engine. As the CSS channel is roughly ten times less costly than v-mail and approximately nine times less costly than the facsimile channel, the savings will quickly justify the cost of the marketing program needed to entice Customers to switch to CSS.

But wait, hold up . . . not so fast. Before going any further, three additional data points need to be brought forward. First, a quick analysis of the nature of the contacts that come in via the v-mail and facsimile channels should be conducted to verify that the CSS channel can adequately deal with those issues. Second, the Customers who presently use the v-mail and facsimile channels should be surveyed to get an understanding of their potential adoption rate to the CSS channel (that is, why are they using these contact modes in the first place?). Third, ascertain from marketing how much a "switch to CSS" awareness program will cost. If cost-prohibitive, the astute contact center manager must get creative and subtly influence the Customer's choice. Again, all financial reports contain sensitive material and should receive limited distribution only.

• Cost to Invoice (bill generation through to A/R resolution). (See Figure 4.20, Data plot, cost per billing channel.)

○ Definition—A measure of the cost to process and collect on an outgoing bill.

○ Unit of Measure—Dollars.

○ Criticality—High.

○ Contributing factors—The target of a well-tuned billing engine is to issue invoices to Customers accurately, timely and economically. In a recurring billing model, such as maintenance contracts paid out monthly, the cost of issuing the bill, which is a constant, should be a small percentage of the bill. There are the hard costs, such as for printing, mailing, receiving, and payment clearing; and there are the soft costs, such as for updating mailing lists, administration of the mailing lists, lost mail (both incoming and outgoing), credits, prorating credits, and overcharges. Suffice to say there are many costs in issuing an invoice.

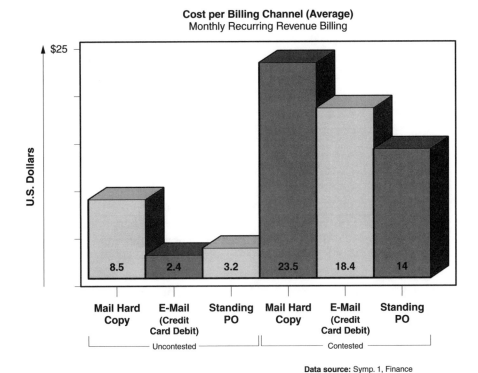

**Cost per Billing Channel (Average)**
Monthly Recurring Revenue Billing

Data source: Symp. 1, Finance
Sample: Billing support, sales order teams
Period: June 2, 2001 to May 30, 2002

**Figure 4.20**   Data plot, cost per billing channel.

Micro-payments and their collection is a massive challenge. Suppose a soft drink is purchased from a vending machine using a wireless handheld to initiate payment. Somewhere, someone is splitting revenue streams between the wireless carrier, credit service provider, software service provider, and soft drink vendor. If the micro-payment to the credit service provider is pennies then the per-transaction cost-to-invoice must be a fraction of those pennies. The problem is not so severe if the user purchases many soft drinks in the course of a paying cycle because the cost-to-invoice can be more readily absorbed over the multiple purchases. But what if the user only buys one? The cost-to-invoice may exceed the revenue—the company can bill themselves to bankruptcy.

There are ancillary contributing factors to an inordinately high collection cost. Probably the most frequent are failures within the data transfer from the corporation's systems to credit card service providers. This can manifest itself in a number of ways that tend to infuriate Customers, such as multiple bill events for one service or slipped decimal places.

Figure 4.20 is divided into two categories, *contested* and *uncontested*. The *uncontested* half of the data plot represents the constant cost by channel to issue an invoice and does not impact the contact center. The *contested* half of the plot does impact the contact center. Each contested invoice event must be drilled-down on, analyzed, and explained to the Customer; and a credit must be issued internally, approved, and issued to the Customer. This represents a huge direct cost and an even greater cost potential to the satisfaction quotient of the Customer base.

○ Application—The plot is an excellent measure of how effective the back-office systems and credit authorization procedures are. If the cost to correct a contested invoice is extraordinary, as it often is, conduct a root cause analysis and ferret out and correct the inadequacies. There are a number of options available for optimizing the interaction between the contact center personnel and the Customer. One of the best examples of this is electronic bill presentment and clearing where the Customer can access their invoice online, post questions, and get a resolution without having to resort to a phone call. The most surprising positive aspect of electronic bill presentment may be the simple fact that the CSR and the Customer are both reading off the same page (figuratively speaking). Both parties are able to view and discuss the exact same "image" of the invoice . . . very powerful indeed.

○ General comment—In the example plot, Figure 4.20, two accounts receivable (AR) aspects are depicted: the cost to collect *uncontested* bills and the cost to collect *contested* bills. An uncontested bill is simply paid by the Customer, no issues or questions. A contested condition indicates that there is an issue with the bill, be it the amount, the terms, an address change, and so on. Again, all financial reports contain sensitive material and should receive limited distribution only.

## Product Metrics

Product metrics detail the performance of the product/service. They are shared and analyzed by the quality and engineering teams with a view to eradicating the top failure modes. The data is mined from the help desk system with data supplied by a repair depot or third party authority (outside of the contact center) that actually repairs the product.

The top failure modes can be understood in two ways: in terms of frequency of contact or in terms of most expensive to resolve. This suggests that a top failure mode may simply not warrant intervention by engineering because the expense to rectify it may outweigh the expense to support it.

As the target audience for product reports are the quality and engineering teams, it is important to clearly indicate the data source. Consider Figure 4.21, Data plot, top failure modes. The discerning quality engineer will want to know the source for the failure modes as there is often a huge difference between what the Customer may claim and what the actual failure mode is. In most support cycles there are three opinion or perspective points on any given failure:

1. What the Customer *claims:* "It's making a terrible noise when I power it up."

2. The CSR *diagnoses*: "It is probably the hard drive, please take the unit into our repair depot."

3. The depot repair technician's *fix:* "One of the front panel control cables was rubbing against the power supply fan. I secured the cable to the panel raiser and the noise went away."

> This is important. Read it again and make sure
> the message is understood and internalized.

In this example there are three separate perceptions of failure modes: noisy, the hard drive has failed, and there is an unsecured cable. Do not assume that the repair technician is right. There very well may be a cable rubbing against the power supply fan, but perhaps the hard drive doesn't start to make noise until it has warmed up for 12 hours.

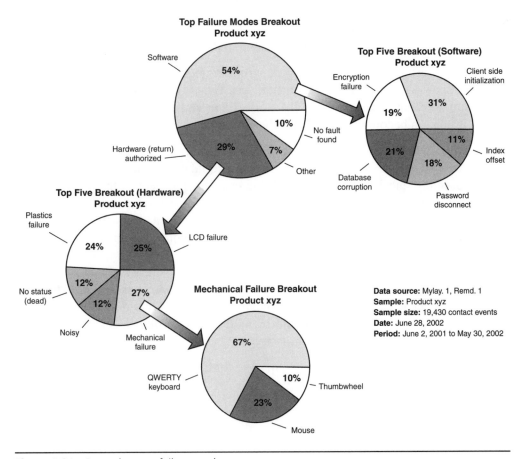

**Figure 4.21** Data plot, top failure modes.

To further complicate matters, all three perspectives are important to report on and analyze as follows:

1. Quality engineer—The quality engineer needs to know that there *may* be issues with securing internal cables. An analysis of the frequency of the issue and an analysis of the potential fixes and their cost implications should be conducted. The quality engineer would also be interested in the Customer's original comment, "terrible noise." An astute quality engineer would be interested in what constitutes a "terrible noise." Quantify and qualify.

2. Contact center—The contact center manager needs to know if additional training is needed, and, as per the quality engineer, an analysis of the frequency of the misdiagnosis is needed. In addition, the knowledge base may need to be updated with a description and action for this failure mode. Get creative, is it possible to isolate the cable noise and sample it as a digital .wav file? The sampled .wav file would provide the CSRs with a reference they could listen to when talking a Customer through the issue. Finally, being that the cost to resolve this issue hits the contact center hardest, a recommendation for a Customer self-fix kit, for those that are inclined, could be made available. A small kit with a tie-wrap, a drawing, and detailed instructions could be produced.

3. Engineering—The engineering department does not give a wit for what the claim was or what the CSR thought it was. The engineer does care that the cables are working loose for both the noise issue and the potential hazard of the insulation becoming eroded and shorting to the metal frame.

To bring closure to this story, the engineer works with the quality engineer and concludes that a $0.0025 tie-wrap is the fix. As the material cost is minimal and the impact on the assembly line is equally minimal, the engineer proceeds with an engineering change notice and any new product rolling off the line is secured.

Perception is often driven by the needs of the audience. Understand the audience and positive change will be smoother and faster and disruption will be minimized.

- Top Five Failure Modes with Breakout. (See Figure 4.21.)

    ○ Definition—A depiction of the top issues the Customer base contacts the contact center in regards to. The granularity of the report is driven by the target audience—the software engineers will want a different set of drill-down points then the hardware engineers.

    ○ Unit of measure—Comparative quantity of total contact volume.

    ○ Criticality—Very high. The data driving this graphic is key to continuous improvement of the product itself. The only exception to this is if the product being supported is mature, robust, and stable, and therefore has the vast majority of the glitches already worked out.

○ Contributing factors—The contributing factors are far too vast to tally as every product has its own unique attributes, failure points, and idiosyncrasies. That said, it is important to note that Customer perception may play a significant role in the top failure mode. It is imperative to listen to the opinion of the Customer. For example, consider the battery life for a personal digital assistant (PDA). The design specification may have called up a target of 48 hours between recharge cycles. The engineering department may have met this target, but if the Customer base resoundingly complains about having to recharge the device every 48 hours then the original specification has to be revisited.

○ Application—This plot is key to garnering an understanding of which product changes/improvements will reap the greatest return on investment (ROI). Product managers, the quality team, and the engineering department(s) will all be very interested in the plots and subsequent detail drill-down exercises.

The plot is a key component of defining what the top $x$ issues are in the contact center. An analysis of the data will indicate what the optimal balance should be between technical staff and nontechnical staff or the mix of skill sets within the technical team. Once the dynamic is understood, staffing levels can be adjusted accordingly.

> In the course of his career, the author has had mixed responses from the senior staff to whom he has delivered top $x$ issues reports. The effective executive embraces the issues and takes corrective action—healthy and smart—the less effective executive goes into denial and tampers with the data—not healthy and smart. Again, know your audience.

○ General comment—The top $x$ issues report is a very powerful report and has a wide audience within the corporation. It is also, however, a very dangerous report (many of them are, but this report is more so than most) that highlights the shortcomings of the supported product. If it was to fall into the hands of a competitor a great deal of damage could be perpetrated on the corporation. This report should be of limited distribution with a registered hard copy only.

• Lifecycle Contact Dynamic. (See Figure 4.22, Data plot, lifecycle contact dynamic.)

○ Definition—This plot depicts the relative contact volume as the product progresses through its lifecycle. The plot looks to the horizon and is forward facing.

○ Unit of measure—The plot is relative.

○ Criticality—Very high. The plot will drive decisions on when to hire and deploy personnel. It is particularly germane in a contact center that supports many products that are in different phases of their lifecycle.

○ Contributing factors—N/A.

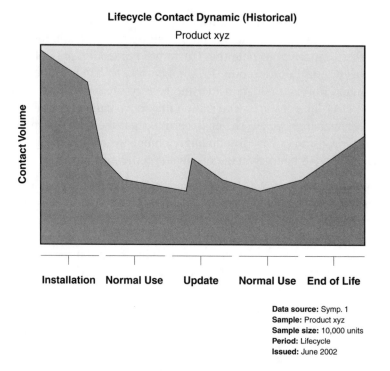

**Lifecycle Contact Dynamic (Historical)**

Product xyz

Contact Volume

Installation    Normal Use    Update    Normal Use    End of Life

**Data source:** Symp. 1
**Sample:** Product xyz
**Sample size:** 10,000 units
**Period:** Lifecycle
**Issued:** June 2002

**Figure 4.22**   Data plot, lifecycle contact dynamic.

○ Application—Resource planning is the first-order application. Use the plot to understand where the greatest support burden is, then resource to mitigate the impact on the Customer base.

The second-order application is to use the plot to plan up-sell and cross-sell campaigns. As the population of the product moves towards the end of its lifecycle, there is opportunity to develop programs to proactively use the contact center to sell the latest generation of the product.

○ General comment—The plot is of more use to a contact center structured as a profit center.

• Call Volume per Event Type. (See Figure 4.23, Data plot, call volume by event type.)

○ Definition—A measure of the increase in outgoing calls, expressed as a percentage increase over a baseline, tied to known events or programs.

○ Unit of measure—Percentage. The baseline is established by sampling the outgoing call volume during periods in which there are no sales/marketing programs (pushes), product updates, or enabling technology failures taking place.

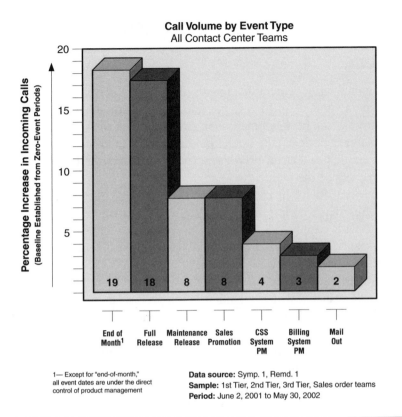

**Figure 4.23**   Data plot, call volume by event type.

- Criticality—High. This data plot is key to managing the timing of events under corporate control.

- Contributing factors—The timing of all but one of the events depicted in Figure 4.23 is directly under the control of the product manager. The one event outside the product manager's control (end of month) is cyclical and may be managed and planned. One contingency not found on the plot is the failure of an enabling technology such as the corporate Internet service provider or a wireless carrier that the technology rides on.

- Application—This data plot is an excellent resource-planning tool. Armed with Figure 4.23 and a tight working relationship with the product manager and the sales/marketing team, the contact center should never be subject to the logistics nightmare of a "full release" (volume up 18 percent) with a "sales promotion" (volume up 8 percent) commencing on August 31 (month-end volume up 19 percent).

# SERVICE LEVEL AGREEMENTS

*Insurance policy.*

An SLA is a container document that details all pertinent performance metrics between a Customer and a vendor. An SLA is put into place to provide a baseline performance metric for a transaction between the issuer and the holder. SLAs bear a number of similarities to insurance policies: the holder pays an annual premium for optimal coverage, the holder is entitled to special privileges, and, most importantly, the holder hopes to never have to exercise the policy.

SLAs are often found in back-to-back configurations where the end user has an SLA with the reseller, who in turn has an SLA with the manufacturer, who in turn may have an SLA with supply-side vendors and enabling technologies providers. Each player in the scenario may also have internal SLAs focused on departments within their organizations that provide services to them.

Entry-level SLAs delineate what the performance targets are. Advanced SLAs detail penalties associated with a violation of the performance targets. Suffice to say, it is a good thing if the business model and the Customer base do not demand penalties. Keeping penalties out of any agreement is optimal for the supplier of the service.

Many businesses have introduced SLAs as a component of their due-diligence process. During the procurement phase, the Customer's procurement officer requests the SLA. Some organizations do not actually review the SLA as it is, in fact, simply a check mark on a list of basic criteria that must be satisfied before the purchase order can be issued. Other organizations have a thorough review process where the SLA is vetted by experts in the field. It is these latter organizations that may put the SLA on the negotiation table as a tactic to either reduce price or exact more performance out of the seller.

The best mechanism to keep penalties off the SLA negotiation table is to provide exemplary service. If there is no history of troublesome performance, the Customer base may be appeased by an SLA that simply details the performance targets. Periodic and sporadic service transgressions are overlooked as a dynamic of business. On the other end of the spectrum, there are mission-critical applications that demand the existence of a concise, tight SLA. In extreme cases there may be litigation protection or risk-sharing clauses within the SLA. Then there are all the companies providing services and product that fall in between these two extremes of mission criticality and laissez faire SLA administration. This section is directed at these organizations.

## Service Level Agreement Web

A service level agreement web (*web* as in multifaceted and interconnected network of dependencies, not as in *World Wide*) is depicted in Figure 4.24, Service level agreement web. As can be clearly seen in the graphic, there are many agreements throughout the corporation. A point in fact is that not all the agreements depicted are known as "service level agreements," but they are, in fact, guarantees on performance and

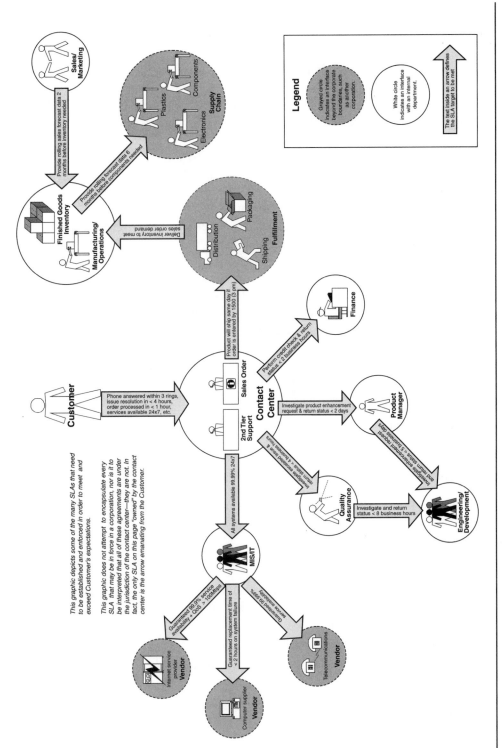

**Figure 4.24** Service level agreement web.

delivery of services—an SLA. Regardless of what they are called, every organization has a web of interconnected agreements to ensure supporting components and products arrive in time.

World-class contact centers map all the key interconnects that are necessary for the contact center to meet its performance goals. As can be seen from Figure 4.24, this is not a trivial task. If a map does not exist, initiate a project to define the dependencies. Start with the first-order dependencies (that is, the obvious dependencies) and then build out to the second- and third-order.

Once the dependencies are mapped, prioritize and rate which have the greatest potential for Customer dissatisfaction. Some of the dependencies may, in fact, require very little management. Good, this frees up resources to concentrate on those dependencies that require a great deal of management.

Construct a team to negotiate the performance metrics of the highest potential dissatisfaction dependencies. Set the teams in motion negotiating performance metrics and time frames with internal and external players. Expect that there may be a degree of education required before the team can begin defining the parameters (which is to suggest that first the team must educate the target owner as to why the process is necessary). Additionally, due to the fact that there is usually some resource burden to the process owner, the benefits will also have to be outlined.

Negotiating with outside factions has challenges. The greatest hurdle is if precedent has been set. That is, in the event the dependency owner has been conducting business with the contact center for some time without an SLA in place, the suggestion of introducing an agreement may be seen as:

- A breach of trust

- A lever to renegotiate terms

- An opportunity to charge more for the services already rendered

Therefore, proceed with caution and obtain the full sanction of the business development team.

## Contact Center Service Level Agreement

Contact centers require SLAs for two main audiences: the Customer and the sales team. The SLA may be extended to become a key driver in incentive and bonus plans for the personnel within the contact center. Internal groups that are good candidates for department-to-department SLAs include:

- Finance—Credit checks, AR appraisals, bad-debt status, credit processing, and so on

- MIS/IT—Support services for the infrastructure including:

  ○ Desktop systems

  ○ Back-office systems (help desk system, ERP, and so on)

- ○ Customer-facing systems (Internet-based tools)

- ○ Telephone system

- ○ Copiers, facsimile, and other sundry ancillary equipment

- Operations—From supply chain management to manufacturing dependencies

- Product management/engineering/development/quality assurance—escalation and enhancement request processing

The list goes on and is unique for every operation. Using the dependencies map as a tool and guide, systemically vet the entire organization for areas that require a more formal structure than the one in place today.

## ENDNOTES

1. See appendix E for contact information for a number of benchmarking organizations.
2. The radar tool is a graph style like a pie chart or bar graph. The radar chart is a very powerful graph style. The author used Excel for the examples, which is to say no special software is needed to generate radar charts.
3. Crystal Reports is an excellent tool and in general use. Note that many system vendors use Crystal Reports within their product, thereby marrying the best of both worlds—built-in reports supported by a COTS engine.
4. Overhang is where the Customer thought they were getting more or superior features than the product contains. Usually it is the sales representative that is blamed for the overhang, but in the author's experience, there are just as many Customers who "hear what they want to hear" as there are unscrupulous sales personnel promising the moon.
5. It is the abandoned to total calls ratio that is important—"five abandoned calls per day" is not as meaningful or actionable as "two percent of all contacts are abandoned."
6. One can postulate that many of the IVR systems in the world today have been mapped by either comedians or practitioners of the Marquis de Sade school of Customer support.
7. The user-friendliness and usability of systems, be they Customer access/assess tools or back-office systems, is a massive challenge in many organizations.

# 5

# Training & Testing

## OBJECTIVE

*Do this right and the contact center will prosper.*

This chapter is not intended to be a comprehensive primer on how to design and conduct training programs. Its very inclusion in this book was questionable, but experience has demonstrated that training is mismanaged time and time again in many organizations. That said, the objective of this section is to drive the concept that training is a key driver to the success of the contact center.

This chapter covers the following topics:

- Training sequence

- Partnering and shadowing

- Lists of questions which will assist contact center management in focusing on, and understanding, the challenges discussed

The initial step is to hire personnel with professional training credentials. Former teachers, newly-trained teachers who do not wish to enter into the public education system, and application trainers are all excellent candidates for the training role. One additional skill that the trainer must possess is the ability to generate training courses

The author was flabbergasted to discover one organization that had entrusted its entire partner training program to a co-op student. The co-op student was, by definition, new to the organization, untrained, had only been on board for six months, had none of the prerequisite skills (the ability to effectively transfer knowledge is not a given, just because you can be taught does not mean you can teach), and had all the discipline and focus one usually finds in a 22-year-old. The criterion that led to assigning the co-op student was simply that the individual needed a project to keep him occupied.

and materials from thin air as, unlike the formal school system, there are no textbooks, no established curriculum, and no standard testing benchmarks.

# TRAINING SEQUENCE

*Just how long is this going to take?*

Figure 5.1, Training sequence, outlines an employee's progression from entry-level new hire to a fully functional CSR. The time line has been left blank as the complexity of both the product/service being supported and the back-office systems is unique to each organization. These complexities will impact the slope of the learning curve and subsequent time to train each new employee. The sequence depicted contains a number of checkpoints on the progress of the new hire. Each session conducted by the training team is followed by a test. The new hire does not progress to the next session until they successfully pass each test.

To be as effective as possible, the tests must be dynamic and subject to near-continuous fine-tuning by the training team. In doing this, the training content and materials will never become obsolete, and the trainees will always receive the most current and relevant content.

The content of the courses and the resulting difficulty of the tests are driven by empirical statistics and metrics. As an example, if the number of contacts that cannot be resolved on the first contact is rising then corrective action needs to be taken to understand why and how to impart the missing knowledge. Or, if the total contact time is rising, say from nine minutes to 12, analyze what has changed, effect corrective action, retrain established CSRs, and adjust the master training materials.

# ANALYSIS OF TRAINING SEQUENCE

*Training sequence.*

Each stage of the training sequence as depicted in Figure 5.1 is discussed in the following section; as are the concepts of new-hire orientation, employee files, employee partnering, and shadowing.

# PRODUCT TRAINING AND TESTING

*What's all this then?*

Product training is the first stage of the training program and is therefore the first opportunity to evaluate the skills of each new hire. This stage is also the first opportunity to correct any hiring miscues.

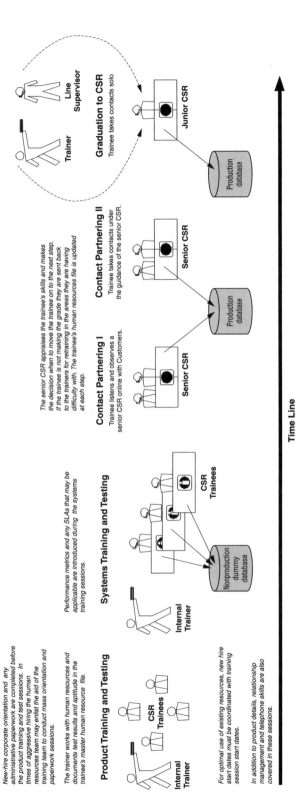

The **I**⌐ icon indicates that the individual is on-line with prospects and/or Customers.

The ⌐**I**⌐ icon indicates that the individual is shadowing the call with prospects and/or Customers.

New-hire corporate orientation and any administrative paperwork are completed before the product training and test sessions. In times of aggressive hiring the human resources team may enlist the aid of the training team to conduct mass orientation and paperwork sessions.

The trainer works with human resources and documents test results and aptitude in the trainee's master human resource file.

## Product Training and Testing

**Internal Trainer**

**CSR Trainees**

For optimal use of existing resources, new hire start dates must be coordinated with training session start dates.

In addition to product details, relationship management and telephone skills are also covered in these sessions.

Performance metrics and any SLAs that may be applicable are introduced during the systems training sessions.

## Systems Training and Testing

**Internal Trainer**

**CSR Trainees**

Nonproduction dummy database

The senior CSR appraises the trainee's skills and makes the decision when to move the trainee on to the next step. If the trainee is not making the grade they are sent back to the trainers for retraining in the areas they are having difficulty with. The trainee's human resources file is updated at each step.

## Contact Partnering I

Trainee listens and observes a senior CSR online with Customers.

**Senior CSR**

## Contact Partnering II

Trainee takes contacts under the guidance of the senior CSR.

**Senior CSR**

Production database

Directly after training, the trainees should be surveyed for ideas to improve the training program.

Representatives from the training team and the CSR's line supervisor will occasionally shadow the CSR. Shadowing is simply listening in on a contact with a view to improving the service by analyzing live contacts.

**Trainer**    **Line Supervisor**

## Graduation to CSR

Trainee takes contacts solo

**Junior CSR**

Production database

### Time Line

The actual time line is determined by how steep the learning curve is for your corporations' product/services and back-office systems.

**Figure 5.1**    Training sequence.

The first target in product training is to "sell" the product/service to the trainees. The objective is to make them believers in the benefits and attributes of the product/service. Render the trainees *evangelists* of the product if possible. Once the trainees buy in to the product/service, they will approach the support of the product in a positive manner. Without trainee buy-in, Customer satisfaction based on the contact center experience is nigh impossible.

If economically and technically feasible, trainees should be given the product, or access to the service, gratis. If they themselves are users, their ability to support the product increases dramatically. Outfitting the CSRs with the product also sends a positive trust and value message.

One of the more effective methods used to achieve early buy-in is to engage one of the star sales personnel as a guest speaker. There is great benefit in delivering the entire sales pitch to the trainees. To secure the trainees' loyalty, an impromptu visit and welcome from a senior staff member (CEO, VP, and so on) is also effective. The message from the senior staff member should focus on the importance of the individual, specifically the trainees, to the corporation's success. Once buy-in is achieved and the trainees have an understanding of how they directly impact and support the success of the organization, it is time to delve into the details of the role they have been hired to fill. In-depth familiarity with the product/service tempered by the activities of the role is the next step. It may be necessary to have different training streams for different roles: for instance, a trainee destined for the sales order team does not need to have an in-depth knowledge of the installation procedure for a software product. Conversely, a trainee destined for the second tier support team does not require a detailed understanding of the pricing and discount schemes. The idiosyncrasies of the product/service, coupled with the services the contact center is to provide, will drive how many training streams are necessary.

Another unfortunate, yet necessary, area to cover during these training sessions is the "abuse standards." Each employee should have a clear understanding of what the policy is and what their recourse is if they find themselves in an abusive situation. See Abuse Standards in the section titled Key Concepts, page 13.

## Top Ten Issues

Regardless of the training stream a new hire is in, an excellent touch point is the top ten issues for the role. The technical stream will have a markedly different top ten issues list from the sales order–processing stream. Each of the top ten issues should be thoroughly dissected for the trainees. The trainee should understand the following for each of the issues:

- Root cause

- Common objections Customers may have

- Scripted responses and approaches that are known to be effective

- Steps to resolution (for instance, return for repair, return to depot, hot swap, and so on)

- An understanding of the latitude they have to resolve the situation (for instance, can CSRs offer rebates or credits?)

The handling procedure for the top ten issues is reinforced by playing back a number of recordings of live contacts that deal with the issues (with the Customer's permission). Practice sessions with the trainees role-playing further internalizes the techniques and protocol.

## Testing

It is necessary to conduct tests to ensure the knowledge transfer has been effective. Be forewarned that the trainees will absolutely detest this part of the process, however, in a merit-based organization, testing is a tool where the stars have the opportunity to shine. For those that have the complaint, "But I don't test well!" it is important they understand that testing is only one tool to gauge their effectiveness—all they must do is pass and then their performance over time will be their measure.

The testing itself can be as rigorous as deemed effective. The most thorough testing is demanded at a start-up where the product/service is just beginning to garner mind and market share. Less rigorous testing is suitable for a mature product that has crossed the chasm to a broader and more general market where the occasional support gaffe does not have the same potential to impact the market's acceptance of the product. The test results are reviewed with a view to answering two questions:

- Is the trainee ready to move on?

- How can the training team improve the training sessions?

In the event that a trainee cannot pass the test, yet peers can, the corrective action is on the hiring process. More screening is needed and a finer understanding of the base skill set is demanded.

Performance metrics and their subsequent enforcement is a very controversial area. Performance metrics should be positioned as Customer-centric and not as a management tool to crush CSRs' spirit. Tread carefully and keep Customer satisfaction as the forefront driver for the metrics and forefront in the employees' mind-set.

On conclusion of the training program, each of the trainees should fill out a survey on the effectiveness of the training. Solicit ideas for improvement from the trainees as they are fresh minds. The surveys serve another purpose as they can be used, with the test results, as part of the review process for the training team.

Before moving on to the next formal step of system training, the trainees are introduced to telephone and relationship management skills.[1] Telephone skills encompass the corporate standards on:

- How to answer a contact

- Opening and closing salutations

- Use of slang

- Where to locate the available scripts and how to apply them

- How to leverage the on-demand availability of management

- How to interpret the abuse standards

Relationship management focuses the trainee on how to:

- Defuse hostile situations

- Apply patience and empathy as tools

- Get to the core issue

- Use and apply open and closed probes and other softer aspects of contact resolution

# BACK-OFFICE SYSTEMS TRAINING

*The back-office sandbox.*

Systems training is a critical component of the training program. This is where the trainee is introduced to the back-office systems and software programs that the corporation uses. The trainee is taught to access and use these systems so that they may fulfill their objective of inducing Customer satisfaction. See Figure 5.2, System(s) training.

Systems training is where any SLA and/or performance metrics the corporation has in place are introduced. Introductions to the performance standards, including how they are measured and how they impact individual CSRs, are presented and discussed.

In preparation for the systems training, the training team must map out what systems and software programs are relevant to the particular type of CSR being training. Next, plot which functions within the systems and software programs the CSRs need to access to accomplish their roles.

There may be systems of such complexity that a phased approach to functions is necessitated. Furthermore, there may be security and trust issues that demand a phased program, for instance, the issuing of credits is not a task for a new hire just out of training. This idea speaks to different levels within each role: junior, intermediate, and senior. Business rules can be established on back-office systems that allow thresholds to be set on what a level can and cannot process. For example, junior personnel can be disallowed from processing a sales order greater than $1000, intermediate personnel can be disallowed at the $10,000 threshold, and the senior level can process up to $100,000 after which the order must be approved by management.

The trainers must anticipate risk areas and/or exposure areas to the business if a new CSR makes a mistake. The type of risk or exposure alluded to is of the subtle and insidious nature. Crashing the sales order system is not what we're talking about here, but rather mis-keying a date, dropping a digit on a credit card number, not capturing the expiration date on a credit card order, or closing a support call at the wrong time.

It may be argued that the previous list of mistakes is all system design and business rule enforcement issues. With proper database constraint–checking these failure modes

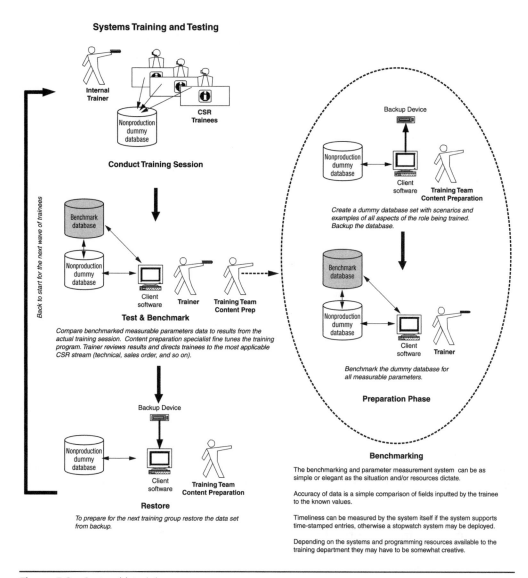

**Figure 5.2**   System(s) training.

could be *designed* out and rendered impossible to commit. No system is perfect, however, and no system can have every contingency designed out. Armed with these three data points—what systems, which functions, and the risk areas—the training team can design programs for each CSR role.

To protect the integrity of the data in the live production systems, all training exercises should be conducted on dummy database sets (aka the sandbox). This isolates new hires from critical databases that are core to the business. If mistakes are made, they are made in a contained, noncritical system.

The following is an example of mistake-proofing a system. All dates should be checked for validity. The first level is easy—all date fields must be in the format MM-DD-YYYY or the system pops up an error to the operator. But consider if a sales order enters the system on 06-29-2001, it is impossible for the requested ship date to be before that time, and it is highly unlikely that a requested ship date of 06-29-2010 is correct. A well-designed system can check for these obvious gaffes. Another example: if a credit card number is keyed in, run a check-sum algorithm to ensure the card number is valid. Better yet, check the card number on an online system to ensure it is valid. Or better yet, if a credit card number is input, make filling in the expiration date field mandatory—simple! One last example: for support calls, enforce a sequence of events that must be followed before the call can be closed.

An additional benefit of the dummy training data set is that the training team can design scenarios where the parameters and metrics of the desired output are known. For example, "sales orders set B" should take an average of two hours to input and should result in:

- The sandbox shipping system receiving fifteen orders for overnight shipment

- The sandbox finance accounts receivable system receiving entries of $11,043

- Four sandbox professional services installation requests

The inputs are known and the outputs are known. Given enough sample trainees, a baseline can be established to work through the scenarios. Each new hire can be measured against the baseline. In a perfect implementation, the scenario testing exercise can be completely administered by computer.

The trainers can gauge the trainees and their own effectiveness over time as wave after wave of new trainees forge through the dummy data set and scenarios. The trainees can be measured on aptitude, timeliness, and accuracy, and be graded accordingly. Placement corrections can be made based on a trainee's empirical performance in the sandbox. Perhaps a trainee with data-input accuracy issues is better suited to first tier support as opposed to sales order processing.

## Contact Partnering Phase I

Contact partnering is the first opportunity for the trainee to interact with prospects and/or Customers. To ensure the Customer base continues to receive optimal support from the contact center, senior CSRs proctor the trainees until the trainee is ready to go solo. This minimizes the risk of prematurely progressing a new hire from training to live. The trainee is provided with the opportunity to observe a seasoned veteran of the contact center making use of the tools and techniques to resolve Customer issues.

In the first phase of the partnering effort, the trainee is in a passive listening mode where they listen to the senior CSR converse with the Customer or prospect but they, the trainee, do not communicate. After each contact the senior CSR can answer any question the trainee may have about the call. Once the senior is satisfied that the trainee can move on to fielding calls, the senior will initiate contact partnering phase II.

As a courtesy, the Customer or prospect should be forewarned that there is a trainee on the contact with the senior CSR. The Customer's permission should be solicited at the start of the contact. It is important to note that the senior CSR is responsible for the conduct of the trainee. It is also important to relax any performance metrics on the senior while engaged in a partnering exercise. In fact, as incentive for providing this crucial service, senior CSRs should be duly rewarded for each trainee they successfully proctor and move into the mainstream. In large organizations, this "proctor" role can be established as a full-time position within the training team.

## Contact Partnering Phase II

Phase II of partnering is similar to phase I. The difference is that the trainee is now engaging the Customer and doing the talking. As with phase I, the Customer's permission regarding the fact that a trainee is handling the call, with a senior monitoring, should be solicited at the start of the call. The senior CSR listens to the conversation and interjects when necessary (the Customer's satisfaction being the driver to interject). After each call the senior provides guidance on how the trainee could have improved the flow and execution of the call. Be sure to mandate that this feedback is not optional, it is part of the senior CSR's responsibility.

The Customer should be provided with an opportunity to comment on the experience. Doing this provides three positive aspects: the Customer is involved in the process and therefore is empowered, this is good in and of itself; the trainee is provided with direct feedback on performance; and the trainers are provided with a continuous improvement opportunity for the entire training program. There are a number of ways to gather the information:

- With the Customer's permission, the senior CSR may conduct a quick, focused question-and-answer session at the end of the call.

- Provide an electronic survey either via e-mail or a secure URL and direct the Customer's attention to it.

- Ask the Customer if they are willing to have one of the members of the training team contact them for their comments and suggestions for improvement.

The optimal approach is to provide all three alternatives so that the Customer has options. An incentive program to secure the Customer's participation has great merit.

Once the senior CSR deems the trainee is ready to move to the next phase, the master human resources file gets updated with comments from the senior. The trainee is now a CSR. The performance probation period begins now.

## Graduation To CSR

Upon graduation, the trainee becomes a junior CSR. As the individual is untried under stress, however, it is best to assign the new representative to a non-peak shift with strong supervision available. It is also highly desirable to position the junior representative in a strong work pod (see the bullet titled "Pods and Furniture" in the "Environment and Culture" section, page 81) where assistance from those with more experience is readily available.

## New Hires—Orientation

It is often the human resources team that takes on briefing new hires regarding corporate orientation, filling out the employment paperwork, and general administration. Human resources often utilizes the professional trainers in the contact center to present the orientation and administration materials, it is, after all, what the trainers do best. This cooperation is particularly rewarding in corporations that are aggressively hiring personnel with large groups of new hires starting each week. If this is the case, it is imperative to manage the stream of new hires and align employment start dates with training session start dates.

## Employee File

In concert with human resources, a file for each new hire should be created. This file follows the employee throughout their career in the corporation. The employee file contains all performance reviews, kudos, test results, and grievances associated with the employee (note that the owner of the employee files is not the trainer, nor even within the contact center, but the human resources team).

## Noncompete/Confidentiality

Confidentiality and noncompete clauses have been a fixture for many years. Traditionally, noncompete and confidentiality clauses were reserved for engineering staff and those in the upper echelons. As contact center personnel are often privy to proprietary data, core technologies, and core incompetence(s), it is prudent to have each contact center employee sign a noncompete and confidentiality agreement (see Exit Interview for further details, page 75).

Engage the legal department and human resources team to write an effective noncompete and confidentiality agreement. Remember that federal, local, and provincial and state jurisdictions all have a say in how restrictive the resultant agreement is. (This is why the legal department must take a stake in the composition of the agreement.)

As a final point regarding noncompete and confidentiality, be sure that the employee understands what it is they are agreeing to when they are hired. More importantly, if an employee leaves the company the noncompete and confidentiality agreement should again be discussed during the exit interview.

## Employee Partnering

Employee partnering is a tool by which a trainee is *partnered* with a subject matter expert. The technique is not limited to the new hire training period, rather it should be leveraged whenever an employee wishes to increase their personal knowledge and skill set. Partnering can also be used as a corrective action directed toward an employee that is not meeting standards.

## Employee Shadowing

Post-training employee shadowing is similar to the activities found in partnering phase I in that there is a passive listener. In this case, however, the listener is a supervisor, manager, or trainer. The reasons to engage in call shadowing include:

- Quality assurance—Listening in on a CSR as they handle a live contact is an excellent way to gauge a CSR's skill and performance.

- Questionable Customers—In the case of difficult or abusive Customers, a shadowing session is an excellent way to validate the origin of the hostility.

- Training, continuous improvement—The training team can run scenarios across the contact center to measure performance on key issues. Corrective action takes the form of more focused training exercises.

The technology that enables shadowing must be nonintrusive. The Customer should not know that a third party is monitoring, and some situations require that the CSR is also unaware of the monitoring activity. Many systems on the market support shadowing whereby a supervisor or manager keys in a code and the phone-system address of the CSR to be shadowed.

The added feature of being able to record shadowed sessions has enormous value (note that recording contacts without the parties' knowledge is illegal in some jurisdictions). It is adamantly recommended that a notification stating that the call may be recorded be posted as part of the standard incoming call greeting and salutation. The reason typically offered for the recording of calls is as a quality initiative to facilitate continuous improvement for both products and support services.

Recorded calls can be used:

- As a formal component of the product improvement process. Playback of actual live comments on the product from Customers has great value for the product management team.

- As an additional tool for training. A trainee can listen to a library of the top issues being handled expediently by the contact center's top performers.

- Situational escalations can be analyzed after the fact by calmer minds. This is both an opportunity for improvement for the CSR who took the call and as background information for the management team member who ultimately deals with the escalation.

Since the beginning of the technological revolution, support personnel have struggled with engineers and software programmers who seemingly speak a completely different dialect than the Customers. There is also the challenge of the continuing dichotomy between what the Customers want in a product and what the engineering folk deem they need. An effective product management team can usually bridge this chasm, that is, unless the product managers are part of the engineering team.

- In extreme situations the recording can be used to exonerate the CSR of any hostility or ill-handling of the Customer. He said/she said claims are immediately quelled in the presence of a recording.

- Playback of Customer comments is useful when faced with the incredulous looks one gets from the software programmers when contact center personnel need support from engineering personnel on attempting to influence feature development.

- The ancillary benefit of announcing that the call *may* be recorded has a calming effect on hostile and potentially abusive Customers.

## Training Adults

Following is a brief section on the unique challenges inherent in training adults. The instructor needs to engage the learner by using principals of adult learning as well as by taking learning styles into consideration in the preparation and delivery of the materials. To accommodate all styles, it is best to: *explain* it, *show* it, and *practice* it.

Typically adult learners want:

- A practical, hands-on approach

- A less theoretical and more conceptual approach

- New material to be related to what they actually do day to day

To meet the objective of turning training into learning, hands-on practice is the optimal tool. Situational examples, practice, and exercises should be provided to allow the trainees to practice the new skills. Training programs must be established to support the employee's initiative. If critical mass and interest is achieved many entry-level training courses can be provided by the corporation on corporate premises. Courses that fit this description include:

- Basic and advanced computer applications such as Word, CorelDraw, Visio, and so on

- Computer technologies such as Linux OS, Cisco routers, Exchange, and so on

In addition, university and college courses can, upon successful completion, be paid for outright or subsidized by the corporation.

## ENDNOTE

1. There are a number of excellent generic training programs on the market that cover telephone and relationship management.

# 6

# Systems and Tools

## OBJECTIVE

*What may be learned in this chapter.*

In order to serve the Customer base, contact center personnel require data points from most, if not all, departments of the corporation. From product enhancements, to billing, to shipping, to return-materials receiving, contact center personnel require visibility and process status. It is the systems and tools that provide the raw data and reports that allow informed decisions to be made in the contact center. This section outlines a number of software/hardware systems that can be applied to capture, maintain, and enhance Customer satisfaction in the contact center context. This chapter covers the following topics:

- Systems and tools available for contact center operations

- The flow of data from the contact center out to all other departments of the corporation

- Purchasing criteria recommendations for contact center systems

- Lists of questions that will assist contact center management in focusing on and understanding the challenges discussed

## DATA SHARING

*Corporate fuel.*

There is a wide range of approaches for sharing data across organizations. Start-ups make do with the cubicle gopher approach whereby the company is so compact that the CSRs pop up over their cubicle and ask the data point owner for status—"Say Jim, did the software update make it to tonight's courier run?" Conversely, there is the megacorporation, in which the help desk and shipping departments are not even in the same country and therefore must rely on real-time status delivered by complex interconnected back-office systems.

# SIZING

*When is a system needed?*

There is no universal rule of thumb used to drive the introduction of a formal data system to an operation. Every contact center, as every business, has unique requirements.

To determine if the operation needs a system to manage data, consider "critical mass" as the main criteria. Critical mass refers to the size and breadth of whatever is under scrutiny. Critical mass is reached (or worse, breached) when the existing systems collapse under their own weight. Consider, for example, a scenario in which the CEO has requested a daily report of call volume in an operation of twenty CSRs supporting an accounting package (that is, there are not many calls, but the calls tend to be of a very long duration). The data can be gathered manually from each CSR and the report can be constructed using a standard spreadsheet program—an automated system is not needed. Critical mass is breached if the operation grows to forty CSRs; it is no longer feasible to manually gather the information and a small help desk is needed.

Alternatively, consider the same daily report in an operation of twenty CSRs supporting a warranty card call-in registration program. In this scenario there are many calls of very short duration. An automated system is needed to generate the daily report, otherwise management will be burning the midnight oil trying to correlate the data and generate the manual reports.

# DATA FLOW

*There's gold in this stream.*

Figure 6.1, Data flow, depicts the flow of data from the contact center to the other departments in a representative corporation. The data-flow exercise revolves around the Customer and begins with the Customer as drawn on the left side of the graphic. The central figure in the graphic, however, is the contact center report writer.

The report writer accesses the data generated from Customer contacts and prepares it for the target audience, which is to suggest that the product manager is interested in different data points than the finance department. Where at all possible, the reports should be standardized in both format and frequency. While there may be times where a given report does not appear to have currency, the existence of the report allows trends to surface and be analyzed and managed. Even in times of relative stability the reports should continue to flow.

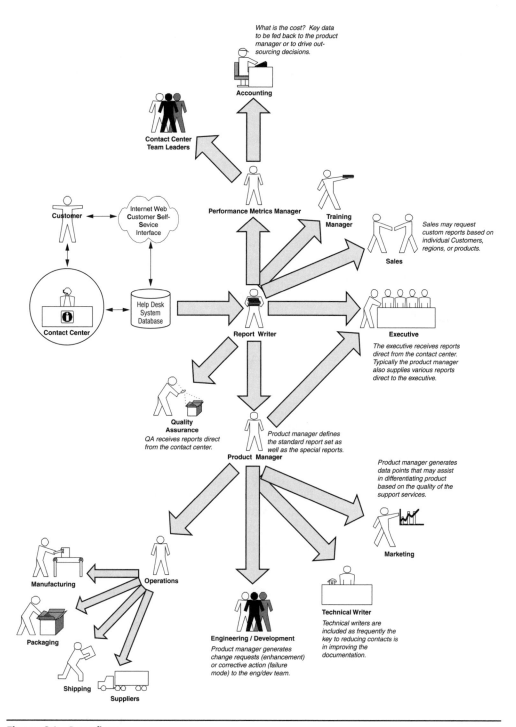

**Figure 6.1** Data flow.

The data dictionary should be published for the more technically-minded team owners so that they may define the reports they need. The data dictionary may also be used as a guide for requesting the addition of fields to the underlying database.

One of the biggest challenges with data and data flow is defining the reports and determining what is meaningful and, therefore, actionable. A large part of this challenge is communication. The marketing manager speaks in business terms—profit and loss and satisfaction—whereas the report writer speaks in terms of fields and records. A request made to a report writer for an analysis of Customer acceptance based on the discount scheme is unlikely to result in what the requester wants. The requester and the report writer must meet somewhere in the middle; the business case–centric speaker must understand the technical writer's world and visa-versa.

Create a custom report request form for the various team owners to use when requesting new reports or one-off drill-down reports. Set up a review protocol to vet the custom report request list for validity and universality. A method for prioritizing which custom reports are to be done first needs to be established. The subsequent priority and target creation date need to be published in a readily accessible place (the corporate intranet).

# DEPLOYMENT

*Scalability, flexibility, stability . . .*

Understand what is needed and deploy systems accordingly. When reviewing the systems needed and those legacy systems available to assist and enhance the contact center, begin with a needs analysis, then fold in deployment effort, and long-term cost of ownership, and execute. Much easier said than done.

Assign a project manager to each system to be deployed. As there is huge overlap in the processes and procedures when deploying new systems, use this commonality to the best advantage. Create a boilerplate checklist to ensure steps are not missed or overlooked. The checklist should include the following features:

- Change management—The target is to introduce the new system in as non-disruptive a fashion as possible. Personnel need to be introduced to the raison d'être for the system[1] and sold on its benefits. Any overlap time between an existing legacy system and the new system will also have to be managed so that the transition is seamless. The issue is change management, but the actionable milestone belongs to the training team.

- MIS/IT—As all systems depend on support from the MIS/IT department, it is prudent to obtain their sanction and buy-in from the very start. Items that are solely in the MIS/IT team's purview (such as procurement, configuration and setup of file servers, infrastructure interconnectivity, and so on) should be time-lined and set as milestones.

- Training—Personnel need to be brought up to speed on the new application. Involve the training department from the start. Creation of a training plan should be an actionable milestone.

- Flexibility—Anticipate requirements that will surface in a month, in a quarter, and during the entire lifecycle of the system. Ensure the new system has the flexibility to incorporate the future expeditiously, economically, and elegantly. This is more of a selection criteria than an actionable milestone, but what can be captured as a milestone, is a long-term support plan. The owner of the long-term support plan is the project manager.

- Scalability—Ensure that the system can be scaled to tomorrow's needs. Consider if the product acceptance, and hence the contact volume, outstrips expectations by 100 percent, 200 percent, and 500 percent. Establish the overload threshold (there is always one) and what needs to be in place to mitigate any disruption of the service caused by the system when the threshold is approached. Like "flexibility," this is a selection criterion and fits into the long-term support plan.

- Reliability, availability, and maintainability (RAM)—Establish benchmark targets for the stability of the system tempered by the mission-criticality of the system. Work in concert with MIS/IT to institute a program for maximizing stability. The creation of the plan underscores the resource planning the MIS/IT department must champion to ensure long-term RAM.

- Open source code versus commercial software—(See appendix A for a definition of open source). Open source is not for every organization, but those that have embraced open source are devoted, almost evangelistic, in their advocacy.

# TOOLS

*Technology alone isn't the grail . . .*

A definitive commentary on the latest cutting-edge hardware and software tools and suites is not the intention of this section. Suffice to say that hardware and software tools are progressing at such a rapid pace that by the time this section were to be complete the whole industry may have changed direction. This section, therefore, covers the tools from a high-level perspective and only outlines a portion of the many tools

> The following is an example of RAM. A fax server can operate quite well from a CSR's desktop, but it is far preferable to position the fax server in the computer room, hooked up to the uninterruptible power supply (UPS) farm and under the existing monitoring protocol established by the MIS/IT department.

that are recommended and available. Comments are limited to the values or philosophy behind tools for facilitating Customer care and not validations or sanctions of the latest technologies.

Systems designed to shape, report on, and enable business processes are necessary in every business. Islands of information are not desirable; each system should be able to access any other system in the corporation that may hold pertinent data (see Figure 6.5, Interim system, page 189, for a graphic showing islands of information consolidated by middleware).

The following list outlines a subset of the systems available to secure and enhance the Customer experience. The list does not contain general-purpose systems (word processing, backup/restore engines, and so on) and applications as they are necessary in any business and not unique to the needs of a contact center. The following sections contain recommended corporate and contact center systems.

## Private Branch Exchange

A basic private branch exchange (PBX) is a telephone network belonging to, and within, the corporation. The alternative to a PBX is to have discrete telephone lines run to every telephone in an organization—hardly cost-effective. World-class contact centers not only have PBXs but, more importantly, they have the software tools that interface directly with the PBXs. The software suites typically reside on a server that links directly to, and controls, the PBX. As these systems can be quite complicated, it is highly recommended to take the user courses offered by the manufacturers of the systems.

PBX software tools provide flexibility to allow:

- Call routing based on:

  ○ Where the call originated from

  ○ Identification codes (such as a contract number)

  ○ Skill set of the available CSRs

- Real-time queue display status drivers for feeding tote board displays or being rolled back into the automatic voice response system (for example, the wait time is currently one minute, we thank you for . . .").

- Flexible report generation tools. Examples of PBX-spawned reports are:

  ○ Figure 4.7 Data plot, pickup time

  ○ Figure 4.8 Data plot, contact duration by function

  ○ Figure 4.9 Data plot, calls over time

  ○ Figure 4.10 Data plot, abandoned call ratio

  ○ Figure 4.11 Data plot, average on-hold time

  ○ Figure 4.13 Data plot, time before escalation

***Baseline.*** The system should support:

- Open standards
- Scalability
- Third-party applications
- Non-proprietary relational database back end
- Flexible report writing tools (many use Crystal Reports' engine)
- Open API and flexible tools for creating custom GUI and applications

***Availability.*** As the PBX is mission-critical to the contact center, it must be robust and have a very high availability rating. I suggest the availability target be greater than 99.99 percent.

***Need.*** Mandatory.

## Customer Relationship Management

Customer relationship management (CRM) is a disciplined approach to managing the most important relationships the corporation has; those with the Customer. A well-designed and implemented CRM system is crucial to the success of any contact center.

CRM systems abound, from entry-level stand-alone versions to enterprise solutions from the top software vendors. There seems to be a new player in the CRM game every second week. All the top enterprise application vendors have a CRM solution.

Considering the islands-of-information syndrome and its undesirability, a strong case is made for deploying the CRM system directly supported by the corporate enterprise resource planning (ERP) or manufacturing resource planning (MRP) system. In the event that the CRM system is the first large system to be deployed, it is prudent to guide the selection of the system by a multidepartmental steering committee.

The CRM system is the central repository for all data related to the Customer base. The CRM system is frequently the data master for Customer information. In the optimal environment, when Customer contact data changes it is the CRM system that is updated first (the master data set). Then, if necessary, the contact data change is disseminated to other databases that rely on this information (billing, shipping, return handling, and so on). The CRM system will contain all contact data, background information, and even personal details regarding the Customer base. CRM systems also serve as a day-timer, reminding contact center personnel to perform callback functions and other time-related events. Some systems provide the ability to task individuals, in the contact center or outside, automatically. The more flexible systems provide sales forecasting capability, marketing/sales program management, report generation, and support modules.

There is a great deal of overlap between CRM and sales force automation systems and tools. The key differentiator is that if the CRM deals with the "Customer," the sales force automation system deals with "prospects." The distinction, however, is loose, and the trend is for old-school sales force automation tools to relabel themselves as CRM.

*Baseline.* The system should support:

- Implementation of business rules with an intuitive scripting interface (as compared to hard coding)
- Open standards
- Nonproprietary relational database back end, flexible report writing tools (many use Crystal Reports' engine)
- Open API and flexible tools for creating custom GUI and applications

*Availability.* As the CRM system is mission-critical to the contact center, it must be robust and have a high availability rating. The availability target should be greater than 99 percent.

*Need.* Mandatory.

## Sales Force Automation

See the section above on customer relationship management.

*Baseline.* See the notes for customer relationship management.

*Need.* Either a CRM or a sales force automation (SFA) system is mandatory. In an organization where both are deployed (CRM for the contact center and SFA for the sales team), the two systems must have a link so that sales personnel have visibility on account activities undertaken by the contact center and vice versa.

## Employee Relationship Management

Employee relationship management (ERM) systems track and report on quotas (for sales), deadlines (regarding project management), individual goals (set during the review process in conjunction with the employee), and any other entity that applies to an individual and can be quantified. ERM systems provide functionality to:

- Track individual performance.
- Set performance thresholds and alarms.
- Allow the employee to (for the most part) self-administer, that is, the data entry burden should be simple enough that the employee enters the data points themselves.
- Provide real-time reports to drive decisions on performance of time-critical functions.

*Baseline.* The system should support:

- Ease of use, by design (as the onus is on the employee to perform their own data entry, the system must be fast, intuitive, and very easy to use)

- Implementation of business rules with an intuitive scripting interface (as compared to hard-coding)

- Open standards

- Scalability

- Nonproprietary relational database back end

- Flexible report writing tools (many use Crystal Reports' engine)

- Open API and flexible tools for creating custom GUI and applications

*Availability.* Once the ERM system becomes entrenched in the organization it will become mission-critical. As the key to ERM is the accuracy and timeliness of the data input by the employee, the system must be very robust or the employees will not embrace the system, and it, by itself, will become the excuse for nonperformance. The availability target should also be greater than 99 percent.

*Need.* Desirable. A prime factor in defining the need for an ERM system is the size of the organization.

## Service Management System

Service management systems (SMS) (in this context) are usually found in organizations that have a hardware repair capability. SMSs provide functionality to:

- Issue service tickets.

- Track and trace returns.

- Control spares and parts inventory.

- Track hard (spares) and soft (personnel) costs.

- Replenish inventory including automatic reorder point calculations and economic order quantity calculations.

The more elaborate systems provide an interface to the Internet where Customers can self-serve on consumable orders and obtain status of returns and repairs.

*Baseline.* The system should support:

- Implementation of business rules with an intuitive scripting interface (as compared to hard coding)

- Open standards

- Scalability

- Nonproprietary relational database back end

- Flexible report writing tools (many use Crystal Reports' engine)

- Open API and flexible tools for creating custom GUI and applications

*Availability.* As the SMS is (probably) not mission-critical to the contact center, it should have an average availability rating. In many operations, however, the repair depot and the contact center are the same organization. In this case, the SMS is probably acting as a CRM system, therefore, the mission-criticality is far higher. The availability target should be greater than 90 percent.

*Need.* An SMS is mandatory if hardware support services are provided. In small operations it may be possible to stretch the capability of the CRM system to encompass some of the functionality provided by SMSs.

## Expert Systems

Expert systems are software applications that, allegedly, mimic the ability of human experts to absorb information and then make decisions based on said information. Expert systems are akin to artificial intelligence (AI) and are still in their technological infancy. The applicability to a contact center is in real-time analysis and subsequent action based on what is happening *now*, which is to strongly suggest that management does not always have visibility on what is driving a contact volume spike and, in fact, may learn of a spike after the fact. If an expert system can process hundreds of contacts in real time and come up with probable root cause, then the contact center can always be on the cusp of an issue. This is the epitome of proactive vis-à-vis reactionary.

*Baseline.* This is impossible to comment definitively on at this time, however, the system would have to be rules-based to allow flexibility. The system would also have to support an innate ability to learn in order to mitigate and alleviate false positives.

*Availability.* Very high as, once operational, the functionality will raise the bar on Customer services and satisfaction to the point where the Customer base will expect CSRs to be near-clairvoyant regarding what is going on *right now*. Once stable and proven, the availability should be greater than 99.9 percent.

*Need.* Highly desirable.

## Document Control

Document control systems are also known as revision control systems and are usually found in the quality assurance/control group.

As the contact center develops and grows, the amount of supporting SOPs, contracts, SLAs, reports, and other sundry documentation will increase radically. Administration of the documentation is best disciplined under a documentation control system. The risk in not deploying a documentation control system is that an obsolete document will inevitably be referenced. This can be a minor annoyance if the obsolete document in question describes how to requisition pencils, but it would be a major risk

Team members can be lax when it comes to documentation control. The author has observed a number of instances in which a sales team member requested a contract boilerplate from the author. The author complied. A number of months later, the same sales representative had the same documentation need but with a different prospect. Instead of requesting the latest revision of the contract, the salesperson simply forwarded the months-old version that they had stored on their notebook computer. The challenge was that the prospect now had a contract in hand that had SLA targets the corporation had relaxed. To the prospect it appeared that we had given preferential treatment to other accounts *and* that we could not meet our own guidelines.

if an old version of an SLA is inadvertently presented to a Customer. Any document that is delivered to the Customer base should be tracked, complete with revision number of the document. The tracking does not take place in the document control system but in the CRM system.

The document control system should:

- Be the central repository of all corporate documentation

- Automatically assign and administer revision levels

- Retain all revisions in safe storage

- Support document locking and archiving

- Support automatic document distribution

- Support security and access rights

*Baseline.* The system should support:

- Open standards

- Scalability

- Nonproprietary relational database back end

- Flexible report writing tools

- Open API

- Flexible tools for creating custom GUI and front-end applications

- All common document formats including Word and Adobe

- Accessibility (secure) from both the intranet and the Internet.

*Availability.* As the document control system is not mission-critical to the contact center it can have a low availability rating. The recommended availability target is less than 90 percent.

*Need.* Desirable.

## Customer Self-Service

A customer self-service (CSS) system is a boon to support services and, in particular, contact centers. The economics of being able to off-load Customer contacts to a self-service portal are self-justifying. The system should also serve, in tangent with the knowledge base, as the access point for frequently asked questions (FAQs).

The Customer satisfaction potential is also very high for those who tend to self-serve, the system will be greeted with relish. For those who do not embrace the technology, there is always the telephone. The CSS system should:

- Either be or link directly into the knowledge base,

- Have a tracking capability to allow assessment of use and satisfaction,

- Be blindingly fast (the time to post a query and get an answer should be seconds)

- Have multiple tiers to support levels of service (potential revenue streams)

- Directly link to VoIP or chat mode in the event the Customer needs a human contact

*Baseline.* The system should support:

- Implementation of business rules with an intuitive scripting interface (as compared to hard-coding)

- Open standards

- Scalability

- Third-party applications

- Nonproprietary relational database back end

- Flexible report writing tools

- Open API

- Flexible tools for creating custom GUI and front-end applications

*Availability.* As the CSS system will become mission-critical to all that use it, it must have a very high availability rating. The recommend availability target is greater than 99.9 percent.

*Need.* A CSS is almost mandatory in 2003. Having one will probably be mandatory by 2004 for high-technology players.

## Knowledge Base

A knowledge base is the cornerstone of a contact center. It is the central repository for all data points, issues, challenges, sales pitches, and comparative analysis summaries in regard to the supported product or service. This includes, FAQs, service bulletins, white papers, and so on.

If the knowledge base is extended to Customers it must be closely linked with the CSS as that is the Customer's conduit to access data found in the knowledge base.

In a perfect world the system would be intuitive and simple enough that once a new-hire is trained to use it they can begin fielding contacts like a product specialist with years of experience. The system should be very easy to search based on very broad criteria, in fact, this is the magic of many knowledge base systems—the ability to search and hit the right information first time.

*Baseline.* The system should be easy to access and update with new information. It should be secure so that information can be disseminated based on security access rights. The system should support:

- Open standards

- Scalability

- Nonproprietary relational database back end

- Flexible report writing tools

- Open API and flexible tools for creating custom GUI and front-end applications

*Availability.* As the knowledge base system is a contact center cornerstone, it is mission-critical and it must have a very high availability rating. The recommended availability target is greater than 99.9 percent.

*Need.* Mandatory.

## Audit Program

An audit program is not a software/hardware application but a continuous quality exercise. An audit program leverages techniques like mystery shopper, blind-testing, and hard data analysis. The deliverable is a report that is a barometer on how well the contact center is performing and where improvement is needed.

*Baseline.* It is preferable if a third party undertakes the audit.

*Availability.* N/A.

*Need.* Mandatory.

## Project Management System

A project management system allows projects to be disciplined. The status of projects is easy to ascertain with a project management system, and project slippage or failure can be mitigated before critical risks surface.

Project management systems are often found in the engineering and quality teams. It may be possible to leverage these existing systems. In fact, it is preferable if the contact center's projects have a great deal of interaction with engineering and quality. Being on the same system provides visibility and solidifies interdepartmental goals.

***Baseline.*** The system should support alarms tied to milestones, provide support for cost analysis, and be intranet-ready.

***Availability.*** N/A.

***Need.*** Desirable.

## Communications Surveillance System

Not a system in and of itself, but usually an add-on to the PBX and e-mail systems. These systems monitor incoming and outgoing contacts and search for key words in the dialog and/or text. If the hit alarms are real-time, management can shadow an "alarmed" dialog and take whatever action is necessary. Non-real-time systems allow management to review the message(s) and the circumstances that spawned the hit.

The system should record and store images of all contacts for a discrete amount of time. These recordings can be used for settling *he said/she said* conflicts and for employee review purposes. Another benefit is the ability to play back Customer comments to interested parties such as product management, engineering, or the marketing team.

It is very important to position this system's function in the right light. It is not a "big brother" engine designed to trap employees. Rather, it is a tool to assist the CSRs by allowing management to intervene in real time and defuse a hostile situation or, at minimum, be aware of an abusive Customer. In some instances it can be used to counter litigation threats. While all businesses are prone to litigation threats, some are more prone than others, for instance, a contact center providing advice on poison control is more likely to be a litigation target than a contact center providing guidance on use of cosmetics.

Note that the Customer must be alerted to the fact that they are being recorded and monitored. This is a legal and moral obligation.

***Baseline.*** The system should:

- Monitor the main channels of communication

- Allow a reasonable archival time for all contacts (such as six months)

- Have a database-driven comprehensive indexing system to allow contacts to be searched and sorted by any number of criteria (such as originating telephone number, CSR identification, time, date, keywords, and so on)

***Availability.*** As a communications surveillance system is not mission-critical to the contact center operation (unless the contact center is providing advice on poison control), it can have a low to medium availability rating. The recommended availability target is greater than 90 percent.

***Need.*** Highly desirable.

## Scheduling Software

Scheduling software is necessary in larger contact center operations, particularly if the operation is twenty-four/seven. The system schedules personnel so that the optimal number of CSRs are available on all shifts. Smaller operations and those running on standard business hours (0900 to 1700) can probably do without a full software suite to schedule personnel. The system is key to meeting SLA obligations therefore links are required to a number of other systems.

*Baseline.* The scheduling software should take into account:

- Contact volume and load
- The skill set of the CSR pool
- Vacation, holidays, sick time
- Shift distribution rules
- Sales/marketing programs, management availability
- Release schedules

The more sophisticated systems link directly into the PBX system for SLA loading, and skill set data.

*Availability.* If the operation is large enough that scheduling software is demanded, the demand will be high. The recommended availability target is greater than 99 percent.

*Need.* Dependent on the size and hours of operation of the contact center.

## Recruitment Software

Recruitment software is more a human resources tool than a contact center tool, but considering the churn rate found in many operations, the contact center may warrant its own system.

Superior systems allow candidates to post their resumes via the Internet. The candidate is instructed to fill in a number of free-form fields and the resume itself can be uploaded or pasted as text. Once the information is in the database, the system sends an acknowledgement e-mail to the applicant, grades the free-form field responses, and searches the resume for keywords and applicability matches to open positions. If a hit is made, a flag signaling staff to review the resume is posted, and the interview process may begin.

*Baseline.* The system should:

- Allow applicants to post electronically from the Internet
- Be database-driven
- Support aging and retiring[2] of resumes over a set time threshold

*Availability.* A recruitment software system is not mission-critical to the contact center operation therefore it can have a low availability rating. The recommended target availability is greater than 80 percent.

*Need:* Desirable.

## Survey Software

Survey software facilitates design, distribution, and analysis of Customer questionnaires and surveys. Survey software is another cornerstone of a world-class contact center. There are a number of excellent survey tools available. The more sophisticated suites support databases, automatic analysis, and real-time analysis and reporting. Internet-based survey tools are becoming popular, but they tend to emphasize negativity as the Customer has come across the survey because they are experiencing problems.

As with any data gathering exercise, it is imperative to understand what you hope to gain from the survey and structure it appropriately. Most survey tools provide guidelines and direction on how to structure and phrase questions in order to capture the data needed without biasing the sample.

There are online survey tools that can be broadcast or directed to specific accounts. Many systems draw on the contact center proper in that the CSRs can solicit answers while online with the Customer base. Alternatively, the contact center can be leveraged to conduct outgoing contacts to proactively gather data from Customers, prospects, and whomever the survey targets as the key audience.

*Baseline.* The system must have:

- A database-driven indexing system to allow survey results to be searched, sorted and correlated by any number of criteria such as:
  - Demographic pointers
  - Originating telephone number
  - CSR identification
  - Time and date
  - Keywords

*Availability.* As a survey software suite is not directly mission-critical to the operation of the contact center, it can have a low to medium availability rating. The recommended availability is greater than 90 percent.

*Need.* Mandatory

## Interactive Voice Response

An interactive voice response (IVR) is a supplemental system and a subcomponent of the PBX. The IVR system is that near-ubiquitous system that requests callers to "dial 1 if you have a . . . , dial 2 if you have a . . ." The IVR system requires close linkage to the CSS and CRM systems and the e-mail/fax infrastructure so that contacts can be qualified and quantified.

The IVR system is the one that most Customers complain about. Cellular phone users find it difficult to navigate (older people detest these systems as many simply wish to talk to a person and not "a machine," younger people have no patience with these systems, and the rest of us just plod on as best as we can).

> Why do contact center professionals insist on deploying these universally-despised systems? The alternative, a farm of receptionists, is not scalable, not economical, and in many ways inferior—that is why.

The system is needed and that is a simple fact of business today. Where many corporations go askew with IVR systems is the mapping, design, and flow of the systems. Keep it simple and straightforward and focus on the raison d'être for the system—to ease contact and to allow Customers and prospects to get to the *right* person in as few motions as possible. Enlist assistance with the mapping from consultants that specialize in this discipline, and be ever conscious and vigilant in keeping the system focused.

*Baseline.* See comments under Public Branch Exchange, Customer Self-Service, Customer Relationship Management, and Knowledge Base Systems earlier in this chapter.

*Availability.* As this supplemental software is mission-critical to the operation of the contact center, it must have a high availability rating. The recommended target availability is greater than 99 percent.

*Need.* Mandatory.

## Automatic Call Distribution System

The automatic call distribution (ACD) system is a supplemental system and a subcomponent of the IVR and PBX systems. The ACD system allows contacts to be routed to the optimal individual based on IVR system responses and CSR availability.

> The author has observed that once other corporate groups learn the contact center has IVR capability, they often attempt to hijack it for their own purposes. Sales wants a "product sales" branch, marketing wants linkage capability to strategic partners, and so on. It is all in the interest of Customer satisfaction, but the end result is one of those infuriating IVR maps that offer you nine options, then seven suboptions, and so on. Keep the system focused and do not attempt to stretch it over the entire corporation. If the need is there, other corporate teams can have their own IVR systems with their separate and discrete access telephone numbers and mapping.

*Baseline.* See comments for Public Branch Exchange, Customer Self-Service, Customer Relationship Management, and Knowledge Base Systems earlier in this chapter.

*Availability.* As this supplemental software is not mission-critical to the operation of the contact center, it can have a medium availability rating. The target availability should be greater than 90 percent.

*Need.* Mandatory.

## E-Mail/Fax-on-Demand Service

E-mail/fax-on-demand is a supplemental system that is part of the PBX (specifically the IVR supplemental system), CSS, and CRM systems and the e-mail/fax infrastructure (assuming the fax service is file server based and not a stand-alone model). E-mail/fax-on-demand allows product brochures, FAQs, and other corporate data to be requested by prospects/Customers and delivered by the e-mail/fax system without any intervention by contact center personnel. The link to the CRM system is to allow tracking of the "on-demand" activity for follow-up purposes (directed at the prospect) and proactive Customer care.

*Baseline.* See comments for Customer Self-Service, Customer Relationship Management, and Knowledge Base Systems earlier in this chapter.

*Availability.* As supplemental software is not directly mission-critical to the operation of the contact center, it can have a medium availability rating. The target availability should be greater than 95 percent.

*Need.* E-mail/Fax-on-demand service is desirable, but not mandatory.

## Automated E-Mail System

An automated e-mail system is a supplemental system that is part of the PBX (specifically the IVR supplemental system), CSS, and CRM systems, and the e-mail system. Auto-response e-mail can be positioned as a service channel on its own.

Responding to e-mail queries is one of the most time-consuming tasks for a CSR. Verbal responses are succinct and to the point, whereas written responses must be vetted for spelling, grammar, and syntax. All this is time-consuming. To bring this into focus consider that, in a contact center supporting a software product, a CSR can respond to an average of fourteen telephone contacts per hour compared to five e-mail queries of similar complexity.

There are a number of software engines on the market that provide automated responses to e-mail inquiries. In the simplest of these systems an incoming e-mail, subject line, and body of the message is scanned for keywords that trigger a standard auto-response.

There are a number of challenges these systems face, not the least being the ambiguity of the English language and its attendant flexibility (for example: to, too, and two). Nuances, from subtle to in-your-face, are also lost on the current generation of auto-response systems. This results in auto-responses that miss the mark, are unsatisfactory, and may cause additional Customer dissatisfaction. Factor in spelling, grammar, and the terse, disjoined syntax often found in e-mails, and the challenge begins to look very difficult.

There is promise of relief in sight. The latest-generation engines tap into natural language process (NLP) algorithms. These systems claim to deduce the meaning and context of the Customer's e-mail. A number of the systems emerging are supplemented by a continuous learning function that "learns" from the CSRs actions and responses.

If and when these systems mature, it is conceivable that e-mail auto-response systems could take the burden of routine queries off the contact center, thereby freeing the CSRs to focus on advanced and difficult queries. The simpler the supported product, the better these systems will operate. If nothing else, an excellent entry-level use of e-mail auto-response is as an information clearing service; interpret the e-mail and direct the Customer to the right resource be it an FAQ section, the manual, or an actual CSR.

*Availability.* As supplemental software is not directly mission-critical to the operation of the contact center it can have a medium availability rating. The target availability should be greater than 95 percent.

*Baseline.* See comments for Customer Self-Service, Customer Relationship Management, and Knowledge Base Systems earlier in this chapter.

*Need.* Highly desirable.

## Voice Mail (V-Mail or Vmail)

V-mail is a supplemental system that is part of the PBX system. V-mail is not a tenable service channel for the average contact center. V-mail for internal correspondence is fine, however, it is not an effective option for Customers calling for support services.

As v-mail usually assumes a callback with the attendant long distance charges, telephone tag matches, and on-hold time, it is often best to set up a disincentive to v-mail. In addition, few v-mail systems can be easily tied to the CRM system, which means a v-mail contact can get lost, thereby spawning a dissatisfaction event.

Finally, v-mails are usually left for individuals. Individuals take vacations, go to training sessions, and move on, in or out of organizations. It is preferable to direct the Customer base to the contact center as a pool of resources and to set up disincentives for Customers calling "individuals." Unless there is a compelling reason to retain v-mail as a service channel *and* unless v-mails are captured by the help desk system, it is probably best to phase out v-mail as a service channel.

*Availability.* N/A.

*Baseline.* N/A.

*Need.* Undesirable.

# SYSTEM PROGRESSION

*System maturity.*

System and application deployment are driven by where the corporation is in its maturity cycle. Start-ups typically have very few disciplined systems in place for Customer care, whereas established corporations that have an existing Customer base and are only releasing a new product/service will have systems in place consistent with the market and Customer needs related to the existing support requirements. This section outlines three different system deployment stages each with its own unique issues and challenges.

As the company progresses through the product and market maturity cycle, pencil and paper are discarded for spreadsheets, which are cast aside for purpose-built stand-alone software packages, which become multiuser systems, which necessitate the introduction of interim data-mining systems, which spawn enterprise resource planning (ERP) systems, and so on.

Corporations deploy software/hardware-based systems to enable personnel to be more efficient and effective. In the best-managed organizations, systems are also deployed to enhance the Customer's experience.

Review Figures 6.2 through 6.5. Figure 6.2 is a depiction of a paper-based system, Figure 6.3 shows a spreadsheet-based system, Figure 6.4 shows a purpose-built system, and Figure 6.5 depicts an example of an interim system. Corporations that have reached full maturity typically deploy (sometimes a number of) ERP systems. There is no graphic outlining an ERP system, but as often as not, the ERP system resembles the interim system with a heavy reliance on data consolidation. Each stage of the progression has its pros and cons.

Paper-and-pencil systems, such as a simple ledger sheet, are simple, always accessible, and can be understood by anyone, however, they are sometimes illegible, often inaccurate, and not very easy to back up or restore. Business rules are enforced by virtue of each employee's memory and personnel integrity.

Spreadsheets and single user databases (such as Microsoft's Access) improve the situation—accuracy increases, backup and offsite storage of the data is possible, and the system remains comprehensible by many. Spreadsheets, however, are only as clever as the macros the user can write (and understand), are difficult to fine-tune to many businesses' particularities, and do not lend themselves to multiple users. So, simple business rules can be checked-and-balanced, but much like the paper-based system, the business rules are enforced by virtue of each employee's memory and personnel integrity.

Purpose-built systems like Accpac accounting, configurable to a number of business models, are often standards-based (generally accepted accounting principles [GAAP] in Accpac's case) and can migrate to a multiuser environment. Business rules can be hard-coded into these systems and enforced. The source code, however, is often not available to the corporation. The organization is then beholden to outside vendors for a mission-critical system. These systems often require a specialist (in-house) and consultants to configure and support it. The system is comprehensible by only a few, and the organization has grown into a series of islands of information—finance, sales,

*Every transaction is recorded on ledgers and forms. Filing is manual and data consolidation is manual. There are so few transactions that the owner knows firsthand how the business is doing. The only reports necessary are financial, typically for tax purposes.*

**Paper-Based**
Small start-up company

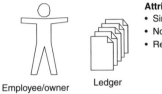

**Attributes:**
- Simple to administer
- No backup
- Reports are manual

Employee/owner    Ledger

*Employees in start-ups tend to fulfill many functions.*

**Figure 6.2** Paper-based system.

*Spreadsheets and small single-user databases (for example, Access) introduced to capture and store data. Reports are necessary but typically custom and purpose designed for the need at hand.*

**Spreadsheet-Based**
Start-up company

**Attributes:**
- Accuracy of data improved
- Backups of critical data
- Analysis of data facilitated
- Reports facilitated

Spreadsheet(s)
& small database(s)

Employees

*Still a start-up but the organization is beginning to grow and hire personnel dedicated to functions previously handed by single individuals.*

**Figure 6.3** Spreadsheet-based systems.

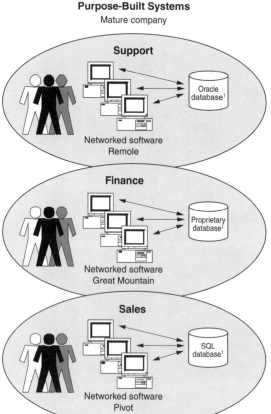

**Purpose-Built Systems**
Mature company

**Support**

Oracle database[1]

Networked software
Remole

**Finance**

Proprietary database[1]

Networked software
Great Mountain

**Sales**

SQL database[1]

Networked software
Pivot

**Attributes:**
- Customers receiving better service overall
- Greater analysis of data facilitated from each data island
- Reports from each data island available
- Systems do not link to each other
- Redundancy of data (that is, Customer address is in three databases which triples the data update task )
- Support contracts are needed with three vendors
- Disparate databases mean higher MIS support costs
- Proprietary database (finance) is a risk factor if the vendor goes out of business

*Departments deploy purpose-built systems to fulfill their business needs.*

[1]Database and application are only examples.

**Figure 6.4**   Purpose-built system.

the contact center, and marketing all have their own systems—none of which share data or information with each other. The worst manifestation of this is when one or more of the databases is in a proprietary format. A proprietary format binds the organization to the vendor. Furthermore, no one individual can see the whole data picture.

Interim systems can assist an organization at the purpose-built stage. These systems can mine data from multiple sources and output comprehensive reports, such as Customer history from the help desk system, cross-referenced with accounts receivable (AR) data

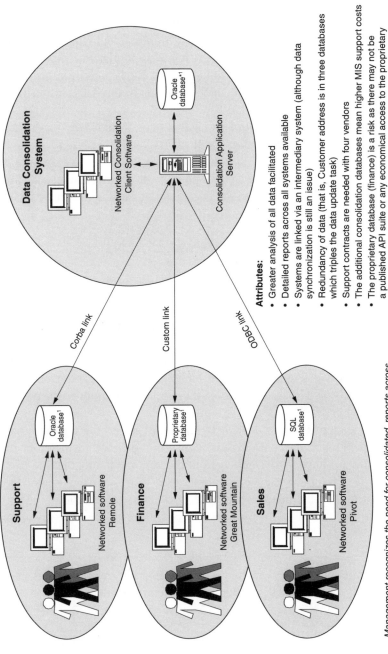

**Figure 6.5**  Interim system.

from the finance system, cross-referenced with last-touch data from the sales system, tempered by demographic filters from the marketing system. The configuration challenges, however, are often enormous as many legacy systems simply were not designed to link to other systems. Be it due to proprietary data structures or absence of open application programming interfaces (APIs), the problem may be insurmountable. Data bridges and middleware links tend to not be economical in initial deployment costs and subsequent support costs. The overhead to support reports and generate new reports is considerable, and the cost to sustain the individual links to the islands of information is often cost-prohibitive as each upgrade to *any* of the systems in the data cluster must now be reviewed in an expanded context.

The final step is the deployment of an ERP system. This is one gargantuan system to be used from finance to manufacturing. It involves CRM, SFA, financial modules, inventory, shipping, and so on. ERP systems, however, are expensive, require dedicated resources to configure and support, and respond to need-for-change with glacier-like speed. And one more thing, no one in the organization can see the entire picture.

# CHANGE MANAGEMENT

*The human element . . .*

One aspect of progression that is not obvious, and is therefore often overlooked, is the human element regarding the use of these systems. Too often, companies expend large sums of money for the technologies but do not give consideration to the personnel that must use them. It is analogous to recognizing a need to procure a corporate jet without also obtaining the services of a pilot, flight crew, ground crew, and support personnel. The corporation ends up with a new state-of-the-art jet that cannot be used because they do not know how.

Whenever a system is introduced it is important to get the right message to the contact center personnel about what is transpiring and how it will affect them. Too many innovations are improperly messaged to the very personnel that are to use them. Far too often the staff views said innovations as a tool for management to exercise more control or reduce the head count, or they otherwise miss the point. If the staff does not buy in to the change, then the change is unlikely to be a positive thing.

---

In one organization, the sales team had a fully configured, comprehensive set of tools built into a state-of-the-art CRM system. The system provided relationship-building tools, forecasting modules, automatic messaging, marketing program tracking, and many other features. The sales team used this CRM system, however, only as a place to record prospects' telephone numbers and addresses. To draw on the jet analogy, the sales team were in fact using the corporate jet as a storage shed.

An immensely powerful technique is to leverage the concept of rumor or other informal channels. Stretching the rumor mill construct yields an efficient mechanism for garnering mind-share among all the constituents the change will touch. In practice: identify the de facto leaders in the contact center—not management, but the cultural leaders—and sell them on the benefits of the idea. This is not a difficult proposition because the idea, if truly a good one, is firmly grounded in a value proposition. If the idea is not a good one then the value of the exercise will be realized by management not being able to sell the idea to the culture leaders; it was bound to fail, it obviously had flaws that were not seen by management. Sow the seeds of the idea to the culture leaders in an informal setting far in advance of the actual rollout of the innovation, then watch as the idea is embraced and personnel start asking when the change will occur.

Some may see this approach as manipulative, but it is, in fact, the same as shopping an idea around, the only difference is that the idea shops itself. The weak link in executing on this idea is that management may not have the relationship currency to gain the trust of the culture leaders. If this is the case then forget about changing anything until the dichotomy of management-to-employee is rectified.

Engage the training and human resources teams in assisting with managing change. Approach changes with the same courtesy as is extended to the Customer base when the product/service undergoes a change.

## ENDNOTES

1. The acceptance of a system by those who will be using it is often overlooked and mismanaged. Engage the users early on in the process and obtain their buy-in, otherwise the project is more susceptible to failure than it need be.
2. Aging and retiring—aging meaning the system should date-stamp when the resume entered the data set, retiring meaning the system should delete the resume after six months.

# Appendix A

# Acronyms and Terms

## PREAMBLE

This section supplies definitions for all the acronyms, terms, and catch phrases used in this book. Due to the number of finance-focused definitions, they have been grouped together in a separate appendix, appendix G—Finance for Contact Center Mangers. While each financial definition has an entry in this appendix, it is only a pointer to appendix G.

## ACRONYMS AND TERMS

*account penetration:* Sales term referring to the portion of users within a targeted account that have embraced the product/service. The task is to persuade the non-users to adopt the product and fully penetrate the account.

*ACD, automatic call distribution:* Technology term. ACD works with incoming contacts and automatically establishes links between a caller and the most appropriate customer support representative. The selection criteria can be based on skill set, priority, product to be supported, or other, often custom, differentiators.

*arithmetic progression:* General term. Used to describe a relaxed growth pattern. Arithmetic progression is expressed by the following series: 1, 2, 3, 4, 5, and so on. Compare with *geometric progression.*

*assets:* Finance term, see appendix G.

*auto-renewal (contracts):* Finance term, see appendix G.

*balance sheet:* Finance term, see appendix G.

*benchmark:* General term. A benchmark in the contact center context usually refers to a process whereby all pertinent metrics are measured and published—the contact center has been "benchmarked"—this provides the contact center management with a snapshot of the performance of the contact center. The benchmark data can be used to drive a gap analysis and set a plan in place to improve the contact center. Benchmarking can refer to the process of comparing one contact center to another to see where improvements can be made.

*boilerplate:* General term. A boilerplate is a blank document template that contains text and formatting information that is reused frequently. Use of boilerplates ensures consistency for contact center documentation. For example, a *contract boilerplate* contains all the legal text, terms, services offered, and contact data for the contact center. When a new Customer requests a contract, the contact center manager opens the contract boilerplate and only has to input the data unique to the new Customer.

*bote:* Blink of the eye. Colloquial term. Very quick. Used as: "I swear the latest restructuring lasted only a couple of *botes*."

*budget:* Finance term, see appendix G.

*burn rate:* Finance term, see appendix G.

*business development:* aka BusDev or BizDev. General term. A relatively new corporate role. The BusDev team searches for opportunities to enhance the corporation and bring added value by aligning with partners. Typically focused on strategic alliances, co-branding exercises, and, less frequently, coopetition. There are a diverse range of value propositions the BusDev team may bring: strategic alliances directly strengthen the sales team's ability to execute; technological alliances facilitate a two-way dialog for the technology players that the product has dependencies on; branding and co-branding bring credibility to the services and the services of your partners; and so on. The relevance to the contact center is in the creative aspect of BusDev; having a full-time resource dedicated to building and nurturing relationships has a very powerful upside. Both those who practice BusDev and those on the outside often confuse BusDev with sales. One litmus test for differentiating the two is that BusDev professionals speak in terms of "deals" where sales professionals speak of "purchase orders."

*business rules:* General term. Refers to the set of dictates or regulations that serve to administer and control how transactions are processed. See the full description devoted to Business rules in the section titled "Key Concepts," page 13.

*business unit:* Finance term, see appendix G.

*capital:* Finance term, see appendix G.

*CATA:* Canadian Advanced Technology Association. Acronym. Benchmark service that provides compensation metrics for high-technology firms. See appendix E for contact information.

*chief executive officer (CEO):* General term. The head of the corporation.

*chief operations officer (COO):* General term. The individual ultimately responsible for all operations in a corporation.

*churn rate:* General term. Churn rate describes the rate at which personnel move in and out of the corporation or within the corporation. A high churn rate resembles a revolving door and is not conducive to long-term success. An inordinate churn rate is a leading indictor of personnel dissatisfaction issues within the contact center. Triggers may be perceived or real and may include pay scale, management style, fairness, and other factors.

*computer-based training (CBT):* Technology term. A CBT program is designed to be delivered on a computer. Usually interactive, and always self-paced, CBT is a worthwhile medium for delivering repetitious training programs. Experience has shown, however, that it is ineffective for some students. Most CBT software applications support testing to ensure the knowledge transfer has taken place.

*computer telephony integration (CTI):* Technology term. In a fully integrated environment, all contacts, regardless of the mode by which the Customer chose to initiate the contact, is fed into and tracked by a centralized system. CSRs respond via the contact method the customer used or requested.

*contact center (CC):* General term. The term contact center evolved from help desk/support desk/incoming correspondence, and so on. The label "help desk" is limited in that it only implies "help," whereas "contact center" implies the handling and clearing of all contacts regardless of the reason or mode of contact. Services found in today's consolidated contact center include: support services, pre-sales, order processing, order tracking, outgoing telemarketing, up-sell, and so on. If, in fact, the operation under study (your organization) does not intend to provide the whole spectrum of services, then it is prudent to label the organization appropriately. If technical support services is the only mandate for the operation, then call them "technical support services." The right label reduces confusion both for the Customers and the sales personnel.

*coopetition:* Business development term. A relativity new term in the business lexicon. Coopetition describes a situation where a company enters into an alliance with a competitor. The driving reasons for this seemly contradictory action are based on the philosophy that there is enough for everyone to prosper so why fight? Key reasons for entering into a coopetition alliance include: opening of new markets, mitigating risks with nascent technology and development efforts, and, most likely, providing products or services to mutual Customers.

*corrective action (CA):* General term. A corrective action is the culmination of a root cause analysis exercise. The corrective action is the *fix* for the root cause of the challenge. To be effective, all departments in the corporation should sanction the corrective action protocol as many corrective actions extend beyond the contact center. Corrective actions should be supported by a standard boilerplate, be serialized, and be subject to review. On occasion it may be prudent to share corrective actions with Customers, particularly in an instance where a Customer demands to know how the corporation is going to ensure the failure never happens again.

*cost of ownership (COO):* Finance term, see appendix G.

*COTS:* Commercial off-the-shelf. Acronym. Usually refers to shrink-wrapped software packages that are generally available through standard distribution channels. It can also be used in a hardware context. COTS packages usually are very easy to configure and seldom have a professional services component attached to them.

*critical mass:* General term. Critical mass is a threshold. When critical mass is reached, the system under scrutiny begins to fail. That is, the system cannot support the mass and has gone critical. Consider a jet—a jet is specified to be able to operate under certain conditions, one of which is the weight of the cargo (mass). If the specified mass is exceeded, the jet is in a breach of critical mass and its performance is no longer guaranteed. In a contact center context, the critical mass can refer to nearly anything that can be quantified, for example, the contact center can handle no more than 750 calls per hour; critical mass occurs at a sustained rate of 751 calls per hour.

*customer relationship management (CRM):* Business term. Usually embodied in a software application that provides a container for all data on a Customer or prospect to ensure they are supported to their satisfaction for the entire lifecycle of their relationship with the corporation. The best-of-class CRM systems hold information on every transaction the Customer has had with the corporation (all teams: sales, contact center, billing, support, shipping, and so on), the Customer's history, and the status of the Customer's questions or concerns. The CRM system is the prime tool for sales and contact center teams. When the CRM system and the sales force automation (see SFA entry) system are the same, the sales team enters the prospect into the system on first contact. The status is updated from "prospect" to "Customer" when the sale is closed and the contact center takes over the relationship.

*customer service representative (CSR):* General term. The customer service representatives are the frontline personnel dealing with Customer issues. Sometimes interchanged with TSR.

*data dictionary:* Technology term. Every database should have a data dictionary associated with it. The data dictionary describes, in detail, the nature of the data (date field, numeric, alpha field, and so on), where the data comes from (auto time-stamped, input at order entry, calculated, and so on), what it is (shipping date, tax status, and so on), what states are supported within the field (open, closed, pending, and so on), related fields (particularly important with a relational database), field size (64 characters, unlimited, and so on), and other pertinent points. The data dictionary is used by report writers to concoct reports for the contact center and other departments that rely on Customer feedback and status. See Figure 6.1, Data flow (page 169) for a graphic depicting the breadth of data required by a corporation.

*deep pockets:* Finance term, see appendix G.

*digital volt ohm meter (DVOM):* Technology term. Diagnostic tool for service personnel. The DVOM is used to measure voltage, current, and resistance in electronic circuits.

*drill-down:* General term. A drill-down is the act of getting more information on a given issue or situation. For instance, a supervisor may be told that a Customer is irate;

the drill-down is performed in order for the supervisor to get all the information surrounding the situation and get to the root cause of the dissatisfaction. A second connotation of drill-down is in reference to reports. Figure 4.21, Data plot, top failure modes (page 144), is an example of a graphic report providing drill-down for areas of interest. The central pie chart provides a macro view of failures. To the right of the central pie chart is a breakout—the active sense of drill-down. The breakout pie chart provides drill-down capability within the larger category of software failure. Likewise, to the left of the central pie chart is a breakout providing additional details on hardware failures, and it has a further breakout depicting mechanical failures.

*employee relationship management (ERM):* An employee relationship management (ERM) system is a supplement to the customer relationship management (CRM), sales force automation (SFA), and enterprise resource planning (ERP) systems. The ERM system does not stand on its own. ERM is focused inward on the management-to-employee relationship. The greatest need for these systems is in sales, manufacturing, and contact center operations where many factors contribute to the performance of the individual. The systems track and report on quotas (sales), deadlines (project management), training progress (training), goals (contact center), and any other entity that can be quantified and applies to an individual. An example of ERM in the contact center is tracking self-study/self-test activity for the personnel; consider that each CSR is to complete two product-focused micro-courses every month, the ERM system can automatically provide a dashboard for management to track progress, raise star performers, and flag those that need assistance.

*failure mode effects and criticality analysis (FMECA):* Quality term. An FMECA is an analysis tool borrowed from the reliability engineering discipline. Traditionally, the FMECA is applied to a product to mitigate risks inherent in that product failing. The FMECA can be used to focus attention on areas that will have an impact on the contact center, the personnel manning the phones, and the business itself. See appendix C, FMECA, for a thorough discussion of FMECA and its applicability to contact centers.

*first contact:* Contact center term. First contact refers to the highly desirable goal of resolving an issue on the first contact, that is, no callback is needed, no research time is required, and the CSR had the answer at hand in real time. Review "Key Concepts," page 13, for further information.

*flextime:* Business term. Flextime allows employees to choose *when* they put in their daily, weekly, or monthly allotment of hours. For example: the employee may be contracted to put in 6.5 productive hours a day. Under flextime, the employee may choose to do so from midnight to 7:00 a.m., or whatever time is convenient to them. Obviously not all functions in a contact center can enjoy the flexibility provided by flextime. CSRs are needed at their posts during peak hours. Alternatively, report writers may actually benefit from working late at night when the call volume is lower and the environment less hectic. In general, flextime works best for those functions that are task-based.

***Fortune 10/100/1000:*** Business term. Refers to a company that has revenue in the top 10, 100, or 1000 U.S.-based corporations. See Global 10/100/1000.

***functional specification:*** Business term. The functional specification is a document that outlines what the engineering/development team is building. The functional specification is often an all-inclusive document complete with milestones and time lines usually depicted on Gantt charts. In most organizations the functional specification document is owned and administered by the product manager.

***Gantt chart:*** Business term. A Gantt chart is a tool for graphically depicting time lines, milestones, and task interdependencies. Microsoft's Project product is used by many organizations to generate Gantt charts (and manage projects).

***gap analysis:*** Business term. Gap analysis refers to the gap between where something needs to be and where it is. For instance: if a dictate is passed down from the CEO that says all incoming calls will be answered in less than 20 seconds (average), the contact center manager needs to ascertain where they currently are (let's say the current average time is 90 seconds), where they need to be, and then formulate how to get there. So, if the target is 20 seconds and the empirical measure is 90 seconds, the gap is 70 seconds. Now the analysis component—how to shave 70 seconds off the time. Obviously, the magic in the gap analysis is not in defining the gap (90 seconds), it is in the analysis on how to overcome the gap.

***generally accepted accounting principles (GAAP):*** Finance term, see appendix G.

***geometric progression:*** Business term used to describe rapid growth. Geometric progression is expressed by the following series: 2, 4, 8, 16, 32, and so on. Growth at a geometric rate can burden even the most robust infrastructures. If planned for, geometric growth can be managed, but if sales are growing at this rate, management can only hope for a plateau or leveling-off in order to catch up. Compare with *arithmetic progression.*

***global 10/100/1000:*** Business term. Refers to a company that has revenue in the top 10, 100, or 1000 globally-based corporations. See *Fortune 10/100/1000.*

***groupthink:*** Business term. Groupthink is a dangerous dynamic that may be observed whenever people join together in teams. In the business world, it is the groupthink dynamic that is often behind some of the poorer decisions that emerge from the boardroom. Groupthink can often be characterized by the phrase "blinded by their own brilliance"—not a good thing at all. Groupthink is when a team sit about, patting each other on the back and ignoring the realities around them. Groupthink can often be akin to "arranging the deck chairs on the Titanic." Wherever there are egos there will be groupthink, and as ego is a prime component of every executive, there is no lack of groupthink in business today. See sycophant, courtier, adulator, or flatter in any dictionary to begin a root cause study.

***hot-link:*** Contact center term. A mechanism that allows a CSR to seamlessly hand off a contact to another corporation's contact center. That is, the host contact center and the target contact center are linked at the PBX level. Usually all that is required is a four-digit code, somewhat like transferring a call internally; there is no need to dial the full phone number, enter a queue, and wait for a representative.

***initial public offering (IPO):*** Business term. When a company wishes to trade on the public stock market they conduct an IPO. The rules governing when, where, and at what price a company issues stocks for their IPO are extensive.

***intellectual property (IP):*** Business term. Not to be confused with *Internet protocol.* Intellectual property consists of the ideas and technologies that are unique to a corporation's product. That is to say, if the competition got hold of the IP they could build the product. IP is also heard in the context of the "secret sauce" of a product. Applying for and being granted a patent protects a company's IP.

***interactive voice response (IVR):*** Technology term. See *mapping* in this section.

***Internet service provider (ISP):*** Technology term. An ISP is a business that provides connections to the Internet to businesses and individual consumers. The ISP may provide connectivity via dial-up modems, ISDN, T1, fiber, cable, or any one of the new connection modes. If the corporation depends on the Internet connection to operate, the ISP should be under an SLA to ensure that it is delivering the bandwidth and reliability the corporation requires.

***IP:*** Technology term. Internet protocol. Part of a suite of protocols governing the mechanisms to manage movement of data on a packet-switched network. This term is usually heard in conjunction with *TCP,* as in *TCP/IP.* Not to be confused with *intellectual property.*

***Java 2 Micro Edition (J2ME):*** Technology term. A small footprint Java extension most commonly found in cellular phones and handheld computing devices.

***kaizen:*** Business term. Japanese term meaning: gradual continuous improvement by doing small things better and continually adjusting to increasingly higher standards.

***loaded/unloaded:*** Finance term, see appendix G.

***liability:*** Finance term, see appendix G.

***Linux:*** See *open source* in this appendix.

***mapping:*** Technology term. Related to the interactive voice response system and refers to the trail one navigates via the telephone touchpad to get to where they wish to be. For example, "Press one for technical support on the THX-1000 product, press two for technical support on the YTR-432 product, press three if you are experiencing an issue with the bill," and so on.

***mean time between failures (MTBF):*** Quality term. Product statistic that states the time between failures of the product. There are theoretical and empirical methods to derive this number. See Benjamin Blanchard's *Logistics Engineering and Management* entry in appendix I, Selected Readings, for a reference to an excellent text on the subject.

***mean time to repair (MTTR):*** Quality term. Product statistics that state the time required to return the product to service. See Benjamin Blanchard's *Logistics Engineering and Management* entry in appendix I, Selected Readings, for a reference to an excellent text on the subject.

*MIS/IT:* Management Information Systems/Information Technology. Acronym. This refers to the team that manages the technology and infrastructure that the corporation runs on. It is often a very powerful group with huge influence in the organization.

*MTWTF:* Contact center term. Denotes Monday, Tuesday, Wednesday, Thursday, Friday (see *SS*).

*mystery shopper:* Business term. A mystery shopper assists in benchmarking the contact center. The mystery shopper assumes the role of a Customer and contacts the contact center but, in fact, they are providing benchmarking data. A regular mystery-shopper program will highlight both objective (rings before pick up) and subjective (product knowledge) improvements in the contact center. There are third parties that specialize in mystery-shopping exercises.

*network operating center (NOC):* Contact center term. The control center for a service provider typically housing all the diagnostic tools that monitor the status and health of the infrastructure. It is from the NOC that failures are first detected and notifications are issued.

*NLP:* Natural language process. Acronym. A set of algorithms which, it is claimed, can deduce the meaning and context of the written word.

*one-off:* Typically this term is found in manufacturing operations. It refers to a singularity, the creation of *one* of a product. In manufacturing and contact center operations, one-offs are to be avoided because they are expensive to create in the first place and then they are even more expensive to maintain in the long term. Similar to an *orphan product*.

*open source:* Refers to software and, in most cases, the underlying operating system. Examples of some of the more popular open-source software programs include the Linux operating system and the Apache web server. The majority of open source is no-charge or at least so inexpensive as to be practically free—one simply downloads the latest version and goes to town. The prime allure of open-source software is its initial cost (minimal if not free), the speed at which patches are provided for late-breaking problems (courtesy of the huge population supporting the code), the ability to tweak the code for a specific application (it is open, therefore highly configurable), and its prowess in large networked configurations (also due to its inherent configurability). On the downside, the MIS/IT personnel supporting open source must be experienced tweakers/hackers/coders as some of the drivers and tools are difficult to set up (without the help of the tweaker/hacker/coders). In addition, many popular programs will not run in open-source environments.

*operating system (OS):* Technology term. The underlying software that instructs a computer that it is a computer. Windows, Linux, and Palm's OS are examples of operating systems.

*original equipment manufacturer (OEM):* Business term. The manufacturer of a product who may not be visibly involved in the sales or service channels. Frequently, the OEM allows their sales channels to brand the product themselves.

***orphan product:*** This term is typically used in software houses. An orphan product is a product that has diverged from the parent product. Consider a software-based tool and assume that there is a standard software code stream; the standard code stream is the parent stream. Now consider a company who requests and pays for changes to the code to fulfill a unique need; the changed code stream is the orphan. The ramifications go both ways. If the parent code is updated with fabulous new features, the company with the orphan code may not be able to upgrade as their code differs from the main stream (parent), and the software provider now has to support and maintain the parent stream (which all Customers use) and all the orphans that they have agreed to. Stay away from orphan code! It is similar to a *one-off* product.

***Pareto analysis:*** Quality term. Pareto was a nineteenth century economist. He formulated the income distribution principle, which stated that the majority of income is controlled by a minority of the population—the few rich compared to the many poor. This distribution dynamic can be applied elsewhere and is generally known as the 80/20 rule. In the contact center context: 80 percent of the call volume is caused by 20 percent of the failure modes. Bring these 20 percent to the attention of the engineering team first.

***peer-to-peer (P2P):*** Technology term. A networking connection option that allow two computers to communicate and interact with each other directly.

***predictive dialer:*** Technology term. A predictive dialer is an add on to a contact center's telecommunications system (the PBX). Predictive dialers are used for outbound telemarketing and telesales teams and are designed to optimize the CSR's time. In brief, the predictive dialer is fed a list of phone numbers of prospects—the list may be a bought list that focuses on a particular demographic or a simple sequence range of numbers—the predictive dialer dials the numbers and is timed such that the CSR's downtome (that is, not on a call time) is minimized. Predictive dialers are responsible for those telephone calls one often gets where there is no one on the line when you pick it up and you get a scripted "please hold for an important opportunity from xyz corporation." Soon after a CSR picks up the line and delivers a sales pitch.

***preventive maintenance (PM):*** Quality term. Any scheduled maintenance activity. Activities performed during PM include hardware validation, diagnostic program execution, file purging, and register flushing. See *remedial maintenance (RM)*.

***principle period of maintenance (PPM):*** Contact center term. The daily period during which the majority of support events take place, usually expressed in 24 hour clock format. Example: A business software tool could be expected to have a PPM of 0800 to 2000 Eastern Standard Time.

***private/public branch exchange (PBX):*** Technology term. The PBX can be thought of as a telephone switch owned by the corporation. The more sophisticated PBXs support software tools that drive many of the contact center's performance metric reports.

***profit and loss (P&L):*** Finance term, see appendix G.

***prospect:*** Business term. A prospect is an entity that has potential to become a Customer. They have not yet bought the product/service and are either still working with the sales team or in the process of ordering. A Customer has purchased the product and is entitled to all the post-sale support services. See *customer relationship management* for further discussion.

***read the frigg'n manual (RTFM):*** Colloquial term. An informal cry of exasperation often heard in contact centers.

***recurring revenue:*** Finance term, see appendix G.

***reference account:*** Business development term. An existing Customer that a prospect may contact that is willing to give an appraisal of the performance of the product. See *strategic account.*

***remedial maintenance (RM):*** Quality term. Like a PM, RM events are scheduled maintenance activities, but RM events are more random and are not planned as far in advance as PM events. For example, a PM schedule is planned far in advance and published as such; but an RM event may be in response to a recent failure, such as a lightning strike. In other words, Customers will know of PM events far in advance, but an RM event could be scheduled at any time.

***responsibility matrix:*** Business term. A matrix that details exactly who is responsible for what. See Figure 2.1, Responsibly matrix example, page 15, for an example of a matrix between a reseller, a Customer, and a contact center.

***return material authorization (RMA):*** Contact center term. This is permission, with tracking, to return a device to the contact center. Also known as RAN (return authorization number).

***return on investment (ROI):*** Finance term, see appendix G.

***revenue:*** Finance term, see appendix G.

***root cause:*** Quality term but has currency in all business units. The root cause is the culprit that is directly responsible for the effect that is being investigated. Root causes are often confused and muddled with *symptoms.* As an example: Western medicine, for a large part, is based on treating symptoms. If you go to see a doctor for upset stomach, the doctor more often than not prescribes medication directed at relieving the discomfort in the stomach. However, the root cause of the upset tummy is the stress this particular contact center manager is dealing with day to day. Prescribing medication to alleviate the discomfort to the stomach only deals with the symptoms and masks the real problem that needs treatment—work-induced stress. If you have been paying attention to this book, you know that the real fix is to investigate why this manager is not dealing with their stress; perhaps a week off is in order, maybe this manager is in need of some mentoring, or perhaps there is a very difficult Customer hounding this manager. Whatever is the source, is the root cause. See appendix D, The Five Whys of Quality, for further reading on getting to the root cause.

***run rate:*** General business term. Run rate refers to the rate at which an entity is performing or is stable, such as: the call volume run rate is 5,500 calls per hour. Run rate is very similar to burn rate, but where burn rate always refers to monetary impact, run rate may refer to anything that can be measured.

*sales force automation (SFA):* Business term. Software application that automates many of the steps sales personnel follow to secure a sale. The SFA system is the prime repository for contact information for prospects. Often the SFA system is the same system used for customer relationship management (CRM); the only difference in the information is that the SFA system is focused on prospects whereas the CRM system is focused on closed sales (Customers, that is). See *customer relationship management.*

*scripts:* Contact center term. A script is a written response to a known issue. The purpose is not for the CSR to read the script to the Customer (as it will sound contrived) but to use the script as a guideline for their own words and phraseology. Scripts should be created for the top twenty issues as well as all common failure modes, particularly endemic failure modes. These scripts ensure consistency of message as well as providing new contact center personnel with a solid basis on which to respond to common issues from the Customers.

*segmentation:* Business development term. An analysis exercise where the market or Customer base is categorized by common characteristics. Consider that to further penetrate the market (marketing-speak for increased sales) it behooves the company to understand its Customer base. Characteristics and attributes, such as demographics related to the product's adoption and success, the buying habits of the prime Customer, and the up-sell propensity of the target Customer, are important to isolate. Market segmentation broadens the segmentation analysis by including trending information on the market in general: Is the market in an economic upswing? Does the market have unique requirements? Is the market dominated by one enabling technology over another (for instance, Oracle database vis-à-vis MySQL)? Does the market have defining environmental characteristics that may impinge on sales or support sales (for instance, if the product is a snowblower you may not require a sales presence in Costa Rica)? and so on.

*service level agreement (SLA):* Business term. An SLA is put into place to provide a documented baseline performance target for any given transaction between the issuer and the holder. SLAs bear a number of similarities to insurance policies—the holder pays an annual premium for optimal coverage, the holder is entitled to special privileges, and, most importantly, the holder hopes to never have to exercise the policy. See the section titled "Service Level Agreements," page 22, for further details.

*service management system (SMS):* Business term. A system that manages the tangible services a company provides, such as: repair, overhaul, and preventive maintenance services. Modules include subsystems for generating service tickets, tracking service calls, and managing spares inventories.

*shadowing:* Contact center term. Shadowing is where a live Customer contact is tapped and listened to by a third party. See the section titled Employee Shadowing on page 163 for details.

***Six Sigma:*** Quality term. Six Sigma is a concept that has as its goal Customer satisfaction by way of reducing errors in processes to no more than 3.4 errors per million opportunities. Sigma is a Greek character ($\sigma$) used in equations to denote standard deviation (variance); the "six" denotes the degree of variance on an exponential scale. It has been suggested that most companies are run at a three to four sigma level, which is tens of thousands of errors per million. Six Sigma exercises are characterized by a scientific approach to analyzing processes; it is very exacting. The key analysis technique is the DMAIC approach, which stands for: *define, measure, analyze, improve,* and *control.* See the reference to further reading material on Six Sigma in appendix I.

***SS:*** Contact center term. Denotes Saturday and Sunday.

***standard operating procedure (SOP):*** Business term. In the best-of-class organizations, the majority of procedures are documented and observed as the SOP. From entering a sale order to authorizing a product return, each procedure is clearly documented. See the section titled "Standard Operating Procedures," page 95, for further discussion.

***strategic account:*** Business development term. An account that for one reason or another is a cornerstone of the product's/corporation's success. See the section titled "Strategic Accounts," page 28, for a full description.

***strike price:*** Business term. Refers to the monetary value an employee pays for company stock. If the corporation is public, the strike price is often the price the shares are trading at on the day the employee starts. If the company is pre–initial public offering (IPO), the price is established as the fair market value.

***subject matter expert (SME):*** Business term. This is an individual who is an expert on a particular topic. They may be intercompany or a hired-in consultant.

***subscription management system (SMS):*** Business term. A system that manages the services any given Customer is enrolled in and entitled to. The more elaborate systems allow Customers to sign up and terminate services without the intervention of a CSR. Examples include services provided by the phone company, the cable company, or some software services providers. McAfee corporation has an excellent Internet-based virus/privacy suite of tools that make use of Customer-initiated subscriptions.

***super-VAR:*** See *value-added reseller.*

***TCP:*** Transport core protocol. See *IP.*

***technical assistance research program (TARP):*** Acronym. See appendix E for contact information.

***telephone/technical service representative (TSR):*** Contact center term. Sometimes interchanged with *CSR.*

***thought-leader:*** General and business development term. In the contact center context, it is the corporation and not the individual that is of interest. The thought-leader is the company that has acted on the latest market intelligence, sussed out the future direction of the market, and put a product/service/mechanism in place ahead of the need. In other words, ahead of the curve, innovating before the Customer base knows they have a need. Being seen as the thought-leader is very valuable. In fact, marketing and business development count on it to a very high degree. The antithesis of a thought-leader is the "me-too" organization—the conservative organization that lets others define the new playing fields and that moves only when the new paradigm is proven. There is nothing wrong with the "me-too" strategy as it has been profitable to many, many organizations.

*top* **x** *issues:* Contact center term. The top $x$ issues is a report that outlines the $x$ most frequent reasons for contacts. The data is used for continuous improvement efforts and to refine the product being supported. Review the section titled "Key Concepts," page 13, for further description. See "Top Ten Issues," page 144, for information on refining and training staff to deal with the top issues. See Figure 4.21, Data plot, top failure modes, page 144, for an example of a graphic plot of top issues.

*tote board:* Contact center term. Tote boards are the large displays often hung in central locations in contact centers that continuously display pertinent metrics such as: number of Customers in queue, on-hold time in seconds, and general SLA data points. Also available are boards displaying system parameters on service-centric businesses, such as routing points and their availability, traffic maps, Web site hit parameters, and so on.

*turnaround time (TAT):* Contact center term. The time it takes to return to the desired state. In the case of a repair, the TAT is the time that elapses between the Customer returning the product and the repair depot sending it back to the Customer. The TAT duration often has a number of modifiers whereby only business hours/days are counted and the TAT is exclusive of holidays.

*twenty-four/seven:* Twenty-four hours/seven days a week. General term meaning full time, 24 hours a day, 365 days a year service and support. Unless otherwise specified in agreements with Customers, it is assumed this includes all holidays. Some businesses are obligated to provide support services on holidays as they may be peak periods for the product/service being supported. For example, a gift of a mobile telephone at Christmastime may necessitate a call to the carrier to have it activated.

*universal resource locator (URL):* Technology term. An address alias for a World Wide Web page. URLs most often take the form of common English rather than the Internet protocol address, for example, http://www.members.rogers.com/jaxschultz/ rather than 122.233.212.022.

*up-sell:* Sales term. Once the organization has captured a Customer and sold product, every time they contact the contact center there is an opportunity to sell the Customer additional products or services; this is an "up-sell." A more proactive approach is to mine the Customer database (as not all Customers may have had need to call the contact center) and initiate an outgoing up-sell program within the contact center. The up-sell is one way a contact center can directly drive revenue.

*value-added reseller (VAR):* Business term. A VAR is a sales channel for a company that does not wish to have a direct sales presence. The VAR takes a portion of the revenue for making the sale and often also takes a portion of the risk in making the sale (returns, high-maintenance Customers, complaint handling, and so on). A VAR agreement can be a close partnership where the company supplying product also supplies sales collateral, training, brochures, return processing, and technical expertise. Alternatively, some VAR agreements have very little interaction between the VAR and the supplier, the supplier only expects the VAR to move product. A super-VAR is a VAR that the supplier wishes to differentiate from the standard VARs. Usually super-VARs have more thorough product training, superior pricing options, on-site expertise, and so on. In order to minimize nuisance contacts in the contact center, all VARs should be subject to a certification process where the supplier ensures that their best interests are being served by the VAR channel. Without certification, the supplier does not have any control over what the VAR channel is claiming to move product. It is the reputation of the supplier that is at stake, as the VAR will just as quickly blame the supplier as they are to make a false product feature/benefit claim.

*virtual private network (VPN):* Technology term. Mechanism whereby personnel can work from home. The VPN allows access to the corporate network through the Internet. The VPN provides remote secure access to the host systems the CSRs most often access. An alternative to VPN is dedicated modem pools and dial-up capability.

*virtual team (V-team):* Business term. Used to describe a team made up of participants from a number of companies (or departments within one company) that seldom meet face-to-face but leverage electronic means. Conference calls, NetMeeting, and videoconferencing are some of the more popular V-team meeting mechanisms. The term has also been used to describe a fluid team whose members are dictated by circumstances—the V-team owner calls in subject matter experts as the situation demands.

*v-mail:* Voice mail. Technology term. System supported by most PBXs where messages can be left for an individual that is not at their desk at the moment. V-mail in the context of a contact center is usually not desirable. As v-mail usually assumes a callback with the attendant long-distance charges, telephone tag matches, and on-hold time, it is probably best to set up a disincentive to v-mail within the contact center. As well, few v-mail systems are tied to the help desk system, which means a v-mail contact can get lost, thereby spawning a dissatisfaction event. Finally, v-mails are usually left for individuals; individuals take vacations, go to training sessions, and move on, in or out of organizations. It is preferable to direct the Customer base to the contact center as a pool of resources and to set up disincentives to Customer calling "individuals." Unless there is a compelling reason to retain v-mail as a service channel, *and* unless v-mails are captured by the help desk system, it is probably best to not offer v-mail as a service channel.

*voice over internet protocol (VoIP):* Technology term. A nascent technology that provides for voice to be carried over an IP network such as the Internet.

*white paper:* The objective of a white paper is to authoritatively outline a product and its associated technologies. In high technology, white papers are to be viewed more as marketing and sales documents vis-à-vis unbiased technical dissertations.

# Appendix B

# Job/Role Descriptions

This appendix outlines each role found in the Contact Center organizational charts. The format is as follows:

*Role:* Description of the role focusing on prime responsibilities.

*Responsible to:* The individual(s) the role is directly accountable to not only from a "reporting to" perspective, but also those who are most affected by the individual's performance and actions.

*Key performance metrics:* A list of measurable metrics used to gauge success in the role. While effort has been made to recommend objective metrics, the more senior roles have a subjective bias. As a result, guidance is provided on the more subjective metrics. The listing is in order of priority with the first being the prime performance metric and so on.

*Focus:* This is typically "Customer-facing" or "back-office." Customer-facing is self-explanatory, back-office refers to support for the infrastructure, tools, and systems used by the contact center personnel.

*Interdepartmental dependencies:* Departments within and outside of the contact center that directly or indirectly impact the potential success of the incumbent.

## EXECUTIVE

### Vice President, Customer Care

(This position is not depicted on organization chart.)

*Role:* The VP is one of the architects of the company vision. This individual looks farthest into the future to ensure that Customer care does not lag the product/service and is prepared for the coming years. The VP frequently visits with accounts and solicits opinion and ideas on how well the operation is meeting the Customer's expectations. The VP is involved with only the most serious of escalations.

***Responsible to:*** Customers, stakeholders in the company, and the executive.

***Key performance metric(s):*** Profit and loss statement, Customer satisfaction quotient, definition and execution of viable vision for the contact center, and culture of the contact center.

***Focus:*** Customer-facing, back-office, and obligations to the executive.

***Interdepartmental dependencies:*** All.

### Director of Customer Care

***Role:*** The director executes on the corporate vision. The role is more tactical than strategic. The director understands the vision and oversees the design and implementation of systems and personnel hiring to support that vision. As with the VP, the director frequently visits with accounts. The director takes an active role in bringing resolution to issues. The director is focused on systemic corrective actions that streamline and fine-tune the support provided to the Customer base.

***Responsible to:*** Customers, contact center, and the VP.

***Key performance metric(s):*** Customer satisfaction quotient, vision to operational readiness (the contact center *readiness* to meet new challenges), and churn rate within the contact center.

***Focus:*** Customer-facing, back-office with obligations to the contact center, VP, and the executive.

***Interdepartmental dependencies:*** All.

# TRAINING

The training department is mandated with training all contact center personnel in the use of systems, technology, product specifics, specifications, deployment, telephone skills, and so on. The training program and subsequent effectiveness testing is continuous; from orientation on day one to system-and-tool updates to skill enhancement courses throughout the employees' tenure. If the contact center is to be effective as a personnel farm for the organization then the training personnel must take the entry-level personnel and give them the skills they and the company need to prosper.

The training team should also train Customers, including partners and vendors, as well as the rest of the organization, in the installation, deployment, and subsequent support of the target products and services. In addition, all non-product training (such as spreadsheet and word processing applications) should also be funneled through the training team. This allows the training team to verify the effectiveness of all training and consolidate all training exercises under one umbrella.

## Manager

*Role:* The manager executes the vision as provided by the director. The manager reviews post-training test results and makes adjustments where necessary. The manager makes recommendations to the director on tools and systems for expediting training services. Analysis on options as to training delivery mechanisms like Internet sessions, computer-based training (CBT), or self-study, will come from the training manager. As training is a value-added service and a product differentiator, the manager of the team may have additional responsibilities regarding revenue stream, expense accountability, and collection activities.

*Responsible to:* Customers, all contact center personnel, director.

*Key performance metric(s):* Profit and loss statement for the team, Customer and internal team satisfaction related to training programs (the data can be gathered from post-training surveys for the Customer base and polling of the manager's peers for the internal training programs), and churn rate of the team.

*Focus:* Customer-facing.

*Interdepartmental dependencies:* Contact center support teams, product management, and marketing.

## Internal Trainer

*Role:* The internal trainer is responsible for ensuring the contact center personnel are effective in the use of the tools and systems provided for them. They also train personnel on the deployment, use, and support of the target product/service. The internal trainer administers effectiveness testing to ensure the training is timely and effective, and that the knowledge transfer process itself is effective.

The internal trainer may also provide training for other departments within the organization. For instance, there is overlap between the training sales personnel required and contact center personnel required. The training team can leverage this overlap and champion the training of both teams. The end result is that the *product message* is consistent from all points within the corporation.

*Responsible to:* Customers, all contact center personnel, training manager.

*Key metric(s):* Satisfaction related to the presentation of training programs the individual has conducted (the data is available by polling the managers of the team the individual has conducted training for).

*Focus:* Customer-facing and internal managers.

*Interdepartmental dependencies:* Contact center support teams and product management.

## External Trainer

*Role:* Provide training services and programs to groups outside of the contact center. This includes Customers, vendors, partners, resellers, and so on. The external trainer is also an excellent source of information about how the product is viewed and accepted from the Customer's perspective.

*Responsible to:* Customers and training manager.

*Key performance metric(s):* Customer satisfaction related to presentation of training programs the individual has conducted (the data can be gathered from post-training surveys for the Customer base).

*Focus:* Customer-facing.

*Interdepartmental dependencies:* Product manager, business development, sales, and marketing.

## Content Preparation

*Role:* Prepare the course materials in the necessary formats (for example: computer-based training, PowerPoint, ScreenCam, and so on). In smaller organizations, the trainers themselves can be counted on to prepare their own materials provided they are reviewed by a single source for consistency (often marketing provides this review service).

The content preparation individuals write the *scripts* used by the contact center. They create scripts for the top twenty issues as well as any common failure modes. These scripts ensure consistency of the message as well as provide new contact center personnel with a solid basis to respond to Customer issues.

The content preparation individual also prepares, and may be the voice for, general access voice messages found on the interactive voice response (IVR) system. This includes notifications of coming preventative maintenance events and unscheduled interruptions of service.

*Responsible to:* Customers, internal and external trainers, training manager.

*Key performance metric(s):* The training team's satisfaction related to the content of the training programs, feedback from contact center managers and Customers on clarity of the prepared scripts, timeliness of scripts, and accuracy of training materials.

*Focus:* Back-office and indirect Customer-facing.

*Interdepartmental dependencies:* Product manager, marketing, and technical writers.

# CONTACT CENTER OPERATIONS

Contact center operations staff is mandated with maintaining the back-office systems and tools that the contact center requires to perform their job functions and ensuring that systems are available to provide the SLA guarantees that exist with strategic accounts.

## Operations Manager

*Role:* The manager executes the vision as provided by the director. The manager understands, in detail, the contractual obligations as defined in all SLAs that exist. The manager understands the support target (for example, calls will be answered in less than 90 seconds) as defined by the product manager and marketing teams. The manager designs the systems to ensure all performance parameters are met. This extends to back-office systems, database administration, backup power, telecommunication trunk capacity issues, redundant systems, desktop computers and tools, communications infrastructure, and so on.

*Responsible to:* Customers, contact center personnel, and the director.

*Key performance metric(s):* Profit and loss statement for the team, contact center effectiveness based on the systems availability, and churn rate of the team.

*Focus:* Back-office.

*Interdepartmental dependencies:* MIS/IT, product manager, marketing, sales, janitorial services, and facilities engineering.

## Report Writer

*Role:* Review Figure 6.1, Data flow, page 169, to get an appreciation of the report writer's role in a successful operation. The report writer pulls data from the databases used by the contact center and then generates reports to allow performance metrics to be measured and analyzed. Reports focused on trends, leading/lagging indicators, and cause-and-effect dynamics are also an important component of the position. The key systems to be mined for data are the help desk and PBX systems. Report packages will be issued on a daily, weekly, and monthly basis with summary reports on a quarterly and yearly basis.

On occasion, the report writer will be called upon to deliver custom reports and must work well across departments. The individual who has requested the report will assist in the definition of the report. The report writer must have an in-depth knowledge of database structures, proficiency in interpreting data dictionaries, and, most importantly, the ability to translate business-centric requests into meaningful report sets. The report writer also submits recommendations for changes and additions to the help desk system.

*Responsible to:* Customers, product manager, performance metrics manager, quality assurance, marketing, and operations manager.

*Key performance metric(s):* Timeliness and accuracy of the reports the individual is responsible to deliver (this data can be gathered by polling the audience for the reports).

*Focus:* Back-office.

*Interdepartmental dependencies:* MIS/IT.

## Infrastructure Support

*Role:* Infrastructure support ensures all systems and feeder technologies are working to specification. Some of the systems that need attention are the electrical plant (wiring), phone system, phone system feed trunk, Internet service provider links, backup power, application servers, backup mechanism, off-site storage of backups, firewall, PBX server, and so on. Daily activities include preventive and remedial maintenance on systems. In addition, there is the near-continuous installation of new workstations and subsequent configuration of users on the system(s). The infrastructure support team works very closely with the utilities (for instance, hydroelectric, telephone company, and so on) and feeder technologies (for instance, Internet service providers, data warehouse) that enable the contact center to operate. The team sets up and polices the SLAs that are in place with said utilities and feeders.

*Responsible to:* Customers, contact center managers, operations manager.

*Key performance metric(s):* Contact center effectiveness based on the systems availability the individual is responsible for.

*Focus:* Back-office.

*Interdepartmental dependencies:* MIS/IT.

## Project Manager

*Role:* The operations project manager position is a generalist role. A project manager is needed for sundry projects or initiatives that surface. This includes anything from the introduction of a new service option to a full overhaul of the systems used by the contact center.

*Responsible to:* Customers, operations manager, contact center managers.

*Key performance metric(s):* Profit and loss statement for the projects the individual has been responsible for, and timeliness of project deliverables (as stated in the project specification Gantt chart).

*Focus:* Customer-facing and back-office.

*Interdepartmental dependencies:* Departments in the organization that are stakeholders in the success of any given project.

## System Maintenance Programmer

*Role:* This role has two discrete focal points. First order is to ensure that the maintenance of the contact center databases is disciplined (this part of the position is oft referred to as a database administrator). The maintenance programmer will also champion database upgrades, data integrity checks, and procedures.

Second order is to affect, test, and then move into production changes to the systems used in the contact center. Changes include: revision or additions to the failure mode codes used by the contact center, additional screens, addition of fields, and so on.

*Responsible to:* Customers, contact center managers, operations manager.

*Key performance metric(s):* Availability of the databases the contact center is dependent on, and accuracy and timeliness of project deliverables including documentation and interdepartmental communications (meaning notification that changes are being effected to online systems).

*Focus:* Back-office.

*Interdepartmental dependencies:* MIS/IT.

# TIER 1 SUPPORT

Tier 1 support is the front line for Customer care. It is comprised, in most contact centers, of generalists. Order input, order fulfillment, shipping, tracking, invoicing issues, and product feature issues are part of the range of issues the first tier is responsible for. The prime performance indicator is Customer satisfaction. Two easy metrics are time-on-call and degree of escalation (the fewer calls the first tier must hand off to the next level the better).

It is the first tier where one finds the highest degree of abuse being levelled at contact center personnel. Intimidation, threats, and general hostility are online every day for this team. It is not an attractive position, and the personnel on the phones deserve the highest respect for being there day after day. Particularly trying are times of endemic failures where call after call has an anxious, often frustrated Customer at the other end. The CSRs are expected to answer each contact with the same optimistic disposition with which they started the day.

## Manager

*Role:* The manager executes the vision as provided by the director. The first tier manager ensures that the Tier 1 team is healthy, staffing levels are adequate, and training is up to standard. The manager frequently shadows his staff with a view to improving services and individual skill sets. The manager takes escalations when necessary. As the contact center takes calls, many with a negative connotation, day in and day out, the manager roles must be filled by individuals with excellent personal and relationship-building skills. The personnel within the contact center look to their immediate managers for support and assistance. It is a demanding proposition. The manager must know how to keep the team motivated and focused.

*Responsible to:* Customers, director.

*Key performance metric(s):* Profit and loss statement for the team and Customer satisfaction with the performance of the team including all SLA-related metrics (for examples of key performance metrics review, see Figure 4.7, Data plot, pickup time; Figure 4.8, Data plot, contact duration by function; Figure 4.10, Data plot, abandoned call ratio; Figure 4.11, Data plot, average on-hold time; Figure 4.12, Data plot, escalation percentage; and Figure 4.15, Data plot, time per function). The churn rate of the team is a key metric.

*Focus:* Customer-facing and back-office.

*Interdepartmental dependencies:* Product manager.

## Line Supervisor

*Role:* The line supervisor, like their fellow supervisors, is focused on the minute-to-minute/day-to-day operation of the personnel under their umbrella. Performance of the team is their prime performance indicator. The line supervisor is the first escalation point for the CSRs. Line supervisors actively take calls when the call/contact volume surges. The line supervisor tracks (within a structured human resources system) sick days, holiday time, and special personnel considerations.

*Responsible to:* Customers, tier 1 manager.

*Key performance metric(s):* Customer satisfaction regarding the performance of the team (for examples of the key metrics see Figure 4.8, Data plot, contact duration by function; Figure 4.10, Data plot, abandoned call ratio; Figure 4.11, Data plot, average on-hold time; Figure 4.12, Data plot, escalation percentage; and Figure 4.15, Data plot, time per function.

*Focus:* Customer-facing.

*Interdepartmental dependencies:* Contact center trainers.

## Customer Support Representative, Nontechnical

*Role:* The nontechnical representative is the first point of contact for the Customer base. Hire the best, be wary of those that only wish to put in their hours, and look for those that wish to move on in the organization. These representatives may be structured to handle all incoming issues and queries or a subset of the issues. The business model and where the contact center is in its evolution will drive the extent of their mandate.

The nontechnical CSR position is an entry point into the organization. The top performers should be allowed to prosper and move on, hopefully within the organization. The less-than-stellar performers should be nurtured and trained to become top performers.

In general, the majority of contacts require 80 percent interpersonal relationship skills and 20 percent technical skills. That is to say that finely-honed telephone skills, patience, skills in defusing situations, and being empathetic to the Customer's needs are far more important than technical ability. Base hiring decisions on the interviewee's interpersonal skills first and on technical abilities second; technology can be learned far easier than how to deal with people.

*Responsible to:* Customers, line supervisors.

*Key performance metric(s):* Whereas the manager and the line supervisor are concerned with the performance of the team as a whole, it is the line supervisor who focuses on the individual's performance. Each employee can be examined on their individual performance in reference to the examples found in Figure 4.8, Data plot, contact duration by function; Figure 4.10, Data plot, abandoned call ratio; Figure 4.11, Data plot, average on-hold time; Figure 4.12, Data plot, escalation percentage; and Figure 4.15, Data plot, time per function. The employee's total performance evaluation should also factor-in their willingness to take on additional responsibilities, provide guidance to junior contact center personnel, sign up for skill set enhancement courses, attitude, and general initiative. Punctuality and tardiness only factor if they are problematic areas with the individual.

*Focus:* Customer-facing.

*Interdepartmental dependencies:* Technical CSRs, infrastructure support.

## Customer Support Representative, Technical

*Role:* This role may not be needed in all contact centers. The focus of this team is technical issues with the product/service. If the product/service is not technology-based, this team may not be needed.

Much the same skill set as for the nontechnical CSR but with a greater depth of experience particularly regarding technologies and technical issues. Community college graduates are an excellent source for candidates for this position. Contacts into this team are often escalations from the nontechnical CSRs.

*Responsible to:* Customers, nontechnical CSRs, line supervisors.

*Key performance metric(s):* Whereas the manager and the line supervisor were concerned with the performance of the team as a whole, it is the line supervisor who looks to the individual's performance on the key performance metrics. Each employee can be examined on their individual performance as referenced to the examples found in Figure 4.8, Data plot, contact duration by function; Figure 4.10, Data plot, abandoned call ratio; Figure 4.11, Data plot, average on-hold time; and Figure 4.12, Data plot, escalation percentage. With the technical staff, accuracy also comes into play, but it is difficult to quantify and qualify. The employee's total performance evaluation should also factor-in their willingness to take on additional responsibilities, provide guidance to junior contact center personnel, sign up for skill set enhancement courses, attitude, and general initiative. Punctuality and tardiness only factor if they are problematic areas with the individual.

*Focus:* Customer-facing.

*Interdepartmental dependencies:* Tier 2 support, infrastructure support, and training.

# TIER 2 SUPPORT

Tier 2 Support is comprised of specialists in technologies intrinsic to the product/service being supported. Their focus is in resolving issues regarding installation, configuration, compatibility, fine-tuning, and platform support (platform usually refers to the operating system [OS], but may also encompass the processor flavor [Intel, Motorola, and so on], the configuration and even the basic input/output operating system). As with tier 1, the prime performance indicator is Customer satisfaction. Two prime performance metrics are time-on-call and degree of escalation.

As with tier 1 support, times of endemic failures are particularly demanding. The second tier CSRs are expected to answer each contact with the same optimistic disposition with which they started the day. Therefore, as with most of the Customer-facing positions, hire individuals that have excellent people skills.

## Manager

*Role:* The manager executes the vision as provided by the director. The tier 2 manager ensures that the second tier team is healthy, staffing levels are adequate, and training is up to standard. The manager frequently shadows his staff with a view to improving services and individual skill sets. The manager takes escalations when necessary.

As the contact center takes calls, most with a negative connotation, day in and day out, the manager roles must be filled by individuals with excellent personal skills. The personnel within the contact center look to their immediate managers for support and assistance and it is a demanding proposition. The manager must know how to keep the team motivated and focused.

*Responsible to:* Customers, director.

*Key performance metric(s):* Profit and loss statement for the team, Customer satisfaction with the performance of the team, (for examples of key performance metrics, review Figure 4.7, Data plot, pickup time; Figure 4.8, Data plot, contact duration by function; Figure 4.10, Data plot, abandoned call ration; Figure 4.11, Data plot, average on-hold time; Figure 4.12, Data plot, escalation percentage; and Figure 4.15, Data plot, time per function. Churn rate of the team is also a key metric.

*Focus:* Customer-facing and back-office.

*Interdepartmental dependencies:* Product manager.

## Line Supervisor

*Role:* The line supervisor is focused on the minute-to-minute/day-to-day operation of the personnel under their umbrella. Performance of their team is their prime performance indicator. The line supervisor is the first escalation point for the CSRs. The line supervisor will actively take calls when the call volume surges. The line supervisor tracks (within a structured human resources system) sick days and holiday time and acts on special personnel considerations.

*Responsible to:* Customers, training, tier 2 manager.

*Key performance metric(s):* Customer satisfaction with the performance of the team (for examples of key performance metrics, review Figure 4.7, Data plot, pickup time; Figure 4.8, Data plot, contact duration by function; Figure 4.10, Data plot, abandoned call ration; Figure 4.11, Data plot, average on-hold time; Figure 4.12, Data plot, escalation percentage; and Figure 4.15, Data plot, time per function. Churn rate of the team is also a key metric.

*Focus:* Customer-facing.

*Interdepartmental dependencies:* Contact center trainers.

## Customer Support Representative, Technical

*Role:* As this team is first escalation for the first tier team, there is overlap in knowledge and expertise with the first tier team. The difference is the degree and depth of knowledge the second tier representatives possess. This begs the question: "Why not have all CSRs at the tier 2 level?" The answer is threefold:

- Economics—Recall that tier 1 is an entry-level position; as a result, tier 2 representatives are paid more than tier 1 representatives. Consider that not as many specialists (tier 2) are required as generalists (tier 1).

- Skill set appropriateness—It is not the best use of the second tier representatives' experience, training, and knowledge to track a package or provide status on an order. Not only will the costs be unjustifiable, but the second tier staff will become disgruntled with the nature of the contacts they are resolving.

- Training—Depending on the complexity of the host company's systems and product/services, it is not always feasible or desirable to take new hires and expose them to all types of contacts. If the first tier team is positioned as a farm team to the second tier team then the learning curve is less steep and the second tier management team has the added benefit of working with known performers.

The 80:20 (interpersonal relationship skills to technical skills) ratio still applies as finely-honed telephone skills, patience, defusing situations, and being empathetic to the Customer's needs remain key aspects of effective support. Depending on the actual product/service, however, the ratio may be adjusted; perhaps 50:50 is a better ratio for the product under support. Consider that the first tier staff may have already defused and gathered the pertinent data; perhaps the second tier need only be detectives, facilitators of the resolution. That said, hire based on incumbent's interpersonal skills first and on technical abilities second; technology can be learned far easier than how to deal with people.

*Option:* In some business models, typically those with less emphasis on high technology, second tier personnel are structured as an internal group that only deal with the first tier team. That is, they do not take contacts direct from Customers but only from Tier 1. This means that the 80:20 (interpersonal skills: technical skills) can be readjusted to 20:80 (20 percent as they still must coexist with their peers in the first tier team).

*Responsible to:* Customers, second tier supervisors.

*Key performance metric(s):* Whereas the manager and the line supervisor were concerned with the performance of the team as a whole, it is the line supervisor who looks to the individual's performance on the key metrics. Each employee can be examined on their individual performance as referenced to the examples found in Figure 4.9, Data plot, contact duration by function; Figure 4.10, Data plot, abandoned call ration; Figure 4.11, Data plot, average on-hold time; and Figure 4.12, Data plot, escalation percentage. A measure of how many entries the individual has made into the knowledge base system is a good measure of initiative. A review of a random portion of the contact documentation the individual has made within the help desk system is a good indicator of the general performance of the individual.

With the technical staff, accuracy also comes into play, but it is difficult to quantify and qualify (speak to the individual's peers if a problem is suspected in this area). The employee's total performance evaluation should also factor in their willingness to take on additional responsibilities, provide guidance to junior contact center personnel, sign up for skill set enhancement courses, attitude, and general initiative. Punctuality and tardiness should only be a factor if they are problematic areas with the individual.

*Focus:* Customer-facing.

*Interdepartmental dependencies:* Tier 1, infrastructure support, training.

## SALES ORDER

The sales order team inputs orders into the corporate order-processing engine. The team is knowledgeable on the key features and benefits of the target product/service. The team provides an excellent opportunity for up-selling prospects on ancillary products or services the company may sell or for promoting complementary products.

The team expends the majority of their time in troubleshooting orders. This may sound like an overstatement to the novice contact center manager, but it is always surprising to observe the creative and innovative ways prospects have of befuddling order forms no matter how straightforward they may be. The team interfaces with prospects to rectify: illegible writing challenges, incorrect credit card information, mandatory fields that were not satisfied, incorrect arithmetic, and a host of additional obstacles to placing an order.

The sales order team may also provide an order status function whereby Customers can call a member of the team and request the status of their order. Many organizations have provided Customer self-service (CSS) tools to allow Customers to check the status of their orders without going through the contact center, but even the most elaborate systems have yet to totally eradicate the need for telephone-based assistance.

The size of this team is related to a number of factors: How many orders are anticipated? Is the nature of the product such that orders will be volume or single orders? Is there a recurring revenue component? How easy is it to actually enter the order into the back-office systems? Suffice to say that this is one area where a close linkage to an Internet-based Customer self-service system yields a very high return in Customer satisfaction. Consider that if the order entry system is such that Customers enter their own data on a Web page, writing legibility, data integrity, and mandatory fields disappear as problems. Fewer problems yield reduced call volume. Furthermore, in off-loading data-entry tasks to the Customer, the clock time for the contact center personnel to process an order is greatly reduced.

## Manager

*Role:* The manager executes the vision as provided by the director. The sales order manager ensures that the sales order team is healthy, staffing levels are adequate, and training is up to standard. The manager frequently shadows his staff with a view to improving services and individual skill sets. The manager takes escalations when necessary.

The Manager must have excellent personal skills. The personnel within the contact center look to their immediate managers for support and assistance, and it is a demanding proposition. The manager must know how to keep the team motivated and focused.

*Responsible to:* Customers, director.

*Key performance metric(s):* Profit and loss statement for the team, Customer satisfaction with the performance of the team (reference examples found in Figure 4.7, Data plot, pickup time; and Figure 4.8, Data plot, contact duration by function). Churn rate of the team is also a key metric.

*Focus:* Prospect/Customer-facing and back-office.

*Interdepartmental dependencies:* MIS/IT, contact center operations, product manager.

## Line Supervisors

*Role:* The line supervisor is focused on the minute-to-minute/day-to-day operation of the personnel under their umbrella. Performance of their reports is their prime performance indicator. The line supervisor is the first escalation point for the sales order team. The line supervisor will actively take calls when the call volume surges. The line supervisor tracks (within a structured human resources system) sick days, holiday time, and special personnel considerations.

*Responsible to:* Customers, training, sales order manager.

*Key performance metric(s):* Customer satisfaction with the performance of the team (reference examples found in Figure 4.7, Data plot, pickup time; and Figure 4.8, Data plot, contact duration by function).

*Focus:* Prospect/Customer-facing.

*Interdepartmental dependencies:* Contact center trainers.

## Customer Support Representative

*Role:* The sales order CSR is the first point of contact for the company's prospects.

As the first point of contact by the prospect base is extremely important to the corporate success, do not allow mediocrity. Hire the best, be wary of those that only wish to put in their hours, and look for those that wish to move on in the organization, perhaps into mainstream sales.

In general, the majority of contacts require 50 percent interpersonal relationship skills and 50 percent product knowledge. The sales order CSR must be able to clearly articulate the salient features and benefits of the product/service. They should be able to crisply differentiate the

> Prospect vis-à-vis Customer: A prospect is an entity that has potential to become a Customer. They have not yet bought the product/service. A Customer has purchased the product.

product/service from the competitor's. Baseline scripts are only the starting point. The successful sales order CSR must be able to deliverer the script in a freely-ranging conversational style.

*Responsible to:* Prospects, sales, line supervisor.

*Key performance metric(s):* Whereas the manager and the line supervisor were concerned with the performance of the team as a whole, it is the line supervisor who looks to the individual's performance on the key performance metrics. Each employee can be examined on their individual performance as referenced to the examples found in Figure 4.7, Data plot, pickup time; and Figure 4.8, Data plot, contact duration by function. With the sales order team, accuracy comes into play and can be measured by ascertaining how many sales orders the individual can process in a given period (accuracy counts as well). The employee's total performance evaluation should also factor-in their willingness to take on additional responsibilities, provide guidance to junior contact center personnel, sign up for skill set enhancement courses, attitude, and general initiative. Punctuality and tardiness should only factor in if they are problematic areas with the individual and corrective action has not already been initiated.

*Focus:* Prospect/Customer-facing.

*Interdepartmental dependencies:* Contact center trainers.

# STRATEGIC ACCOUNT

The strategic account team is responsible for maintaining a very high degree of Customer satisfaction for strategic accounts. Each and every member of the strategic account support team is the epitome of empowerment. They can, and do, make decisions on a daily basis to secure the highest degree of Customer satisfaction possible. That said, some businesses do not have strategic accounts; all accounts are on equal footing and there is no preferential treatment available for any account. If this describes the product/service then a team to take *special* care of strategic accounts is unnecessary. If you recognize, however, that some of the Customers have special status then instigate a strategic account team.

## Manager

*Role:* The manager executes the vision as provided by the director. The strategic accounts manager ensures that the strategic accounts team is healthy, staffing levels are adequate, and training is up to standard. The manager frequently reviews each strategic account with a view to ensuring the Customer's expectations are being exceeded.

The manager frequently visits with management at the strategic accounts. Occasionally the manager takes along the CEO, contact center VP, director, the responsible strategic account representative, and whoever else is deemed necessary to retain and sustain satisfaction.

As the individuals in the strategic account team require less hands-on management, the manager is, by definition, a hands-off manager. The manager must be shrewd in hiring the right individuals, or promoting from within, so that the manager is afforded the opportunity to be hands-off. The manager must be comfortable with interfacing at senior levels of management within the strategic accounts. The Manager takes escalations when necessary.

*Responsible to:* Strategic accounts, customers, director.

*Key performance metric(s):* Profit and loss statement for the team, satisfaction of the strategic accounts with the performance of the team, churn rate of the team.

*Focus:* Customer-facing (specifically strategic accounts) and back-office.

*Interdepartmental dependencies:* All.

## Team Leader

*Role:* The team leader oversees the team and ensures that there is consistency among the services proffered by the team. The team leader reviews Customer performance metrics with the individual team members and initiates corrective action when necessary. Because the manager of this team is often traveling, the team leader keeps their travel to a minimum. The team leader is the first line for escalations. The team leader must know how to keep the team motivated and focused.

*Responsible to:* Strategic accounts, customers, strategic accounts manager.

*Key performance metric(s):* Satisfaction of the assigned accounts with the performance of the team. As this team supports a subset of the Customer base, custom reports may be needed to ascertain individual performance. For examples of the key metrics see Figure 4.8, Data plot, contact duration by function; Figure 4.10, Data plot, abandoned call ration; Figure 4.11, Data plot, average on-hold time; Figure 4.12, Data plot, escalation percentage; and Figure 4.15, Data plot, time per function.

*Focus:* Customer-facing (specifically strategic accounts).

*Interdepartmental dependencies:* All.

## Sales Order Clerk

*Role:* The sales order specialist clerk focuses on issues with product/service orders and fulfillment. Sales order specialists will have strategic accounts assigned to them so that the strategic accounts can call directly into a knowledgeable representative at the first sign of a glitch.

This individual's responsibility is to ensure that every order placed by the strategic accounts they are assigned to be executed within the time frame parameters set out in the SLA. If the SLA does not specify performance parameters for orders, fulfillment, and invoicing, then the representative must deliver these services within informally negotiated timelines.

In the absence of an SLA, a set of baseline benchmarks for these soft services must be delineated in a formal document and brought to the strategic account's procurement, accounts payable, and other interested parties' attention.

*Responsible to:* Customers, strategic accounts, strategic accounts team leader.

*Key performance metric(s):* Satisfaction of the assigned accounts with the performance of the individual. Employees can be examined on their individual performance as referenced to the examples found in Figure 4.7, Data plot, pickup time; and Figure 4.8, Data plot, contact duration by function. With the sales order team, accuracy comes into play and can be measured by ascertaining how many sales orders the individual can process in a given period.

The employee's total performance evaluation should also factor-in their willingness to take on additional responsibilities, provide guidance to junior contact center personnel, sign up for skill set enhancement courses, attitude, and general initiative.

*Focus:* Customer-facing (specifically strategic accounts).

*Interdepartmental dependencies:* MIS/IT, finance/accounting, all contact center personnel.

## Technical Specialist

*Role:* The strategic account technical specialist focuses on technical issues with the delivery and daily operation of the product/service. Technical specialists will have strategic accounts assigned to them so that the strategic accounts can call directly into a knowledgeable technical representative at the first sign of a challenge. From initial installation to end-of-lifecycle retirement procedures, the technical specialist is the point person for the strategic accounts they are assigned to.

This individual's performance metrics are governed by the parameters set out in the SLA. In the absence of an SLA, a set of baseline benchmarks for these technical services must be delineated in a formal document and brought to the strategic account's technical staff and other interested parties' attention.

*Responsible to:* Customers, strategic accounts, strategic accounts team leader.

*Key performance metric(s):* Satisfaction of the assigned accounts with the performance of the individual. The nature of technical support for strategic accounts makes it very difficult, if not impossible, to generate reports from the system on the individual performance. It is therefore imperative to poll the accounts assigned to the individual to garner review and satisfaction quotients. An additional source of information on the individual is to conduct a peer review.

*Focus:* Customer-facing (specifically strategic accounts).

*Interdepartmental dependencies:* MIS/IT, QA, all contact center personnel.

## Service Level Agreement Analyst

*Role:* The service level agreement analyst ensures that the performance metrics, as defined in the SLA, are being met. The analyst gathers statistics from the back-office systems and compares the run-time results with the published goals. The analyst delivers reports direct to the Customer, in this case "strategic accounts," as well as to the contact center management. The goal for the analyst is to be the catalyst for continuous improvement across the entire organization.

An equally important role for the analyst is to define what services are feasible and can be provided under the auspices of an SLA. When negotiating any given SLA, the analyst must scrutinize all parameters that extend beyond the standard offering. The analyst must take into account the physical feasibility (that is, can the back-office systems provide the needed data points to deliver the extended service) and the economics of these parameters. As noted previously, the contact center's best interests are served by having as few of these "specials" as possible, each special requirement represents not only an operational burden, but an administrative one as well.

The analyst will initiate root cause analysis exercises and the subsequent corrective action(s) on challenges and problem areas. This is not a passive role as the analyst will not only identify the shortcoming but also make recommendations on the remedy. The analyst's recommendations will not be limited to contact center standard operating procedures but will extend to systems and the actual product/service being supported.

*Responsible to:* Customers, strategic accounts, team leader.

*Key performance metric(s):* This is a difficult position whereby if the individual is a star performer, management may not even be aware of their existence, let alone their stellar performance. However, reviewing achievements over time, peer review (interdepartmental in this case), and reviewing the changes and projects the individual has championed will provide performance metrics.

*Focus:* Back-office.

*Interdepartmental dependencies:* MIS/IT, contact center operations, product management.

## DEFINITION OF EXPANDED ROLES

*More, more, more.*

The following role definitions relate to a contact center that has need of extended services and discipline in the services provided. Review the organizational chart found in "Figure 2.6, Expanded contact center structure." If the anticipated call volume for the contact center does not warrant personnel dedicated to the following roles, consider that the functions provided by these roles are still needed. The majority of the roles in this expanded contact center organizational chart are necessary if the goal is to provide world-class support services. Therefore, understand the following roles and assign responsibilities as appropriate to the existing personnel. Some of the expanded roles have common characteristics with the generic organization chart.

## PERFORMANCE METRICS

Performance metrics consolidate performance measurement, enforcement, and corrective action across the entire contact center. Where the generic contact center had one individual focused on metrics (strategic account, service level agreement analyst), the expanded contact center has an entire team dedicated to measurement, analysis, and improvement.

## Manager

*Role:* The manager executes the vision as provided by the director. The performance metrics manager ensures that the performance metrics team is healthy, staffing levels are adequate, and training is up to standard. On a regular basis, the performance metrics manager reviews performance metrics with all contact center managers with a view to continuous improvement of the services each manager is responsible for. Particular attention is paid to strategic accounts and the SLAs in force. The performance metrics manager seldom travels but may on occasion to present results and corrective actions to key and strategic accounts. The manager takes escalations when necessary.

*Responsible to:* All contact center managers, strategic accounts, Customers, director.

*Key performance metric(s):* Profit and loss statement for the team, churn rate of the team.

*Focus:* Customer-facing and back-office.

*Interdepartmental dependencies:* All.

## Performance Metrics, Cost Analysis Clerk

*Role:* The cost analysis clerk is an accounting/finance function within the contact center. The clerk analyzes the costs associated with all functions within the contact center. The costs are based on a number of factors including the burden rate (salary), capital costs, back-office systems, overhead, and so on. The clerk should be able deliver detailed reports on where the contact center budget is being spent. This includes not only the obvious per-contact cost but also cost analysis on warranty costs, sales programs, and marketing initiatives.

The Clerk will report on costs associated with continuous improvement and corrective action initiatives. For example, if the contact center call analysis identified the installation routine as a top ten contact generator, this fact should drive a modification to the installation procedure (championed by the product manager). This should, in turn, result in a reduction in contacts on this issue, which should manifest itself by a reduction of cost related to the installation routine. The clerk provides the monetary proof of the cost reduction.

*Responsible to:* Contact center managers.

*Key performance metric(s):* Delivery of accurate reports in a timely fashion. Cost reduction initiatives spawned by the individual is also a good barometer of the individual's performance.

*Focus:* Back-office.

*Interdepartmental dependencies:* MIS/IT, contact center operations, product manager.

## Specialist

*Role:* The performance metrics specialist is in fact a *generalist* in the metrics arena. Special programs and initiatives that have a relatively short lifecycle fall under the specialist mandate. This individual champions short-term programs where extenuating circumstances demand attention but not changes to the contact center's standard operating procedures.

Consider the introduction of a Customer self-service module. The specialist would assist with the initial alpha and beta test of the service and report back, with a specialized set of metrics, to the owner of the initiative. Once the Customer self-service module has been tuned and fine-tuned and in full production, the attention of the specialist is no longer needed as they have ensured that the necessary data hooks and links have been established and been added to the mainstream metrics package.

*Responsible to:* Contact center managers.

*Key performance metric(s):* Success of the projects championed is the key metric. Efficiency innovations, cost reductions, and Customer satisfaction retention are barometers of the individual's performance.

*Focus:* Back-office.

*Interdepartmental dependencies:* All.

## Survey Specialist

*Role:* The performance metrics survey specialist is the champion for Customer and prospect surveys. The survey specialist defines what the target question to be answered is, understands what data is necessary to provide insight to the answer, designs the optimal survey, launches the survey, collects the data points, runs the analysis on the subsequent data gathered, and delivers the final report summarizing the data.

*Responsible to:* Contact center managers, product manager, marketing.

*Key performance metric(s):* Delivery of meaningful reports based on surveys conducted.

*Focus:* Customer-facing and back-office.

*Interdepartmental dependencies:* Marketing.

# HUMAN RESOURCES

Human resources play a key role in the lifecycle of a contact center. The needs of contact center personnel are different than those found in other parts of an organization. The fact that the contact center is operational twenty-four/seven, attracts entry-level personnel (that is young, minimum salary, and often inexperienced), typically has a high employee churn rate, and subjects the CSRs to hostile and often negative Customers day after day means the human resources team must not only champion the hiring but also be available to assist with the nurturing of the contact center personnel.

The human resources team works very closely with the management layer of the contact center to ensure personnel are motivated and generally psychologically healthy. The contact center human resources team often finds themselves more akin to high school guidance counselors than career development specialists. Contact center personnel are typically young and may be on their first venture into the working world.

Fair rules of behavior need to be published and understood by the personnel in the contact center. Even with clear, concise, published, and well-known rules of behavior, grievances will surface. The human resources team needs to be prepared to assist in coaching the management layer and in getting directly involved in issues centered on perceived slights, preferential treatment, relationships among personnel, harassment, and every other issue you can anticipate, when you throw one hundred or so young people together.

## Manager

*Role:* The manager executes the vision as provided by the director. The human resources manager ensures that the human resources team is healthy, staffing levels are adequate, and training is up to standard. On a regular basis, the manager reviews churn rate and staffing levels with all contact center managers.

*Responsible to:* All contact center managers, strategic accounts, customers, director.

*Key performance metric(s):* Profit and loss statement for the team (for the most part this is a measure of effectiveness of the dollars spent on recruitment programs, advertisements, and so on), churn rate of the contact center in general, churn rate of the team.

*Focus:* Back-office.

*Interdepartmental dependencies:* All.

## HR Specialist

*Role:* There are three distinct areas that require attention from the human resources specialist: hiring, nurturing, and termination.

*Hiring*—The specialist works with the managers, team leaders, and supervisors to identify which roles are needed in the contact center and at what staffing levels. The specialist defines and documents the minimum criteria and generates job descriptions for each position. The specialist champions the posting (internal and external) of the job descriptions, the subsequent review of respondents, and, typically, the first round of interviews (via telephone).

It is a good idea to align the company's job descriptions with industry standards. The job descriptions should be posted where all contact center personnel can review them (the intranet is a good place) and apply for the positions. There are many organizations (see appendix E) that provide guidelines on job descriptions, pay scale, and incentive plans. The best guidelines correlate the pay scale numbers based on company size, location, industry, and other parameters.

*Nurturing*—The specialist works with the managers, team leaders, and supervisors to ensure the contact center personnel are motivated. Like a morale officer, the specialist arranges the small delight events such as: pizza on a particularly high call-volume day, movie passes, sporting event passes, and so on. The Specialist also champions the more formal initiatives such as a merit-based bonus plan and career and advancement counseling.

***Responsible to:*** All contact center managers.

***Key performance metric(s):*** Hiring the right people and not having too many hiring corrections to make is the performance barometer.

***Focus:*** Back-office.

***Interdepartmental dependencies:*** All.

# ESCALATIONS

One can only hope that the supported product/service is so robust as to not require an entire team dedicated to issue escalation. The wild-card variable is the user base—the Customers. No matter how well-designed and thought-out the product/service may be, there will be a component of the Customer base that finds something to take umbrage to. Be it the tone or demeanor of a CSR, the perceived nonperformance of the product/service (". . . your sales guy told me it sliced bread as well as . . .") or a bona fide failure of the product. There will always be Customers who demand to speak to the CSR's supervisor, or the manager, or the CEO, "Whoever is in charge," and so on.

While there is huge value in the CEO and other executives to, on occasion, take calls direct from the Customer base, the frequency of these contacts must be managed and controlled. As effective as the CEO may be at defusing situations and restoring Customer satisfaction, the CEO must focus on the functions the CEO was hired to perform. Furthermore, once a Customer has the ear of the CEO it is very difficult to stop the Customer from contacting the CEO every time they have an issue. The CEO's gesture to support the situation backfires and the CEO finds more and more of their time consumed dealing with Customers they have built a rapport with.

Another aspect of escalations is that when an executive is pulled into a situation they need to be fortified with the relevant facts and figures. Enter the escalation team. The escalation team handles Customer issues that cannot, for one reason or another, be resolved by the standard contact center channels. Typically the Escalation team deals with situations that have intensified to the point where the Customer demands to speak to "someone who can help them." The team prepares briefing material for executives who are pulled into these situations. The team can also prepare detailed histories for personnel (sales or otherwise) who are visiting with accounts and require the historical support data.

## Manager

*Role:* The manager executes the vision as provided by the director. The escalation manager ensures that the escalation team is healthy, staffing levels are adequate, and training is up to standard. The manager ensures that the escalation team generates a continuous stream of root cause analysis exercises and the subsequent corrective actions. This manager is focused on putting his team out of work. That is to suggest that if the escalation team is conducting quality root cause analysis and the corrective actions are executable, then, barring new failure modes, escalations will diminish over time. The manager takes escalations from the team.

*Responsible to:* Customers, all contact center managers, strategic accounts, director.

*Key performance metric(s):* Profit and loss statement for the team, Customer satisfaction with the performance of the team, churn rate of the team.

*Focus:* Customer-facing and back-office.

*Interdepartmental dependencies:* All.

## Escalations, Team Leader

*Role:* The team leader's role is to consolidate the efforts of the escalation team and ensure there is minimal overlap on root cause analysis and corrective actions. The team leader takes escalations from the team.

*Responsible to:* Customers, escalations manager.

*Key performance metric(s):* Customer satisfaction with the performance of the team, timeliness of resolutions, and accuracy of data supplied to other players in supplying services to the escalated accounts are the prime performance indicators.

*Focus:* Customer-facing.

*Interdepartmental dependencies:* All.

## Escalations, Specialist

*Role:* This is the individual actually taking the hot handoff[1] from the CSRs in the contact center proper. The number of specialists needed is driven by how many issues surface, how effective the first and second tiers are at defusing situations, and, to a large degree, the nature of the product/service. The escalations specialist is particularly adept at defusing situations and getting to the core of the issues the Customer is having. The specialist is a world-class listener and an expert at using open probes to get the data they need. Empathy with the Customer is desirable but the specialist must also be able to deliver an answer that the Customer may not like or want—a fine line.

The Specialist initiates root cause analysis exercises. It stands to reason that since the specialist must drill down to satisfy the escalated Customer, the specialist is uniquely positioned to assess if the situation demands a permanent solution or if the challenge was a singularity. Once the root cause analysis has been conducted and documented, the specialist hands it off to the corrective action specialist.

*Responsible to:* Customers, team leader.

*Key performance metric(s):* Customer satisfaction with the performance of the individual including ability to empathize and bring about a satisfactory (to the corporation as well as the Customer) resolution to issues.

*Focus:* Customer-facing.

*Interdepartmental dependencies:* Contact center proper.

### Corrective Action, Specialist

*Role:* The corrective action specialist is the clearinghouse for all root cause analysis exercises. The specialist reviews the recommendations presented in the root cause analysis and champions the execution across all departments. The specialist may contact the Customer directly to clarify points or issues. There may be some travel to Customer sites, and certainly visits to other contact centers (partners, vendors, noncompetitors, and even competitors if possible) have value.

*Responsible to:* Customers, escalations team, escalations manager.

*Key performance metric(s):* Initiatives completed and the resulting increase in Customer satisfaction are the barometers for this individual's performance.

*Focus:* Back-office and Customer-facing.

*Interdepartmental dependencies:* All.

# INSIDE SALES

The inside sales team has a degree of functional overlap with the sales order team, however, the two teams serve different purposes. Please review the role description for the sales order team.

In many organizations the inside sales team is part of the sales department and is not in the contact center. However, as they have need of many of the same systems and tools as the contact center, many organizations have positioned inside sales within the contact center. Either way has pros and cons. Within the contact center the inside sales personnel can facilitate an up-sell and be a natural promotion step for CSRs that wish to make the transition to sales.

Inside sales personnel are the support staff for the organization's outside sales staff. Unlike most teams in the contact center, the inside sales team is mandated to initiate outgoing contacts. The team has very close alliances with the outside sales team and, in fact, may be divided into the same territories as the sales team.

Compensation for inside sales is a complicated and delicate matter. The majority of the contact center employees are salaried, whereas sales personnel are often on a performance incentive or commission-based compensation package. If the inside sales are *making* sales they will expect the same incentives as the outside sales team which may cause an issue with their salaried coworkers. Tread with caution on the compensation issue and ensure there is a clear, concise, and well-documented compensation package.

## Manager

*Role:* The manager executes the vision as provided by the director. The inside sales manager ensures that the inside sales team is healthy, staffing levels are adequate, and training is up to standard. The manager ensures that the team is productive and meeting sales targets and/or quotas.

*Responsible to:* Prospects, Customers, director.

*Key performance metric(s):* Profit and loss statement for the team, Customer satisfaction with the performance of the team, churn rate of the team.

*Focus:* Prospect/Customer-facing and back-office.

*Interdepartmental dependencies:* Sales, marketing.

## Inside Sales, Team Leader

*Role:* The team leader(s) structure mimics the outside sales team with one team leader assigned to each territory. The team leader ensures the inside sales are complementary to the outside sales team and not in conflict or contention. The team leader works very closely with their corresponding outside sales representative to set goals and quotas for the team.

*Responsible to:* Sales, inside sales manager.

*Key performance metric(s):* Customer satisfaction with the performance of the team. Orders processed, prospects contacted, prospects closed, and accuracy and timeliness of orders entered are key. If a sales quota is established then meeting the quota becomes the prime performance metric.

*Focus:* Prospect/Customer-facing.

*Interdepartmental dependencies:* Training, sales, marketing.

## Inside Sales, Customer Support Representative

*Role:* Sales opportunities come into this team. Prospects contact the team and may have questions or request clarifications. The individual team members field the contacts, supply the answer, and take the order. A solid understanding of the product/service key benefits and differentiating factors is mandatory knowledge. The ability to deliver the benefits message is also mandatory—not everyone has the sales gift. This role is an excellent training ground for the organization's outside sales personnel and is an excellent source of new, albeit junior, sales personnel.

*Responsible to:* Team leaders, corresponding outside sales representative.

*Key performance metric(s):* Number of sales closed and accuracy and timeliness are the key performance indicators.

*Focus:* Prospect/Customer-facing.

*Interdepartmental dependencies:* Contact center, sales, marketing.

# NEW PRODUCT RELEASE

The new product release team is focused on preparing the contact center for the release of a new product. The new product release team works in concert with the training team to ensure the contact center is equipped with the knowledge they need to perform.

There are few things that drive down the performance of a contact center more than having inadequate product knowledge. As obvious, simple, and fundamental as this idea is, many companies do not adequately manage product releases. The smaller the enterprise the more likely the introduction of a new product/service will be mismanaged. There are documented cases of products being introduced to Customers without the contact center's involvement or knowledge. Software patches have flown from the developer's desktop direct to the user base; features have crept into the product stream with no documentation, zero training for the support staff and, in the worst case, no testing.

Typically, new product release procedures fall under the auspices of the product manager. If the product manager has a good handle on what needs to be accomplished to ready the contact center and the organization is small enough, the product manager can champion readying the contact center. Larger organizations, however, require dedicated resources within the contact center to ensure the contact center is prepared for the release of any new product.

## Manager

*Role:* The manager executes the vision as provided by the director. The new product release manager ensures that the new product release team is healthy, staffing levels are adequate, and training is up to standard. The manager ensures that the team is always ahead of the new product release curve.

The new product release manager works very closely with the training team. The new product release team uncovers the data points the contact center needs to perform their job, but it is the training team that disseminates the message across the contact center.

*Responsible to:* Customers, contact center managers, director.

*Key performance metric(s):* Profit and loss statement for the team, Customer satisfaction with the performance of the team, contact center readiness to respond to new innovations made to the product/service, nondisruptiveness of product introduction programs, and churn rate of the team comprise the top performance indicators.

*Focus:* Customer-facing and back-office.

*Interdepartmental dependencies:* Training, product management, marketing.

## New Product Release, Planner

*Role:* The planner must anticipate and schedule a number of activities before the new product hits the commercial market, including: contact center familiarization, alpha/beta testing, analysis of alpha/beta data points, failure mode effects and criticality analysis (FMECA—see appendix C), contact center training and certification, and partner/vendor training and certification.

The planner works very closely with the product management team. The planner starts with reviewing and influencing the functional specification documentation set. The planner works backwards from the release date in functional specification time line and creates a contact center–centric Gantt chart detailing time lines for preparation of the contact center.

*Responsible to:* Customers, contact center managers, new product release manager.

*Key performance metric(s):* The contact center's ability and general readiness to provide services related to product innovations or release of a new product is the prime performance indicator.

*Focus:* Back-office.

*Interdepartmental dependencies:* Training, product management, marketing.

## New Product Release, Alpha/Beta Champion

See appendix F, Alpha/Beta Testing, for a short primer on alpha and beta testing.

*Role:* The alpha/beta champion works closely with the new product release planner and the product management team. The champion coordinates the various test exercises and conducts analysis on the results. Upon conclusion of a beta test, the champion makes recommendations on the impact of the product's release to the contact center. Included in the recommendations are staffing requirements, training, Customer satisfaction, exposure and risk areas, tools, and systems impact.

*Responsible to:* Customers, contact center managers, new product release manager.

*Key performance metric(s):* Customer satisfaction with the performance of the individual, Customer satisfaction recovery, and initiatives based on the recommendations to smooth new product transitions for the contact center.

*Focus:* Back-office.

*Interdepartmental dependencies:* Training, product management, marketing.

# NOTIFICATIONS

Personnel dedicated to service disruption notifications are applicable in businesses that provide services. Consider electrical utilities, telecommunications service providers, Internet service providers, or an application service provider—these all provide infrastructure services that, when working properly, are completely transparent to the subscriber. If one of these service providers was to experience an interruption in service, they are obligated to provide notification of the service disruption.

A product-centric business has less need of dedicated notification personnel. The company may, however, have a need for an occasional broadcast for a recall condition or perhaps a new feature.

## Manager

*Role:* The manager executes the vision as provided by the director. The notifications manager ensures that the notifications team is healthy, staffing levels are adequate, and training is up to standard. The manager ensures that the notifications, in general, are timely and accurate.

The notifications manager works very closely with the team that is administering the actual service and/or infrastructure (the engineers and technicians in the network operating center or NOC). The manager may arrange for one of the notification team members to be stationed in the NOC. The reason behind this redundancy is that when the NOC suffers a failure, the NOC personnel are focused on restoring operation, not on getting a timely notification out to the user community. The attending notification team member in the NOC also provides the NOC personnel with insight into the Customer-facing part of the organization.

*Responsible to:* Customers, contact center managers, director.

*Key performance metric(s):* Profit and loss statement for the team, Customer satisfaction with the performance of the team, churn rate of the team.

*Focus:* Customer-facing and back-office.

*Interdepartmental dependencies:* MIS/IT, contact center operations.

## Notifications, Customer Support Representative

*Role:* The notifications CSR is the individual that actually posts/sends the service disruption notifications. Consider that the crucial part of the role is to issue notifications when an unscheduled event occurs; but also that the role is charged with issuing preventive and remedial maintenance notifications. The dependence of the core product on technology partners may drive a notification pass-through component.

The position is marked by periods of *non-notification* work such as assisting on the help desk. When a failure does surface, the notification CSR must get a clearly articulated notification (technical writing skills) out via numerous channels (various technologies including e-mail, IVR voice message posting, Web posting, intranet posting) to a number of audiences (Customers, strategic accounts, sales, partners/vendors, and contact center personnel) each of which have different data granularity requirements. All this must be accomplished in real time; not a trivial task. Once service is restored, an all-clear notification should also be issued by the notifications CSR.

Administration of the notification distribution lists alone is a full-time job let alone the technical writing and actual broadcasting functions.

*Responsible to:* Customers, notification manager.

*Key performance metric(s):* Customer satisfaction with the performance of the individual (however, being that this individual is continually the bearer of bad news, some latitude must be shown), timeliness and accuracy of the actual notifications.

*Focus:* Customer-facing.

*Interdepartmental dependencies:* MIS/IT, network operating center.

## Notifications, Vendor Liaison

*Role:* This role provides the glue that bonds the organization and the enabling technology partners/vendors. The role is similar to a technical account manager but with a real-time component and sense of urgency driving the role.

The individuals in this role are responsible for the timeliness, accuracy, and veracity of the incoming notifications from the partners/vendors. They are part of tight, cross-company virtual teams (V-teams) ensuring that communication channels are open between the companies and that all parties are satisfied that they are getting the data needed to perform their jobs.

The open communication is not limited to preventive, remedial, and corrective action notification events but may also include planning data such as forecast information like "units deployed over time," loading information like "expected increase in bandwidth requirements over time," peak usage data based on seasonal impact, and so on.

Frequent travel is required to partner/vendor sites to keep the communication lines as lubricated and effective as possible. Expect the role to host frequent in-house meetings and tours with partners and vendors. Depending on the degree of dependence the business has on a partner's/vendor's technology, this role may be a full-time off-site role; that is, a resident at the partner's/vendor's network operating center.

*Responsible to:* Contact center managers, partners/vendors, notification manager, business development team.

*Key performance metric(s):* The effectiveness of the lines of communication is the barometer for this individual's performance.

*Focus:* Back-office.

*Interdepartmental dependencies:* MIS/IT, networking operating center.

# TRAINING

The mandate for the training team in an expanded contact center is the same as for the generic contact center.

There is only one addition to the Training team found in Figure 2.6, Expanded contact center structure. Larger operations may require a dedicated staff member to prepare scripts.

## Training, Scripting

*Role:* Prepare the scripts used by all contact center personnel. The scripts are guidelines to be used by the contact center staff. The scripting specialist ensures that any and all messages the contact center delivers are consistent with the company philosophy, marketing spin, sales literature, and general culture. The scripting specialist works closely with the product manager and marketing personnel to ensure consistency. Notifications may also be rolled into the script writer's mandate which means tight relationships with the notification team and a need to be available twenty-four/seven.

*Responsible to:* Customers, prospects, contact center managers, training manager.

*Key performance metric(s):* Accuracy and timeliness of the scripts are key, but even more so may be the quality of the writing in terms of clearness, brevity, technical veracity, conciseness, and friendliness.

*Focus:* Back-office and Customer-facing.

*Interdepartmental dependencies:* Sales, marketing, notifications team.

# CONTACT CENTER OPERATIONS

The mandate for the expanded contact center operation is the same as for the generic contact center.

There is only one addition to the contact center operations team found in Figure 2.6, Expanded contact center structure. Larger operations may require a dedicated resource to generate schedules.

## Operations, Scheduling Manager

*Role:* The scheduling manager is a team of one that affects the majority of contact center personnel. As the title implies, the scheduling manager is in charge of the master schedule for all staff.

A scheduling manager is required in those environments that are operational on a twenty-four/seven basis and some of the larger, standard business hours operations. The scheduling manager draws up the master schedule for all contact center teams. The SLA (internal and external) drives the staffing levels, personnel and shift overlap, training schedule, and skill set assessment.

There are the obvious components of the scheduling task such as planning around vacation time, sick time, and training time, and there are the less obvious factors that impact the contact center that need to be managed. The scheduling manager must be aware of and respond to, any sales and marketing initiatives that may impact contact volume. New product releases, patches, and updates must also be factored into the master schedule. If the operation has an overflow mechanism (see the bullet titled "Call Overload Insurance," page 37), it is the scheduling manager who interfaces with the management of the overflow mechanism.

*Responsible to:* Customers, contact center mangers, operations manager.

*Key performance metric(s):* Contact center readiness to respond to normal and special loads is the chief metric.

*Focus:* Back-office.

*Interdepartmental dependencies:* Sales, marketing.

# ENDNOTE

1. Hot handoff is the transfer of the contact from the CSR that took the original contact and has requested an escalation. Note that from a Customer satisfaction perspective a hot handoff is far superior to a warm handoff, that is: Customers do not like to hear "someone will call you back."

# Appendix C

# FMECA

An FMECA (failure mode effects and criticality analysis) is an analysis tool borrowed from the reliability engineering discipline. Traditionally the FMECA is applied to a product to mitigate risks inherent in that product failing. The author has used a subset of FMECA to focus attention on areas that will have an impact on the contact center, the personnel manning the phones, and the business itself (liability). In preparation for an FMECA program, a boilerplate FMECA form should be designed. Table format is the optimal structure for a contact center FMECA. Figure C.1, FMECA boilerplate example, is an example of a table-based FMECA.

Following are the definitions for the columns used in Figure C.1:

- *Ref:* Unique reference number assigned to each failure mode line entry. For failure modes that are related, the reference numbers can extend to as many decimal places as needed (for example, 1.1.0).

- *Failure mode:* Short description of the failure mode. Key on the prominent failure dynamic and use very exacting language.

- *Effect:* Short description of the consequence(s) of the failure. In the contact center context this almost always includes the Customer's perspective on the failure.

- *Dependency/Team:* Dual-focus column that delineates who is involved, who owns the failure resolution, and, when appropriate, situation recovery.

- *Response:* This is not the remedy to the failure (the remedy is found in the knowledge base) but is a cross-reference to the appropriate scripts and procedures to recover from the failure.

- *Notify list:* A listing of who is to be notified when the failure mode occurs. Depending on the severity of the failure mode, this list could include Customers, sales, and members of the executive.

- *Severity:* A measure of the impact the failure has on Customer satisfaction and the contact center.

| Ref | Failure Mode | Effect | Dependency/ Team | Response | Notify List | Severity |
|-----|--------------|--------|------------------|----------|-------------|----------|
|     |              |        |                  |          |             |          |
|     |              |        |                  |          |             |          |
|     |              |        |                  |          |             |          |
|     |              |        |                  |          |             |          |

**Figure C.1**   FMECA boilerplate example.

Figure C.2, FMECA example, is an example of the boilerplate filled in for a contact center supporting a handheld device that has a dependence on a wireless carrier. Reference items 1.0 to 1.3 are relatively severe failures affecting large portions of Customers. The FMECA then jumps, for illustration, to reference 8.2. Reference 8.2 is an example of a less dramatic failure that only affects a small portion of the Customer base.

Once the FMECA is completed the contact center management team can start planning for the contingences listed. If the list of failures is so vast as to be unmanageable, additional criteria may be added to the FMECA to focus energies on those areas in most need. For instance, the addition of a "probability of occurring" column will assist in setting priorities. Referencing Figure C.2, the addition of a probability column will influence the sequence of actions significantly. Reference 1.3 could have such a low probability of occurring due to redundancies and crisis control mechanisms the carrier has in place that the contact center may not need to plan for this contingency.

To start a contact center FMECA program follow these steps:

1. Solicit support from all departments—Divide departments that have multiple disciplines into appropriate subgroups. A high-technology product manufacturer could have the following groups and subgroups:

Engineering

   Software

   Client side

   Server side

   O/S

Hardware

   General (plastics, and so on)

   Recharge brick

   LCD

   Keyboard

| Ref | Failure Mode | Effect | Dependence/Team | Response | Notify List | Severity (1 = Very, 5 = Not Very) |
|---|---|---|---|---|---|---|
| 1.0 | **Carrier outage** | **Handheld rendered inoperative in area where outage occurs.** | | | | |
| 1.1 | Single radio tower outage | 1. Zero data traffic to handhelds in region serviced by radio tower. 2. Potential ancillary effect: neighboring towers may become saturated and congested. | 1. Vendor management team for affected carrier. 2. Vendor's strategic account support team. 3. Contact center strategic account team. 4. Contact center notification team. | 1. Ascertain area affected. 2. Ascertain fix ETA. 3. Ascertain restore of normal service ETA. 4. Scripts: 1222 and 1230. 5. IVR script: 1119. | 1. All strategic accounts that utilize services from the affected carrier. 2. Sales. 3. Post notify on IVR—clear on restoration of service. | 3—severity increases with the duration of downtime. 3 is < 1 hour, 1 hour to 4 hours is 2, and > 4 hours is 1 |
| 1.2 | Router node failure | 1. Multiple radio tower outage. 2. Zero data traffic to handhelds in regions serviced by radio towers. 3. Potential ancillary effect: neighboring routers may become saturated and congested. | 1. Vendor management team for affected carrier. 2. Vendor's strategic account support team. 3. Contact center strategic account team. 4. Contact center notification team. | 1. Ascertain region affected. 2. Ascertain fix ETA. 3. Ascertain normal service ETA. 4. Scripts: 1283 and 1230. 5. IVR script: 1001. 6. Request carrier to issue corrective action notification. | 1. All strategic accounts that utilize services from the affected carrier. 2. Sales. 3. Finance. | 1—outage will cause call volume to spike for the duration of the outage, spike density driven by the actual area affected (population is in direct proportion to the spike intensity). |
| 1.3 | Network operating center failure (fall-back mechanism unsuccessful) | 1. All data traffic to handhelds ceases. 2. All data traffic interfaces cease. | 1. Vendor management team for affected carrier. 2. Vendor's strategic account support team. 3. Contact center strategic account team. 4. Contact center notification team. 5. Vendor's executive team. | 1. Ascertain fix ETA. 2. Ascertain normal service ETA. 3. Scripts: 1000. 4. IVR script: 1000. 5. Request carrier to issue corrective action notification. | 1. Executive distribution list. 2. All strategic accounts that utilize services from the affected carrier. 3. Sales. 4. Finance. | 1—massive outage will cause the call volume to spike for the duration of the outage plus a settle time estimated at 50 percent of outage duration. |
| 8.2 | Battery compartment clip catch broken | 1. Battery clip falls off | 1. QA | 1. Offer replacement batter clip. | None | 5 |

**Figure C.2** FMECA example.

Finance

    Billing

    Accounts receivable

    Credit processing

Operations

    Shipping/receiving

    Packaging

    Return processing

Vendor management

    Carrier issues (service level agreement, and so on)

2. Have representatives from each department identify the top ten failure modes that have an impact on the contact center from the perspective of their discipline—the engineers will have no problem understanding the data points that are needed, but finance may require some guidance as to what is required. These items become the main reference categories such as "1.0."

3. Drill-down—With the appropriate representatives, investigate each main reference and define the decimal point failure modes such as "1.1 and 1.2."

4. Weight the risk regarding each failure mode. Assess the impact to Customer satisfaction and the contact center itself and assign a weighting.

5. Assign probability[1] of occurrence for each failure mode. This may be added as an additional column to the FMECA.

6. Prioritize the failure modes by risk and probability (Pareto principle).

7. Generate FMECA document. Distribute FMECA document to all participants for review and comment. Include the contact center managers and supervisors in the review exercise. Act on the comments and fine-tune the document.

8. Define structured responses to each failure mode (control plan). The FMECA can be divided among the appropriate team managers and supervisors. Review the input, fine-tune, and execute the plan.

Like so many other procedures outlined in this book, once finished with the steps above, do it again, and again, and again. Regardless of how well the FMECA exercise is conducted, expect to undercover failure modes that were not anticipated.

# ENDNOTE

1. Probability—When assigning a probability weighting it is interesting to note that there are, at least, two different flavors of probability. The first is "abstract" and is characterized by the rolling of dice—the distribution of numbers is a probability of nature. The second is "subjective" and is characterized by foretelling how a human is going to respond to a situation— the distribution of responses is subjective probability. It is often the latter dynamic that is of interest in the contact center. There are no guidelines as to how an individual is going to respond to a given set of circumstances, as humans are often anything but rational.

# Appendix D

# The Five Whys of Quality

I learned of the five whys from a colleague at one of the high-technology corporations for which I worked. I have searched for the source of the five whys on the Internet and mentioned the technique to many Quality professionals I know. As I have come up dry on the search for the source, I thank Les McPhee for this simple but effective technique.

Root cause analysis tool. To kick off this section, let us review the meaning of root cause from appendix A:

> Root cause—Quality term but has currency in all business units. The root cause is the culprit directly responsible for the effect that is being investigated. Root causes are often confusing and muddled with symptoms. For example: Western medicine, for a large part, is based on treating symptoms. If you go to see a doctor for an upset stomach the doctor more often than not prescribes medication directed at relieving the discomfort in the stomach. However, the root cause of the upset tummy is the stress this particular contact center manager is dealing with day to day. Prescribing medication to alleviate the discomfort to the stomach only deals with the symptoms and only masks the real problem—the real cause is work-induced stress. If you have been paying attention to this book you know that the real fix is to investigate why this manager is not dealing with their stress. Perhaps a week off is in order; maybe this manager is in need of some mentoring; perhaps there is a very difficult Customer hounding this manager. Whatever is the source, is the root cause.

The technique of the five whys may be applied to many activities, it is not just a quality-centric tool. The five whys stipulates that when delving into a root cause of an event, the investigator needs to ask the question "why" ad infinitum (or five, whatever comes first) until the root cause becomes apparent. This is probably best illustrated by a simple dialog:

Investigator: Why was order *xyz* shipped late? [first why]

Investigatee: Because the order entry system was unavailable and hence the order could not be entered.

Investigator: Why? [second why]

Investigatee: Because the database needed to be re-indexed.

Investigator: Why? [third why]

Investigatee: Because the uninterruptible power supply (UPS) didn't cut over during this afternoon's electrical brown-out and the server suffered an ungraceful shutdown.

Investigator: Why? [fourth why]

Investigatee: Because the batteries in the UPS had discharged.

Investigator: Why? [fifth why]

Investigatee: Because the UPS is not part of MIS's monthly preventive maintenance routine.

The root cause is that the order was shipped late because the MIS department had missed a key component in its preventive maintenance program. The remedy is to include the UPS in the preventive maintenance program and to conduct an additional investigation to ascertain if any other key components have been missed.

In analyzing the flow of the dialog it is obvious that there is more than one person in the dialog. The true root cause and its remedy take an interesting trip through departments and seniority levels. The trip and the owner of the various questions and answers are captured in Figure D.1, Five whys.

To bring closure to this example: the Customer would be called back and informed that the root cause was identified and corrective action has been initiated so that it will not occur again. The MIS department has two actions in that they need to include the UPS in

| Sequence | Who Is Asking | Who Is Responding |
|---|---|---|
| First why | Spawned by an irate Customer who called his sales representative, the question "Where's the order?" It is sales who ask the first why. | Contact center order entry supervisor |
| Second why | Contact center order entry team supervisor. | MIS department technician |
| Third why | Contact center order entry manager. | MIS department technician |
| Fourth why | Contact center general manager. | MIS department manager |
| Fifth why | Contact center general manager. | MIS department manager |

**Figure D.1**  Five whys.

the preventive maintenance program and they need to conduct an investigation to ensure the preventive maintenance program has missed no other mission-critical components.

Some would suggest that the five whys could be done away with if the right question was asked in the first place. The answer to that is that hindsight is 20:20. It is difficult to know what the *right* question is when the root cause is not self-evident.

Others may suggest that it is not the question but the answer that needs to be fleshed out. Better answers could cut the five "whys" to two "whys." The rebuttal is it is difficult to know to whom to ask the question until the root cause is known. The sales team member certainly wouldn't have known to contact the MIS manager because an order was late, nor would the order entry supervisor get a satisfactory answer to the re-index root cause question.

In addition, the answers personnel give are often filtered by their roles and personalities. Would an order entry supervisor even know what a UPS is? There is also the depth of the answer to manage. It is similar to the experience of asking an engineer what you believe to be a simple question and receiving in response the history of silicon and integrated circuits (much like having the entire workings of a clock explained when all you wanted to know was the time).

# Appendix E

# Organizations

There are a number of organizations of interest to contact center and support professionals. There have been a number of organizations that have designed their own quality criteria, but it is difficult to imagine any better underlying criteria than those offered by the Baldrige or Canadian Quality systems. Why invent a quality program when there are ready-made programs that carry with them national recognition and panache. The author strongly recommends a thorough review of the Baldrige criteria and the Canadian Quality criteria. Some of the more interesting and relevant organizations are listed as follows.

## ASQ—American Society for Quality

The ASQ is focused on becoming the authority on issues relating to quality. Their monthly magazine, *Quality Progress,* is an excellent source for ideas and leading-edge articles on quality methods, systems, and tools.

Internet: www.asq.org

## ASAP—Association of Strategic Alliance Professionals Inc.

ASAP is a nonprofit organization focused on the needs of strategic alliance professionals (such as business development team members). Their objectives are to:

- Nurture and support the professional development of its members and corporate sponsors.

- Raise awareness of strategic alliances in general.

- Sponsor, conduct, publish, and disseminate research related to best practices in alliance creation and maintenance.

Internet: www.strategic-alliances.org

## Baldrige National (U.S.) Quality Program

The Baldrige program[1] is one of the most effective and thought provoking programs as it places the Customer in the forefront of all business procedures and decisions. If its principles were adopted and applied the organization would certainly succeed.

In order to be most effective the Baldrige approach should be applied across the entire organization and not just the contact center. However, entrenching the Baldrige philosophy in the contact center is a good start to introducing the criteria to the entire organization. The sooner the executive of the organization embraces the criteria the better. Become a Baldrige champion and expound on its benefits frequently to anyone who will listen.

The U.S. Department of Commerce is responsible for the Baldrige National Quality Program and the Baldrige Award. The mandate, in brief, is to help improve organizational performance practices, and capabilities, specifically:

- Facilitate communication and sharing of best practices information among U.S. organizations of all types.

- Serve as a working tool for understanding and managing performance; and guiding, planning, and training.

### Baldrige Criteria for Performance Excellence Goals

The criteria are designed to help organizations enhance their performance through focus on dual, results-oriented goals.

Goals:

- Delivery of ever-improving value to customers, resulting in marketplace success

- Improvement of overall organizational effectiveness and capabilities

### The Key Constructs in the Baldrige Criteria

- Leadership

- Strategic planning

- Customer and market focus

- Information and analysis

- Human resource focus

- Process management

- Business results

### Canadian Quality Award

The Canadian Quality Award[2] has many similarities to the Baldrige program and everything said previously applies here as well. The Canadian program differs slightly in that the strong onus on the Customer is supplemented by a focus on continuous improvement.

The key points in the Canadian system are:

- Support quality principles.

- Review the quality criteria.

- Take quality tests.

- Develop an improvement plan.

- Spread the quality message.

- Enact the improvement plan.

- Monitor the improvement plan.

- Retest for quality.

- Maintain gain(s).

- Continue improvement.

## CATA—Canadian Advanced Technology Association

Internet: www.cata.ca

## Help Desk Institute

Internet: www.helpdeskinst.com

## Fortune 1000 Database

Internet: www.fortune.com/sitelets/datastore/index.html

## ISO 9000

Internet: www.iso.ca/iso/en/isoonline

## Six Sigma

Not an organization as such, but a quality concept and methodology. Six Sigma sets a goal of no more than 3.4 defects per 1,000,000 events. While its initial focus was on manufacturing operations, its theories and methods to reduce variability in processes translates well to the contact center environment. See the reference to further reading material on Six Sigma in appendix I.

## Software Publishers Association

Of particular note is the their excellent Technical Support Survey document.

Internet: www.spa.org

# ENDNOTES

1. *Malcolm Baldrige National Quality Award 2000 Criteria for Performance Excellence,* Gaithersburg, MD: National Institute of Standards and Technology, 1999.
2. *The Roadmap to Excellence,* National Quality Institute of Canada, 1997.

# Appendix F

# Alpha/Beta Testing

Alpha and beta tests are controlled, real-world tests conducted on new products. Alpha and beta tests are always conducted under controlled circumstances. The success of the test is gauged by comparing the real-world performance with a set of known targets, goals, and metrics. The product manager designs the testing protocol and key metrics to be measured and analyzed.

The contact center is involved only in the execution of the alpha and beta tests. The value to the contact center is huge in that they get the opportunity to observe the new product firsthand and prepare the contact center resources accordingly. Alpha and beta exercises often go through multiple iterations before the product is deemed ready for release. Each iteration of the alpha/beta test is tweaked and performs better than the previous. Each Pareto analysis on the failure modes yields tighter results until the product is deemed ready for commercial release.

## Alpha Test

The testers are staff members. Very low risk and very controlled. The new product is given to staff members that are representative of the target audience. For instance, if the target is MIS/IT professionals, include the second tier support personnel in the test; if the target is the average consumer, include the sales order and administration personnel in the test population. The prime benefit to the contact center personnel is that they are provided with hands-on experience with the new product and have the opportunity to directly influence the product's evolution.

## Beta Test

The final test before a product is released to the commercial market. Beta testers are existing Customers. Two criteria to be included in the beta test program: the Customer must be friendly and be forthcoming with feedback. The Customers in the beta program must be fully aware that they are taking part in a "pre–commercial release" test program. The beta program should be contained within a time frame. Often the beta product is recovered once the test is completed. This allows a further degree of testing and review. The benefit to the contact center personnel is that they are provided with prerelease experience with the new product and have opportunity to gauge the product's impact on the contact center (contact volume, contact duration, nature of contact, and so on).

# Appendix G

# Finance for CC Managers

Finance is a very structured and disciplined component of business. This section provides a 35,000-foot view of finance as it relates to the contact center.[1]

Regardless of what the underlying structure of the contact center may be, profit or cost center, every contact center manager should have a firm understanding and working knowledge of a number of financial terms and concepts. There are four fundamental elements that are of concern:

- Assets—All that which has value and is owned by the corporation. From capital assets (desktop computers for example) to intellectual property (patents and ideas for example) to real estate (land and building for example).

- Liabilities—Amounts owed by the corporation. In the contact center context this includes rent, leases, and capital expenditures that may be paid for over a term (for example, PBX and IVR systems, however, once paid for, the liabilities becomes an asset).

- Revenue—Incoming funds. In the contact center context there are a number of possible revenue streams: maintenance contracts, accelerated support premiums, per call revenue, training services, and so on.

- Expenses—The cost of conducting business. In the contact center context this includes training cost, travel and living cost, telephony costs, and so on.

In addition to the four fundamental elements, there are a number of terms and concepts that are of interest.

*auto-renewal:* Many maintenance contracts have auto-renewal mechanisms whereby when the term of the contract comes up, usually after one year, the contract automatically renews itself unless the user intercedes. An up-rider on an auto-renewal provides the service provider with an opportunity to adjust the price of the contract to the user.

***balance sheet***—The financial state of the corporation is captured on a balance sheet. The balance sheet has relevance to the astute manager in that an understanding of the profitability of the entire organization can be discerned from the balance sheet. Questions such as Is more cash being generated than spent? and Is the revenue generated sufficient to support long-term growth? can be assessed by reviewing the corporate balance sheet.

The key difference between the balance sheet and a profit and loss statement is that the balance sheet is a snapshot whereas the profit and loss statement is linked to a time frame or specific term.

***budget***—Budget is a general term that needs no explanation, however, in the context of a contact center the budget defines the *burn rate*.

The managers within the contact center deliver their budgets for the coming year to the director or VP who then consolidates, adds additional universal expenditures not captured by any single manager, ascertains budgetary costs from IT/MIS and finance, and submits the budget to the executive. In a typical budget round, the budget numbers are negotiated with the executive and agreed upon, sent back for revision, or flatly rejected.

Budgets should include capital costs (soft and hard), recruiting expenditures, new hire ramp up costs, skill enhancement training programs, bonus and incentive funds, operational programs and costs, upgrades to systems and desktops, and contingency funds.

In terms of the four fundamental elements mentioned earlier, budgets touch upon liabilities, revenue, and expenses.

***burn rate***—This term refers to the cost of keeping a corporation running. As in "burning through money." As the term is informal there are no hard and fast rules as to deriving the burn rate. The burn rate can be a loaded or unloaded number; usually, in practice, the number is unloaded and exclusive of capital costs. See Figure 4.18, Cost per contact, page 138, for a burn rate calculation. In terms of the four fundamentals, the burn rate is an expense.

***business unit***—Business units are found in corporations where the functional areas of the corporation have been divided into separate units with their own responsibility and accountability for budgets and profit and loss. A high-level organizational chart is shown in Figure G.1.

***capital costs (hard and soft)***—*Capital* refers to money. In the context of a contact center, capital costs are those costs associated with equipping personnel with all the tools, systems, computers, application licences, and telephony equipment the staff require to perform their jobs.

Capital cost may also include the *soft* costs incurred by the IT or MIS departments to support the personnel in the contact center. For example, the standard CSR's desktop has a *hard* capital cost of $3000, amortized over three years, plus a *soft* capital cost of $1200 per annum to support, maintain, and update that desktop.

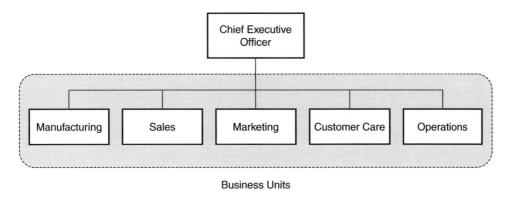

Figure G.1 Business units.

Therefore, the hard plus soft capital cost for each desktop computer is $2200 per annum ($3000/3+$1200).

The capital cost typically is delivered to the contact center manager by the IT or MIS department. In terms of the four fundamentals, capital costs are an expense.

*COO*—Cost of ownership (or chief operations officer, but it is ownership we are concerned with here). The cost of ownership are the ancillary, often hidden, costs associated with a product or service. COO includes the less-than-obvious costs found in the definition of loaded and unloaded costs. There are even more subtle costs taken into account when reviewing COO.

For example: the executive finally gives approval to purchase a PBX recommended in the last budget round. The PBX is procured and installed. Everything is working to specification and adequate budget was allocated for the discovery, implementation, training, and deployment phases (collectively known as professional services). However, the MIS department discovers that the addition of the new PBX to the equipment room has driven the ambient temperature of the room to well over 100° causing many of the other systems in the room to shut down due to thermal overload. The fix is to procure and install a new dedicated 20-ton air conditioning unit on the roof of the building. The landlord is not willing to bear any of the cost, therefore, not only must the contact center bear the cost of the new air conditioning unit but also the sky crane and installation costs, and bear the inconvenience of the systems shutdown in the interim. The cost of the new PBX had nearly doubled once the dust had settled.

*deep pockets*—An informal term meaning the corporation has a great deal of capital (money) in the bank. A corporation with deep pockets can support a high *burn rate* for quite a long time before the product actually starts returning revenue.

*GAAP*—Generally accepted accounting principles. Guidelines developed by the Accounting Standards Committee that govern how businesses report their financials. In the contact center context, GAAP is not a huge concern as long as the astute manager is aware that there are standardized accounting rules. However, balance sheets and profit and loss statements are subject to the rules set forth by GAAP. An example of a GAAP rule:

> Cost principle: assets are recorded at the actual purchase price. This price is never adjusted during the lifecycle of the asset.

*loaded/unloaded costs*—A loaded cost is where the less obvious costs have been included in the cost. Consider a CSR: the obvious cost is salary. Less obvious is the cost of the desktop computer system, the telephone system, the software applications, and so on. Even less obvious is the cost of the cubicles, desks, and lunchroom refrigerator; and even less obvious is the cost of the air conditioning, real estate fees, rent, utilities, parking lot upkeep, and so on.

In practice, finance usually supplies a factor that the employee's salary is multiplied by to obtain the loaded cost. The accuracy of the resulting loaded number is not at issue as it is accepted as an approximation. What is included in the factor is not written in stone; the manager needs to ascertain exactly what is included. For example: Are capital costs and MIS/IT costs included? If not, the manager needs to ascertain these numbers from MIS/IT to build his budget.

Loaded cost is also known as "fully burdened cost." Real-world examples of loading factors are "1.4" and "2.2." A sample equation follows to illustrate the use. Assume:

$$CSR \; salary = \$35,000$$

Loading factor = 2.2 (includes all administration, support, and ancillary costs)

Therefore,

$$loaded \; cost \; per \; CSR = \$35,000 \times 2.2$$

$$loaded \; cost \; per \; CSR = \$77,000 \; per \; annum$$

If the budget uses loaded costs, $77,000 per CSR is needed for next year. If the budget uses unloaded costs (most do) $35,000 is needed, but then another budget line is needed to capture training costs and other direct soft costs. See Figure 4.18, Cost per contact, page 138, for an example of using loaded costs.

*pass-through*—A business model where a transaction is processed by one entity on behalf of a silent entity. Revenue is passed-through to the silent entity untouched by the corporation processing the transaction. Frequently the entity processing the transaction will apply an administration fee or appropriate a portion of the revenue collected.

***profit/cost center*—**A profit center is a business unit that directly drives revenue. A cost center is a business unit that does not directly drive revenue and only diminishes the bottom line.

Sales is an example of a direct driver of revenue; sales is a profit center. The shipping department is an example of a cost center. It can be argued that all business units drive revenue one way or another for what is the use of a sale if the product cannot be shipped to the Customer?

If at all possible do not structure the contact center purely as a cost center. If the business model is such that support is gratis and there is no direct revenue, then find a way to assign monetary value to Customer satisfaction. Alternatively, arrange a system of charges to internal departments per support event.

Traditional revenue streams for contact centers include maintenance contracts, upgrade programs, and up-selling programs. Billing events could be driven by fixed fee per support event, fee based on length of contact, or a flat fee for all support events regardless of length. Less tangible revenue streams include Customer satisfaction value and Customer retention value.

***profit and loss statement (P&L)*—**In many organizations it is this report that defines the success and/or failure of the business units, therefore, the profit and loss statement is the most important financial report for the contact center management team.

One aspect to the profit and loss, which surfaces frequently, is the fact that the P&L is firmly grounded on financial tangibles. As Customer satisfaction does not have a hard-set value association or dollar value, how can the contact center management justify the cost to retain, build, and improve Customer satisfaction? The answer is assigning a tangible value to Customer satisfaction in much the same way value is associated with intellectual property. Enlist the marketing, business development, and sales teams in the exercise to assign value to Customer satisfaction.

The P&L statement reconciles sales, costs, and the subsequent profit or loss over a set term. Quarterly P&L statements are the industry norm but annual P&L statements are also popular. The downside of only one P&L statement (per annum) is that it only provides one opportunity per year for corrective action.

The P&L statement is typically delivered to contact center management by the finance department. The contact center P&L is rolled into the corporate P&L to provide an overview of the entire business.

***pro forma*—**A term borrowed from Latin. In general, a pro forma document is provided in advance so as to outline form or list items. In a business context, pro forma invoices are often extended so that the buyer can initiate the process within their organization's accounting department to procure a product or service.

***ratio (business or finance)*—**Financial ratios depict the relationship between two elements from the corporate balance sheet (or income statement). Ratios are typically used to evaluate financial performance. The most popular financial ratios pit assets against liability and provide an understanding of the liquidity position of the corporation (that is, do they have enough cash and cash flow to cover expenses?). Perhaps the most prudent time to delve into a corporate financial ratio(s) is just prior to accepting a position with the corporation to review their liquidity and financial stability.

***recurring revenue***—The best kind of revenue . . . it just keeps coming. Revenue from a maintenance contract is an example of recurring revenue. The frequency may be monthly, quarterly, or annually. See *auto-renewal.*

***ROI***—return on investment. When making a pitch to the executive for funds, present the ROI story first. The ROI assumptions and calculations outline the tangible gain to the corporation.

The pitch:

> "If $100,000 is allocated to update the telephony system to provide an automatic call distribution capability then the contact center will be able to distribute issues by skill set. This will result in relating support resources to the issues they are best able to handle. As an example: the corporate Cisco-certified support engineers will no longer be burdened with questions about desktop applications and can therefore concentrate on router and firewall issues. Desktop issues will, through the automatic call distribution system, be routed to the entry-level CSRs. This, in turn, will allow management to adjust the ratio between entry-level and certified support engineers without affecting Customer satisfaction (in fact it may enhance satisfaction). As the loaded cost of a certified support engineer is three times that of an entry-level CSR, the $100,000 will be recouped in four months. The personnel overhead savings continue beyond the four-month period for the entire life-cycle of the automatic call distribution capability.
>
> Furthermore, utilizing the tracking and accounting links (that is, A/P and micro-payments) within the automatic call distribution engine provides the contact center with potential revenue streams. For example: "A rider premium of $2.00 per minute to access our top support engineers, with a Customer adoption rate of 20 percent, will yield approximately $12,000 per month in additional revenue."

Compare return on investment with cost of ownership.

## ENDNOTE

1. Attempting to encapsulate "finance" in a brief appendix is no less audacious than if the author attempted to encapsulate engineering in few sentences. For further information see "Finance for Technical Managers" referenced in appendix I.

# Appendix H

# SOP Template

The standard operating procedure (SOP) template is to be used by all procedure owners to document the sanctioned routines and techniques to counter common occurrences. One of the prime features of introducing an SOP template is that all documented procedures will have a similar look and feel.

The SOP documentation template is divided into two sections, text and graphics. The notes in the italic font provide direction to the personnel filling out the template. Reference to other documents assumes a naming convention of CC-xxxx, where CC means the document is owned and administered by the contact center and xxxx is the document serial number.

The *repository* refers a central documentation storage and administration mechanism. The librarian is the administrator of the repository. There are a number of excellent software packages that simplify this task. Contact the engineering and quality departments as they may already have a documentation control tool that the contact center can leverage.

## CC-0004—SOP TEMPLATE

Use this template to document new procedures or processes. See "CC-0011 Documentation Guidelines" for detailed instructions on how to use this template.

*Team:* Open text field, 24 characters. The contact center team name that this procedure applies to goes here. Use the team name as found on the latest version of "CC-0003 Organization Chart."

*Procedure Title:* Open text field, 64 characters. Descriptive name for the procedure. Please see "CC-0011 Documentation Guidelines" for a description of the rules for creating procedure titles. Also check the document repository to ensure the title you have chosen has not already been used.

*Scope:* Open Text field, 64 characters. The area covered by the procedure.

*Purpose:* Open text field, 64 characters. Why is this procedure needed?

*Ref:* Locked field. The repository librarians fill in this field once the document has been approved.

*Author:* Open text field, 24 characters. Put your name here.

*Companions:* Open text field, 24 characters. Document the name(s) of companion documents such as the flowchart document name.

*Date:* Locked field. This is an auto field, do not overwrite the meta-tag.

*Keywords:* Open field, 64 characters. Each keyword must be followed by a comma. Insert keywords for search and reference navigation. See "CC-0011 Documentation Guidelines" for suggestions on optimal keyword usage.

*Comments:* Open field, unlimited. Put any comments related to the procedure here.

*Reviewed:* Locked field. This field is filled-in automatically via the review process.

*Approved:* Locked field. This field is filled-in automatically via the review process.

*Graphic Flow:* Insert graphic flow of procedure here in *.wmf format. See "CC-0011 Documentation Guidelines" for guidelines for the flowchart symbols and tools.

The remainder of this appendix presents an example of a fully completed procedure.

*Team:* Sales Order Entry/Finance.

*Procedure* Title: Credit Check.

*Scope:* Applies to all standard process sales orders processed with the contact center.

*Purpose:* This procedure establishes the prospect is a reasonable credit risk.

*Ref:* CC-0102

*Author:* Tom Harkins, inside sales order manager.

*Companions:* C-0102 process flow.vsd

*Date:* June 28, 2002

*Keywords:* Credit, sales order, credit risk

*Comments:* This procedure was tested and introduced in June 2002. Highly recommend that, as the product line expands and discounting plays a larger role in the average sale, this procedure be reviewed frequently (each quarter).

*Reviewed:* Garry Schultz, VP contact center and Scott Wial, comptroller (finance department).

*Approved:* Garry Schultz, VP contact center and Scott Wial, comptroller (finance department).

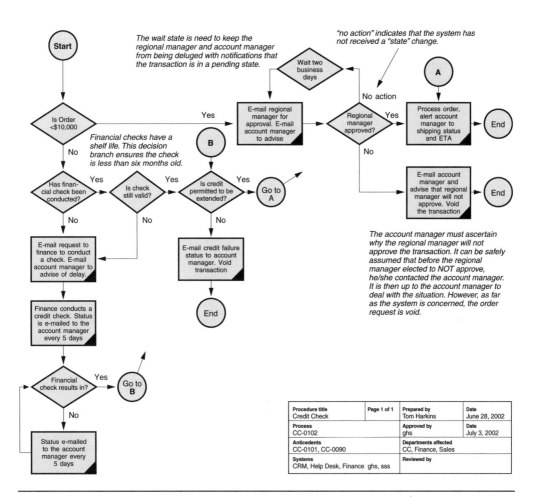

**Figure H.1**   SOP example.

# Appendix I

# Selected Readings

Bergeron, Pierre G. *Finance for Non-Financial Managers* (Scarborough, ON: Nelson Canada, 1990).

Blanchard, Benjamin S. *Logistics Engineering and Management* (Englewood Cliffs, NJ: Prentice Hall International, 1992).

Brown, Stanley A. *Breakthrough Customer Service: Best Practices of Leaders in Customer Support* (Etobicoke, ON: Coppers & Lybrand, 1997).

Coleman, Richard M. *The 24 Hour Business: Maximizing Productivity through Round-the-Clock Operations* (New York: Amacom, 1995).

De Bono, Edward. *Six Thinking Hats* (Markham, ON: Penguin Books, 1985).

———. *Po: Beyond Yes and No* (Markham, ON: Penguin Books, 1972).

Gale, Bradley T. *Managing Customer Value* (New York: The Free Press, 1994).

Harry, Mikel, and Richard Schroeder. *Six Sigma, the Breakthrough Management Strategy Revolutionizing the World's Top Corporations* (New York: Doubleday, 2000).

Hayes, Bob E. *Measuring Customer Satisfaction* (Milwaukee: ASQ Quality Press, 1998).

Lapin, Lawrence L. *Statistics for Modern Business Decisions* (San Jose State University: Harcourt Brace Jovanovich, 1990).

Moore, Geoffrey A. *Crossing the Chasm* (New York: Harper Business, 1991).

Reichheld, Frederick F. *The Loyalty Effect* (Boston: Harvard Business School Press, 1996).

Stamatis, D. H. *Failure Mode and Effect Analysis* (Milwaukee: ASQC Quality Press, 1995).

Vavra, Terry G. *Improving Your Measurement of Customer Satisfaction* (Milwaukee: ASQ Quality Press, 1997).

Weinberger, David, Doc Searls, Christopher Locke, and Rick Levine. *The Cluetrain Manifesto: The End of Business As Usual* (Cambridge, MA: Perseus Books, 2000).

# About the Author

Garry Schultz was born in Ottawa, Canada in 1958. From 1958 to 1982 nothing really remarkable happened other than the sort of antics one would expect from someone growing up in those years. It was during these years that a love of music developed and, in turn, Schultz studied the guitar—classical, folk, rock, and jazz. But as many others have discovered, music does not pay the bills.

Schultz has been active in the high-technology sector for over 20 years. Starting as a field engineer with oscilloscope in one hand and a DVOM in the other, Schultz troubleshot and repaired mainframe class computers. The computers in that day were large monoliths enshrouded in their own rooms; 1k memory planes were on 12" × 12" circuit boards and cost more than a small car does today, and 10 megabyte disk drives were the size of dishwashing machines.

Early in his career Schultz realized that field engineering and his focus on circuit level repair were going the way of the dinosaur. He concluded that to continue being prosperous he needed to change his focus from pure technology and get into an aspect of high technology that wouldn't be rendered obsolete every three years. General management was the direction he decided to pursue.

He prospered. First as a technical manager, then as a general manager. He eventually secured a director position, was promoted to VP of professional services, and further progressed to VP of business devolvement.

Schultz has built a number of world-class teams and organizations. Interesting highlights of his career include being in Saudi Arabia as a guest of the Kuwaiti Government-in-exile just prior to the Gulf War (prior meaning hours before); travels in areas marked by civil strife such as Sri Lanka and Nicaragua; travels in areas of great beauty including Uruguay, Brunei, and New Zealand; and visits to the metropolitan centers of the world: Hong Kong, New York, Singapore, Bangkok, and North Gore, to name just a few.

He has been happily married for 20-some years to Jackie, has one daughter, Jenna, and a friendly, loving dog named Jazzmine.

# Index